The Political Economy of European Banking Union

The Political Economy of European Banking Union

David Howarth and Lucia Quaglia

OXFORD
UNIVERSITY PRESS

OXFORD
UNIVERSITY PRESS

Great Clarendon Street, Oxford, OX2 6DP,
United Kingdom

Oxford University Press is a department of the University of Oxford. It furthers the University's objective of excellence in research, scholarship, and education by publishing worldwide. Oxford is a registered trade mark of Oxford University Press in the UK and in certain other countries

First Edition published in 2016

Impression: 1

Published in the United States of America by Oxford University Press
198 Madison Avenue, New York, NY 10016, United States of America

British Library Cataloguing in Publication Data
Data available

Library of Congress Control Number: 2016931111

ISBN 978–0–19–872792–7

Printed in Great Britain by
Clays Ltd, St Ives plc

Preface

In June 2012, the euro area heads of state and government agreed to 'complete' Economic and Monetary Union (EMU) by creating an 'integrated financial framework' which was later labelled 'Banking Union', and which was to be based on four main components: a single framework for banking supervision; a single framework for the managed resolution of banks and financial institutions; a common Deposit Guarantee Scheme (CDGS); and a common backstop for temporary financial support. Banking Union was to make use of the European Union's (EU's) Single Rulebook on banking (notably, capital and liquidity rules). Between June 2012 and the end of 2015, three of the four components were negotiated and agreed, while negotiations on the common deposit guarantee scheme were launched in late 2015.

This book examines the making of Banking Union, explaining why two decades after the agreement on EMU, the euro area heads of state and government decided to embark on the transfer of significant powers over banking supervision, financial support, and resolution to the supranational level. Our study also explains why Banking Union took the shape it did and why other possibilities were not chosen. Above all, our study focuses on national government preferences on Banking Union, and we explain the outcome of intergovernmental negotiations as an uneven balance of these preferences. German preferences were most influential, but German policy-makers nonetheless had to compromise on a number of important issues.

Having both worked on EMU, central banking, and financial regulation in the EU, and on national banking systems, we were very well (if not uniquely) positioned to study Banking Union, which requires a good understanding of all these subjects. Oxford University Press was very supportive of our project from the very beginning, and we began working on the different chapters of the book in earnest.

While writing this book, we were faced with several challenges. First, Banking Union was a moving target and our content had to be repeatedly updated. As the book was sent to press, not all the Banking Union elements had been agreed—notably, the creation of a common DGS—or put into place, which means that our analysis of certain issues is necessarily provisional. Second, we wanted to write a book that could be both of interest to, and accessible to, economists, political scientists, and public policy and EU scholars. This required striking the (hopefully correct) balance between economic and political science analysis. For some chapters, this ambition was more difficult to achieve than for others. Third, there was a trade-off between analysing all the main elements of Banking Union and achieving a detailed analysis. Clearly, individual book-length studies can be written on each of supranational banking supervision and EU supervisory rules, resolution, deposit guarantee, fiscal support, and the EU Single Rulebook. We opted for broad coverage, and hence in each chapter we had to be selective as to the material included. We adopted a similar structure for each of the empirical chapters: we provide an overview of negotiations regarding the Banking Union element under discussion, and then we apply our analytical framework focused on how banking system configuration and moral hazard concerns shaped national preferences.

Our research was in part funded by the Luxembourg Fonds National de la Recherche through an INTER mobility-in fellowship (PEBU—ID 7555123), which financed Lucia Quaglia's year-long research stay at the University of Luxembourg. She wishes to thank the University of Luxembourg for hosting her during the 2014–15 academic year and the University of York for granting her research leave.

The primary research for this book could not have been completed without the help of many practitioners and experts in EU institutions, national governments, banks, and interest organizations. We were able to benefit from a large number of helpful interlocutors, who generously gave us their time despite busy schedules. We are very grateful to all of them. It was agreed with all the interviewees that, although we would likely use the information they provided us, they would not be identified. All errors, omissions, and interpretations in this book are ours.

In writing this book we drew on the research undertaken for a number of journal articles and book chapters that we published over the past four years on Banking Union and related subjects, including, notably: Howarth, D. and Quaglia, L. (2016), 'Internationalized Banking, Alternative Banks, and the Single Supervisory Mechanism', *West European Politics*; (2014) 'The Steep Road to Banking Union: Constructing the Single Resolution Mechanism', *Journal of Common Market Studies Annual Review*, 50 (s1); and (2013) 'Banking Union as Holy Grail: Rebuilding the Single Market in Financial Services, Stabilizing Europe's Banks and "Completing" Economic and Monetary Union', *Journal of Common Market Studies*, 49 (s1): 119–41.

From the start of our research, several academics generously offered their advice, and several commented on parts of the book, conference papers, and other academic publications in which some of the findings of our research have been presented. In particular, we would like to thank Michele Chang, Shawn Donnelly, Kenneth Dyson, Henrik Enderlein, Ian Hardie, Dermot Hodson, Patrick

Leblond, Huw Macartney, Manuela Moschella, Ivo Maes, Renate Mayntz, George Pagoulatos, Uwe Pütter, Charlotte Rommerskirchen, Sebastian Royo, Tal Sadeh, Joachim Schild, and Amy Verdun.

We further benefited from a range of comments offered by participants at various conferences of the University Association for Contemporary European Studies, the European Union Studies Association, the British Political Studies Association, and the European Consortium for Political Research. We also wish to thank the four anonymous reviewers of the detailed book proposal. At the University of Luxembourg, Jakub Gren provided outstanding research assistance for data collection and the compilation of the bibliography; Moritz Liebe regularly provided information of interest and assisted with chart formatting; and Agnes Darabos efficiently copy-edited and formatted the manuscript. Last but surely not least, we wish to thank the series editor, Aimee Wright, for her prompt interest in and unfaltering commitment to our project.

Professors David Howarth and Lucia Quaglia,
Luxembourg and York,
May 2016

Contents

List of Figures

List of Tables

List of Acronyms

ABI	Italian Banking Association
AQR	Asset Quality Review
BBA	British Bankers' Association
BCBS	Basel Committee on Banking Supervision
BaFin	German Federal Financial Supervisory Authority
BIS	Bank for International Settlements
BPCE	Banques Populaires et Caisses d'Epargne
BRRD	Bank Recovery and Resolution Directive
CACIB	Crédit Agricole Corporate and Investment Bank
CEBS	Committee of European Banking Supervisors
CEECs	Central and Eastern European countries
CME	Coordinated Market Economy
CMU	Capital Markets Union
CRD	Capital Requirements Directive
CRR	Capital Requirements Regulation
DGS	Deposit Guarantee Scheme
EBA	European Banking Authority
ECB	European Central Bank
ECOFIN	Economic and Financial Affairs Council
EDIRA	European Deposit Insurance and Resolution Authority
EDIS	European Deposit Insurance Scheme
EDP	Excessive Deficit Procedure
EFC	Economic and Financial Committee
EFSF	European Financial Stability Facility
EFSM	European Financial Stabilisation Mechanism
ELA	Emergency Liquidity Assistance
EMF	European Monetary Fund
EMS	European Monetary System

EMU	Economic and Monetary Union
EP	European Parliament
ERM	Exchange Rate Mechanism
ESA	European Supervisory Authority
ESM	European Stability Mechanism
ESRB	European Systemic Risk Board
EU	European Union
EU-27	the 27 EU member states prior to Croatia joining on 1 July 2013
FBF	French Banking Federation
FSA	Financial Services Authority
FSAP	Financial Services Action Plan
FSB	Financial Stability Board
FSCS	Financial Services Compensation Scheme
G20	Group of Twenty
GDP	gross domestic product
HLEG	High-Level Expert Group on Reforming the Structure of the EU Banking Sector
HSBC	Hong Kong and Shanghai Bank of Commerce
IMF	International Monetary Fund
LCR	liquid capital ratio
LLR	Lender of Last Resort
LTRO	Long-Term Refinancing Operation
MEP	Member of the European Parliament
MFI	monetary financial institution
MOU	Memorandum of Understanding
MPS	Monte dei Paschi di Siena
NCA	National Competent Authority
NFC	non-financial company
NSFR	net stable funding ratio
OCA	optimal currency area
OECD	Organisation for Economic Co-operation and Development
OMT	Outright Monetary Transactions
QMV	Qualified Majority Voting
RBS	Royal Bank of Scotland
SGP	Stability and Growth Pact
SMEs	small and medium-sized enterprises

SMP	Single Market Programme
SRB	Single Resolution Board
SRF	Single Resolution Fund
SRM	Single Resolution Mechanism
SSB	Single Supervisory Board
SSM	Single Supervisory Mechanism
TARGET	Trans-European Automated Real-Time Gross Settlement Express Transfer System
TEU	Treaty on European Union
TFEU	Treaty on the Functioning of the European Union
UK	United Kingdom
US	United States

1

Introduction

In June 2012, EU heads of state and government agreed upon the need to create a 'genuine' EMU as called for by the four presidents (European Council 2012a).[1] This involved the construction of an 'integrated financial framework' which was later labelled 'Banking Union' and was to be based on four components: a single framework for banking supervision; a single framework for the managed resolution of banks; a common DGS; and a common backstop for temporary financial support (Council 2012; see also Van Rompuy 2012a, b). This backstop is related to the function of Lender of Last Resort (LLR) even though LLR was never officially presented as a component of Banking Union. Finally, there was the Single Rulebook in banking, which was a main underlying element of Banking Union, even though it applied to all EU member states.

From June 2012, three of the components of Banking Union were discussed and adopted. The regulation for the establishment of a Single Supervisory Mechanism (SSM) was adopted in October 2013, followed by the Bank Recovery and Resolution Directive (BRRD) in June 2014, and the regulation on the Single Resolution Mechanism (SRM) in July 2014. New requirements for national Deposit Guarantee Schemes (DGSs) were finalized in June 2014. In November 2015, the Commission launched a proposed regulation for the creation of a European Deposit Insurance Scheme (EDIS). The European Stability Mechanism (ESM)—which was established by an intergovernmental treaty finalized in 2012 to replace the temporary European Financial Stability Facility (EFSF)—began operation in September 2012. In June 2012, the euro area member states envisaged that, subject to certain conditions, the ESM could provide financial support to ailing banks as well as to the governments of countries experiencing severe financial difficulties (Euro Area Summit 2012). The adoption of EU capital requirements legislation in April 2013

[1] The four presidents were the presidents of: the European Council, Herman Van Rompuy; the European Commission, Jose Manuel Borroso; the European Central Bank, Mario Draghi; and the Eurogroup (the ministers of finance of the euro area member states), Jean-Claude Juncker.

reinforced the Single Rulebook—although considerable national discretion and many lacunae remained.

The proposal for Banking Union amounted to a radical initiative to rebuild financial market confidence in both banks and sovereigns—especially in the euro area periphery—to stabilize the national banking systems exposed directly to a vicious circle between the international financial crisis and the euro area's sovereign debt crisis, and to reverse the fragmentation of European financial markets. Banking Union was also to bring about a significant transfer of powers from the national to the EU (to be precise, the Banking Union) level.[2] The decision to create Banking Union represented a major development in European economic governance and European integration history more generally. At the same time, the form of Banking Union eventually agreed amounted to a considerable dilution of the vision presented in the so-called 'four EU presidents report', 'Towards a Genuine Economic and Monetary Union', of December 2012 (Van Rompuy 2012b).

Banking Union was also significant because not all EU member states joined: as of June 2016 it included only countries participating in the euro area even if other EU member states were able to opt in. Hence, Banking Union increased the trend towards differentiated integration in the EU (Dyson and Sepos 2010; Schimmelfennig 2016), which in itself posed a major challenge to the EU as a whole and to the opt-out countries—first and foremost the United Kingdom (UK), given the size of its financial sector and its interconnection with the euro area.

This book is informed by two main questions. First, what was the rationale behind the move to Banking Union in 2012? Second, why was a certain design for Banking Union agreed?

The Argument

A two-step explanation is articulated in this book. We first explain the economic rationale of Banking Union by building on the concept of the financial trilemma, and examining the implications of EMU for both euro area member states and non-euro area countries. The book takes as a starting point Dirk Schoenmaker's 'financial trilemma' (2013), which examines the interplay of financial stability, international banking, and national financial policies, arguing that any two of the three objectives can be combined—given the rise of globally systemic important banks—but not all three: one has to give. For Schoenmaker, the international financial crisis of 2008–9 provided

[2] For a range of articles on the creation of supranational banking supervision, see the special issue of *West European Politics* (2016), guest edited by David Howarth and Huw Macartney.

clear evidence of the trilemma. We argue that in the EU, the trilemma was made particularly acute for those member states which adopted the single currency. On the one hand, EMU reinforced financial (banking) integration in the euro area. On the other hand, monetary union undermined national financial policies because the function of LLR could no longer be performed at the national level. Moreover, national resolution powers were constrained by euro area fiscal rules.

Consequently, for euro area member states that sought to maintain the currency union, the safeguard of financial stability could best be achieved at the supranational level—as demonstrated by the sovereign debt crisis. Euro area member states agreed (in some cases with great reluctance) to move to Banking Union, which was to replace the third element of Schoenmaker's trilemma, namely 'national financial policies', principally regulation, supervision, and resolution. The UK was positioned differently with reference to the trilemma because the UK did not participate in monetary union; thus, British policy-makers had less reason to seek participation in Banking Union.

Central and Eastern European member states of the EU that were not part of the euro area faced competing rationales. On the one hand, their banking systems were dominated by foreign-(principally euro area) headquartered banks—albeit with significant variation across countries, ranging from just over 50 per cent to almost 100 per cent of total bank assets and retail market share (Spendzharova 2014). These member states thus had an incentive to join Banking Union because they were less able to safeguard financial stability domestically. On the other hand, the high level of foreign bank penetration gave policy-makers in these countries an incentive to promote the development of domestic banks (a form of 'banking nationalism'), which could be better achieved by retaining national control over banking supervision and remaining outside Banking Union (Mero and Piroska 2016; Spendzharova 2014).

Second, we seek to explain the design of Banking Union through an examination of national policy-maker preferences on the core Banking Union components. Indeed, the countries that faced the trilemma in its most acute form because they were euro area members had different preferences on the various elements of Banking Union. We develop a comparative political economy analysis to understand the preferences of national policy-makers in key member states as stemming principally from the configuration of the national banking system. We also examine the concerns of policy-makers in certain member states regarding the moral hazard for banks and sovereigns potentially created by the different elements of Banking Union. This two-part political economy analysis is necessary in order to understand the position of national policy-makers on the allocation of direct supervisory powers in Banking Union (to the European Central Bank [ECB] or

National Competent Authorities [NCAs]), the allocation of resolution powers and deposit protection (Banking Union or national level), and the provision of financial assistance to governments and ailing banks (source, limits, and conditions).

The configuration of national banking systems—and, in particular, the internationalization of the activities of banks headquartered in the six member states (including the 'domestic reach of internationalization'), foreign penetration, as well as systemic patterns in banking activities—shaped the preferences of national policy-makers on the SSM, the SRM, and the common DGS. Those countries in which the reach of internationalization into the national banking sector was relatively limited were keen to exclude purely domestic banks (generally, smaller 'alternative'—that is, public, savings and cooperative—banks) from the scope of the SSM and SRM. They also opposed a common DGS. We also argue that there is a direct link between the national banking system and moral hazard concerns. The preoccupation of national policy-makers with moral hazard derived in large part from the 'manageability' for governments of real and potential bank losses—i.e., the 'manageability' of the sovereign–bank nexus. Moral hazard was of greater concern for policy-makers in countries that were less likely to need financial support in Banking Union because their banking system was in sufficiently rude health and/or because these governments had a sufficiently strong fiscal position that would enable them to withstand real and potential bank losses. Moral hazard was less of a concern for policy-makers in countries that would likely need to access external financial support in Banking Union because their banking system was in poorer health and/or their domestic fiscal position was weaker. Policy-makers in countries concerned about moral hazard—notably Germany—sought to establish clear limits to their financial assistance to ailing banks and governments in countries hit by the sovereign debt crisis. These concerns help to account for the limited scope of the SRM agreed, the delay to an agreement on a common DGS, the limited amount of ESM funds made available, and the strict conditionality attached to their use.

Finally, the asymmetric distribution of bargaining power during the Banking Union negotiations, which were skewed in favour of Germany, accounts for the prioritization of certain components of Banking Union rather than others. Germany was a 'constrained veto player' (Bulmer and Paterson 2013): agreement to do nothing on supervision, fiscal support, and resolution was not a possibility. This inability to accept the status quo gave other euro area member states a degree of influence over the design of the SSM, the SRM, and the ESM. As of July 2016, it remained to be seen if the German government could resist the pressure of a number of member states, the European Commission and the European Central Bank on the creation of the EDIS. The assumption of asymmetrical influence results in our decision to examine the preferences of policy-makers in the five euro area member states (France, Germany, Italy, the Netherlands, and Spain) with the largest economies and banking systems, plus the UK. Whereas Germany was reluctant to accept Banking Union, France, Italy, and Spain were strongly in favour, with the Netherlands keen on supervision but cautious on funding mechanisms. The UK is included as the main non-euro area country with a large financial sector outside Banking Union—as Begg (2012) puts it, the UK was 'the elephant in the room'. The preferences of British policy-makers were less relevant to the design of Banking Union; however, British preferences were reflected in support for but aloofness from the SSM, the SRM, and the use of ESM funds.

Our political economy analysis of Banking Union thus has, as a secondary focus, the intergovernmental and inter-institutional bargaining on the different components. Ours is not an analysis of EU policy-making per se. Rather, we focus on explaining the preferences of policy-makers (notably governments) of the five euro area member states with the largest economies and banking systems. Our specific focus on the preferences of German policy-makers stems from the assumption that the German government had the greatest influence over the final agreement but that it did not have veto power.

The Structure

This book is structured into two parts. The first consists of three chapters that set out the background to Banking Union and the building blocks of the analytical framework. The second part of the book consists of five chapters that apply the analytical framework to examine the main components of Banking Union.

Chapter 2 begins by reviewing the literature on the politics and economics of EMU, asking to what extent the explanations put forward with reference to the establishment and the design of EMU might have explanatory power with regard to the establishment and the design of Banking Union. This chapter then reviews the literature on Banking Union. It elucidates the two-step analytical framework underpinning this study of national preferences: namely, the concept of the trilemma, which explains the functional drive towards Banking Union; and the main features of national banking systems which, together with the concern for moral hazard, account for the preferences of national policy-makers on the Banking Union's main components. These factors combined with an asymmetric distribution of bargaining power, resulting in an asymmetric design of Banking Union.

Chapter 3 examines the causes and consequences of the international financial crisis (2007–9) and the euro area's sovereign debt crisis (from 2010), which set the background to the intergovernmental negotiations on Banking Union, and which largely explain its timing. It is argued that the sovereign debt crisis created a doom loop between the instability of national banking systems, which needed to be bailed out in a number of euro area member states, and the fragility of public finances, which were becoming unsustainable in much of the euro area periphery. The crisis thus brought to the fore the financial trilemma, which was made particularly acute by monetary union.

Chapter 4 discusses the configuration of the EU's six largest banking systems: notably those of Germany, France, the Netherlands, Italy, Spain, and the UK. The key features of national banking systems that explain national preferences on Banking Union and its specific elements are outlined. These key features include the degree and form of the internationalization of the activities of nationally based banks and foreign bank penetration. The 'manageability' of the sovereign–bank nexus—notably explained in terms of the health of national banking systems and the state of public finances—explains varying national preoccupation with moral hazard.

Chapter 5 presents two main arguments regarding national preferences on the establishment of the SSM. First, moral hazard concerns pushed otherwise disinterested governments—notably, the German government—to accept the need for supranational supervision, especially over banks in member states in need (or potentially in need) of financial support for banks. Second, the internationalization of national banking systems explains interest in supranational supervision. Countries in which the 'domestic reach of internationalization' was high—mainly through consolidated and semi-consolidated groups of 'alternative' banks—favoured a low threshold for direct ECB supervision (and the reverse). For EU member states not participating in the euro, the incentive to join the SSM depended on the degree of 'internationalization' and 'Europeanization' of their national banking systems, and also on the level of banking nationalism.

Chapter 6 examines national preferences on the BRRD that applied to all EU member states, and on the SRM, which was the second component of Banking Union. Moral hazard concerns—linked to the 'manageability' of current and possible bank losses—and the degree of internationalization of the national banking system, including the 'domestic reach of internationalization', explain German and Dutch preferences on the BRRD (bail-in followed by bail-out), and reluctance on the SRM and the use of the ESM as a common fiscal backstop for resolution. Spanish and Italian preferences stemmed from limited concern for moral hazard—thus, a reluctance to accept bail-in and an interest in building confidence by mutualizing risk through a large Single Resolution Fund (SRF).

Chapter 7 examines the inconclusive discussions on a common DGS, starting with the revision of the 1994 directive on the harmonization of national DGSs. We argue that the difficult harmonization of national schemes and the failure to agree to create a common DGS were due to different national preferences stemming from two main factors. First, the different configurations of existing national DGSs were linked to the different configurations of national banking systems. Second, German moral hazard concerns stemmed from concerns related to the ex-post design of most euro area national schemes and the fear that well-funded pre-existing German schemes would inevitably be called upon to cover the deposits of foreigners in foreign banks. The Italian and Spanish governments insisted, again, that all member states would benefit from increasing the confidence of financial markets by mutualizing bank risk.

Chapter 8 explores national preferences on the fiscal backstop in Banking Union and the related issue of LLR for both banks and sovereigns. The chapter first analyses the central role performed by the ECB in boosting stability during the international financial and sovereign debt crises—despite EU treaty provisions banning bail-outs for governments. It then examines the creation and design of the temporary EFSF and its permanent successor, the ESM, both established to help tackle the sovereign debt crisis in the euro area. National preferences regarding the operation of the ECB and the establishment of these support mechanisms were shaped by two competing rationales: the desire to prevent the break-up of EMU, and the need to limit moral hazard created through intervention to help sovereigns and banks.

Chapter 9 discusses the 'regulatory' element of Banking Union: namely, the Single Rulebook in banking. It first discusses the main preferences of national policy-makers in the negotiations on the Basel III accord, which set new capital and liquidity rules for internationally active banks. It then examines the transposition of Basel III into the EU's Capital Requirements Directive (CRD IV), arguing that some of the compromises on the definition of capital, the leverage ratio, and liquidity rules reached in the Basel III negotiations were reopened in the EU negotiations because of the application of the rules to all EU banks. The chapter also discusses the recent EU legislation on bank structural reform. Overall, we show that considerable national discretion with regard to the so-called Single Rulebook in banking regulation and supervision remained because of different preferences stemming from the configuration of the national banking system.

The concluding chapter summarizes the main findings of the book, outlines the main challenges ahead for Banking Union (including its potential implications for EU member states that do not participate in the euro area), and puts forward proposals for further research. It also discusses the 'Five Presidents' Report' (2015) entitled *Completing Europe's Economic and Monetary Union* which stated several objectives. One of these was a 'Financial Union' for euro area member states, which was to consist in large part of a problematically labelled Capital Markets Union (CMU) to apply to the entire European Union.

2

Understanding Economic and Monetary Union to Understand Banking Union

This chapter begins by reviewing the literature on the politics and economics of EMU, asking to what extent the explanations put forward regarding the establishment and the design of EMU might have explanatory power with reference to the establishment and the design of Banking Union. It then reviews the literature on Banking Union, which, with some notable exceptions, so far has mainly focused on the economic and legal aspects of the Banking Union's main components. Finally, the chapter elucidates the analytical framework underpinning this study—namely, the concept of the trilemma, which explains the functional drive towards Banking Union; the main features of national banking systems which, together with the concern for moral hazard, account for the different preferences of national policy-makers on the Banking Union's main components; and the asymmetric distribution of bargaining power among member states. The factors provide a convincing explanation of the asymmetric design of Banking Union agreed between 2012 and 2014.

Lessons from the Literature on Economic and Monetary Union

The extensive corpus of scholarly work on the establishment and the design of EMU is reviewed concisely in this section (see also Sadeh and Verdun 2009). Theoretically, the purpose is to tease out the main explanations for EMU put forward by scholars in political science and political economy, asking to what extent these accounts can be applied to explain the establishment and the design of Banking Union. We seek to position the analytical approach adopted in our study in relation to this previous work. Empirically, the aim of this section is to explain how in several ways Banking Union can be seen as the completion of EMU. Controversial issues that were papered over or side-stepped in the negotiations on EMU re-emerged forcefully once the final stage of EMU began in 1999, generating different types of 'asymmetry'.

By and large, the explanations for EMU in political science can be grouped under three main headings: neofunctionalism, constructivism, and intergovernmentalism. Moreover, there are political economy approaches that have investigated EU member state preferences on the main components of EMU—namely, monetary policy, exchange rate policy, and fiscal policy—as well as the 'winners' and 'losers' from EMU. These explanations are considered in turn.

A small number of academic studies adopt neofunctionalism to explain the establishment of EMU (see, e.g., Verdun 2002; Wolf 2002). Neofunctionalism, which is the oldest theory of European integration, dating back to the 1960s, is based on three main tenets. Neofunctionalism predicts an 'ever closer union'—that is, the deepening of political and economic integration in Europe over time. It emphasizes the concept of economic and political 'spillovers' from previous integration and from one policy area to another. Finally, it assumes the shifting of the loyalty of interest groups from the national level to the EU level. In the early 1990s, neofunctionalism was partly subsumed into the 'supranational governance' approach (Sandholtz and Sweet 1998), which was less over-deterministic than neofunctionalism about the final integration outcome, and emphasized the role of supranational actors in pushing integration forward.

The few studies that explain the establishment and design of EMU from a neofunctionalist perspective mainly argue that EMU was the result of spillover from previous integration, first and foremost the Single Market and European monetary integration. For these studies, the turning point was the establishment of the European Monetary System (EMS), specifically the Exchange Rate Mechanism (ERM) that set in place a system of semi-fixed exchange rates among the participating countries.[1] Furthermore, the studies that adopt a supranational governance approach to the establishment of EMU (Sandholtz and Sweet 1998) point out the strategic role of the Commission in driving the project forward (see also Jabko 1999).

Economic spillover was itself the core element of the official European Commission justification for EMU. The Commission and a number of federalist-minded economists insisted that the gains of the Single Market could not be optimized without a single currency—notably, in the influential publication *One Market, One Money* (European Commission 1990; see also Emerson, Gros, and Italianer 1992). Following similar reasoning, some federalist-leading

[1] The literature on the EMS is extensive: see Buiter, Corsetti, and Pesenti (1998), De Grauwe and L. Papademos (1990), Fratianni and Von Hagen (1992), Giavazzi and Giovannini (1989), Giavazzi, Micossi, and Miller (1989), and Gros and Thygesen (1998).

economists, building on the Mundell–Fleming 'unholy trinity' of fixed exchange rates, full capital mobility, and national monetary policies, added the Single Market to the trinity, which then became an 'inconsistent quartet' in the EU (Padoa-Schioppa 1982). Like the Commission, a number of economists also stressed the instability of the ERM of the EMS (Eichengreen et al. 1993)—especially given currency speculation—and the functional need to move from the ERM's semi-fixed exchange rate to EMU.

A number of academic studies forward an ideational or constructivist approach to understanding the establishment and the design of EMU. There are several variations of constructivism, but what they all have in common is the explanatory power assigned to ideas or 'policy paradigms' (Hall 1993), defined as a set of causal beliefs concerning a certain policy area, rather than material (mostly economic) interests. Constructivist accounts generally emphasize the importance of socialization in international or EU fora as a way to facilitate ideational convergence. Some authors (e.g., Schmidt and Radaelli 2004) point out the role that 'ideational entrepreneurs' play in paradigm change and in diffusing new ideas. Others investigate the presence and activity of 'epistemic communities', defined as a set of actors sharing the same 'episteme' or world view (Haas 1992).

Some ideational approaches to the establishment and design of EMU focus on the role of central bankers as an epistemic community supporting a stability-oriented design for EMU, based on central bank independence and anti-inflationary goals (Marcussen 2000; Verdun 1999). Other works consider a broader set of actors, not only central bankers, in the ideational convergence towards EMU. McNamara (1998, 1999) traces the 'currency of ideas'—that is, the spread of the stability-oriented macroeconomic paradigm from Germany to other member states (see also Quaglia 2004). McNamara argues that this ideational convergence among macroeconomic elites across the EU explains why it was possible to reach an agreement on EMU as well as the specific 'sound money' and 'sound public finance' (Dyson 1994) design chosen for EMU. The stability-oriented design agreed for EMU in the Maastricht Treaty (Treaty on European Union [TEU]) of 1992 was remarkable, if compared to previous blueprints for EMU put forward in the Werner report (1970) or the MacDougall report (1977), which had a strong Keynesian imprint.[2]

The majority of scholars have adopted implicitly or explicitly an intergovernmentalist approach in order to explain the establishment and the design of EMU (see, e.g., Moravcsik 1998; Sadeh 2009). There are various versions of intergovernmentalism; their common denominator is the focus on national interests and the decision-making power of national governments negotiating

[2] Furthermore, some authors also consider identity, especially a Europeanized identity among the elite, as a factor in promoting or hindering EMU support in the member states (Risse et al. 1999).

in intergovernmental fora. Intergovernmental accounts of EMU investigate the (often competing) interests of the member states that had to be reconciled in EU negotiations, which often resulted in convoluted compromises. Intergovernmentalist accounts also consider the different bargaining power of the member states, and generally focus on the main member states.

The basic intergovernmentalist argument for the establishment of EMU mostly builds on economic analyses of the functioning of the EMS. In the ERM, the German currency (the Deutsche mark) was the 'anchor' of the system and the German central bank (the Bundesbank) could freely set its monetary policy objectives. The other participating countries had to 'adjust' their monetary policy by following Bundesbank policy decisions (Bini Smaghi 1992; Bini Smaghi and Micossi 1990). The main line of division in the ERM was between strong and weak currency countries.

'Weak currency' countries, such as Italy and France, were countries that tended to have higher inflation—with rates significantly above those in Germany—and normally ran balance of payments deficits which undermined the value of their currency. 'Strong currency' countries, first and foremost Germany, maintained low inflation and considerable surpluses in their balance of payments; hence, their currencies had a tendency to appreciate. According to intergovernmentalist explanations, the establishment of EMU was a way for 'follower countries' (notably, France and Italy) to end the German dominance of the ERM. The macroeconomic logic for these 'weak currency' countries was to escape having to follow the monetary policy of the leading 'strong currency' country in the ERM, namely Germany. In EMU, they would gain a say in the making of a single monetary policy and a seat at the ECB (Howarth 2001; Moravcsik 1998).

German policy-makers, especially top central bankers in the Bundesbank, were reluctant to agree to EMU because the enterprise was fraught with risks (Kaltenthaler 1998, 2002). The German mark was the anchor currency of the ERM; thus only the Bundesbank had full policy-making autonomy in pursuing its low inflation goal. Moreover, in the late 1980s and early 1990s, the majority of German public opinion was opposed to EMU, given the stability of the Deutsche mark and the comparative strength of the German economy. However, large German exporters supported EMU. The move to a single currency could give them a competitive advantage thanks to comparatively low German inflation, which would lower the cost of German products in relation to French and Italian products (Hefeker 1998).

The German political elite agreed to EMU, mainly for political (rather than economic) reasons. However, they imposed most of the EMU design, centred on an independent central bank located in Frankfurt and stability-oriented macroeconomic policies (Heisenberg 1999; Kalthenthaler 1998, 2002; Loedel

1999). The issue of moral hazard (the concept is explained later in this chapter) was very important in the design of EMU: the main concern of stability-oriented countries was to avoid establishing a system that would create perverse incentives to increase the risk-taking behaviour of member states—notably, should a bail-out mechanism be included. In order to reduce moral hazard in EMU, German negotiators insisted upon inserting a 'no bail-out' clause and a 'no monetary financing' clause in the TEU (Dyson and Featherstone 1999; Heipertz and Verdun 2012). They opposed any step towards fiscal federalism or 'transfer union', fearing that Germany would end up becoming the main contributor, as it always had been in total net terms to the EU budget. German policy-makers also successfully demanded convergence criteria that countries had to fulfil in order to be able to join EMU and then, in 1994, proposed the Stability and Growth Pact (SGP), designed to avoid excessively loose fiscal policies in EMU (Heipertz and Verdun 2010).

The EMU design established by the Maastricht Treaty was asymmetric, whereby full monetary union was not accompanied by full economic union (Dyson 2000; Verdun 1996). Several (mainly US) economists were critical of this design for EMU (Feldstein 1997), arguing that the euro area was not an optimal currency area (OCA) (Mckinnon 1963; Mundell 1961): it lacked adequate adjustment tools to cope with asymmetric shocks and therefore it was unwise to give up the exchange rate as an instrument of adjustment (see also Sadeh 2006). At the same time, the ECB would be unable to run a 'one size fits all' monetary policy suitable for all euro area countries (De Grauwe 2012; Howarth and Loedel 2005). In order to cope with these shortcomings, fiscal transfers or automatic stabilizers were needed (De Grauwe 2012; Eichengreen 1997; Obstfeld and Peri 1999), but they had deliberately been left out of EMU because of German opposition (Dyson and Featherstone 1999).

By combining intergovernmentalism and domestic politics in a two-level game (Putnam 1988), Dyson and Featherstone (1999) explain how German public opinion and macroeconomic elites (first and foremost in the Bundesbank) constrained the 'win set' of German policy-makers negotiating at the EU level. This limited 'win set' and the German government's strong bargaining power made Germany the pivotal country in the agreement on and design of EMU. The two-level game was at play, albeit in a different guise, for other countries. In Italy, the 'technocrats' at the Bank of Italy and Treasury supported their country's membership of the EMS first and EMU later as external constraints on domestic macroeconomic policies (Dyson and Featherstone 1996, 1999). In the late 1980s, some Italian economists pointed out the benefits of tying one's hands through exchange rate policy by de facto following the monetary policy of Germany, and borrowing 'credibility' and 'reputation' from the Bundesbank (Giavazzi and Pagano 1988). A similar reasoning would also apply to other weak currency countries, such as Spain, and countries with a heavy debt load, including Belgium.

For French policy-makers, EMU was the coronation of the 'franc fort' policy and the drive to improve the competitiveness of the French economy by driving down inflation—the policy of so-called competitive disinflation (Fitoussi 1993; Howarth 2001). Yet, in comparison with the Germans, French policy-makers had different preferences as to the design of EMU, as demonstrated by their frequent calls for 'gouvernement économique' (Howarth 2001, 2007) and their hope of reflationary stimulus in EMU, which was rebuffed by Germany. In the ERM, several follower member states, first and foremost France and Italy, complained about the deflationary tendencies of this mechanism of semi-fixed exchange rates and the lack of an engine of growth in the European Community, which worsened macroeconomic imbalances (Vona and Bini Smaghi 1988).

In the case of the UK, the economic and political rationale to support the move from the ERM to EMU was less powerful. From the mid-1980s, the Conservative government maintained a steady exchange rate with the Deutsche mark in order to bring down domestic inflation and saw ERM membership (from 1990) in similar terms. However, unlike Southern European governments, the British did not see EMU as a crucial external constraint upon macroeconomic policy. Most importantly, the political elite and public opinion opposed the idea of a single currency, which was widely seen as an unacceptable step towards a federal Europe (Thompson 1996). Economic elites, first and foremost in the financial sector, were better disposed towards EMU (Eglene 2011; Talani 2000), but this was insufficient to overcome the political obstacles to it.

A handful of authors have investigated the domestic political economy of EMU in the main member states (Eglene 2011; Eichengreen and Frieden 1994; Frieden 1996; Hefeker 1998; Talani 2000; Walsh 1994, 2000), teasing out the main 'winners' and 'losers' from EMU among national economic and socio-economic interests, and hence the main supporters and opponents of the project. By focusing on the preferences of domestic interest groups regarding the main components of EMU (monetary policy, fiscal policy and exchange rate policy), these authors uncovered the social bases underpinning (or in certain cases, undermining) EMU, complementing the elite-focused account of the intergovernmentalist approaches summarized above.

One of the most influential of these political economy studies (Frieden 1996) argued that the economic sectors exposed to international competition (mainly manufacturing and internationally tradable services, including finance) were those that suffered most because of, and that were 'disciplined' by, the (semi-fixed) exchange rate and 'hard currency' policy of the

EMS. Firms in these sectors were most likely to support the move to full EMU and the stability-oriented macroeconomic policies enshrined in the project, including the external constraint on national fiscal policy, which was wielded mainly to the benefit of those sectors not exposed to international competition (notably, certain domestic services and the public economic sector).

Overall, from the literature on EMU, it is possible to tease out at least three main explanations for Banking Union. A neofunctionalist argument, combined with supranational governance, would be that Banking Union was a spillover from the incomplete EMU, and supranational institutions—notably the Commission and the ECB—performed a crucial role in promoting Banking Union (see, e.g., Epstein and Rhodes 2016; Ioannou, Leblond, and Niemann 2015; Schimmelfennig 2016; Verdun 2015). A constructivist or ideational analysis would examine the policy paradigm underpinning Banking Union, arguing that the Banking Union was the result of shared (or converging) ideas about how to deal with the sovereign debt crisis. An ideas-focused analysis could also seek to gauge whether an epistemic community or ideational entrepreneurs were at work. An intergovernmentalist analysis would focus on the converging, or at least compatible, preferences of the main member states, also investigating the domestic national politics and political economies shaping those preferences (see Howarth and Quaglia 2015a; Schild 2015; Schimmelfennig 2015; and, for a 'neo-realist' take on Banking Union, see Donnelly 2014).

The approach we adopt in this study recognizes some 'functionalist' pressure in the form of spillovers from EMU—the 'financial trilemma' (which is discussed in the following section) was made more acute in the euro area by the introduction of the single currency. Our study also explores the role of important supranational actors—namely the Commission, the ECB, and the main transnational banks—in the construction of Banking Union. The bulk of our analysis, however, takes an intergovernmentalist approach, examining the preferences of the main member states and investigating the domestic political economy of Banking Union. In so doing, our analysis aligns well with and builds upon the political economy work on 'winners' and 'losers' from EMU (see Frieden 1994; Hefeker 1998; Walsh 2000). Here the focus is specifically on the 'winners' and 'losers' in the banking sector; hence, our analysis is narrower than the full-scale investigation of the domestic political economy of EMU undertaken by the above-mentioned authors. However, the scope of Banking Union—which first and foremost concerns the banking sector—is also narrower than that of EMU. Moreover, our analysis of national preference formation includes 'redistribution' considerations, principally in the context of moral hazard, but also with reference to different banking groups.

Lessons from the Emerging Literature on the Establishment and Design of Banking Union

Unlike the well-established literature on EMU, the literature on Banking Union is in its infancy. So far, it has mainly been developed by economists (e.g., Allen, Carletti, and Gray 2013; Beck 2012) and lawyers (Boccuzzi 2015; Busch and Ferrarini 2015), who have tended to focus on the specific components of Banking Union, namely the SSM the Single Resolution Mechanism (SRM), the CDGS, the ESM, and the LLR in the euro area. This builds on earlier work focused upon cooperation and coordination in the EU on banking supervision, support, and resolution (see, e.g., Dragomir 2010; Kremers, Schoenmaker, and Wierts 2003; Masciandaro, Nieto, and Quintyn 2009).

The SSM, which was the first element of Banking Union to be agreed, has been the subject of extensive legal analysis (see, e.g., Alexander 2015; Ferran and Babis 2013; Wymeersch 2014), which has examined the SSM structure and powers (see also Véron 2012). Several economists have pointed to the need to transfer banking supervision to the euro area level (see, e.g., Masciandaro and Nieto 2014; Sibert 2012; Valiante 2014; Véron 2012). Gros (2012b) calls for the establishment of the SSM, stressing the tendency of national banking supervisors to 'ring fence' the banks they supervised by encouraging national banks to reduce their cross-border exposure. At the same time, national supervisors also encouraged the transformation of foreign branches into (fully capitalized) subsidiaries. These supervisory actions increased the Balkanization of the euro area's financial markets, worsening the international financial and then sovereign debt crises (Gros 2012b).

Similarly, the need for 'European solutions' to problems arising in cross-border banks is stressed by Allen et al. (2011), who examine the different channels through which the sovereign debt crisis put pressure on banks' balance sheets. These authors explain how the growth of cross-border banking in the EU posed significant challenges to financial stability. In their words, the EU faced a 'fundamental choice'. It could 'either continue on the path of cross-border banking based on the Single Market, or retreat to national banking with 27 segmented banking markets in the EU' (p. 91). A similar point was made by the chairman of the Financial Services Authority (FSA), Lord Turner, who in a well-known FSA report issued in the wake of the international financial crisis, argued that either 'more Europe' or 'less Europe' was needed (FSA 2009).

To date, not much has been written with reference to the SRM and the CDGS, which has not yet been agreed. Some authors, such as Gros and Schoenmaker (2012, 2014), call for the creation of a European deposit insurance and resolution fund in order to break the 'diabolical loop' in the euro area (Pisani-Ferry [2012] writes of the 'vicious loop'). In this loop, weak domestic banking systems damaged sovereign fiscal positions, and weak sovereign positions threatened domestic banking stability. Since banks generally held a large number of government bonds, the sovereign debt crisis weakened the capital position of banks, increasing their funding costs on the market, while the 'fragility of the banks undermined the borrowing status of the sovereign that [had] to stand behind them' (Begg 2012: 15). Overall, while economists mostly point out the need to complement the supranationalization of banking supervision with the supranationalization of resolution (Carmassi and Herring 2013; Véron and Wolff 2013), legal analyses of the SRM (see, e.g., Alexander 2015; Zavvos and Kaltsouni 2015) are mainly critical of the complexity of the decision-making process of the SRM and the financial capacity of the SRF (for a different view, see Huertas and Nieto 2014).

The ESM has mainly been analysed from a legal perspective (Adam and Parras 2013; De Witte 2011, 2012; De Witte and Beukers 2013) given its rather unusual legal set-up, which is discussed in Chapter 8. Several legal scholars discuss the case brought before the European Court of Justice, which was asked to rule on the legal foundations of the ESM.[3] Moreover, analysis of the ESM can be linked to analysis of the LLR in the euro area, because the mechanism was established to provide financial support to sovereigns and, potentially, banks.

In approaching the start of the final stage of EMU in 1999, there was an intense debate as to whether the ECB would be able and willing to act as LLR in case of crisis (Begg et al. 1998; Buiter 1999; Dyson 2000; Goodhart and Eric 2000; and on the operation of LLR in general, see Goodhart 1995, 1999). The main assumption at that time was that the ECB might need to act as LLR to the banking sector, which is what the ECB in fact did during the international financial (banking) crisis of 2007–9. When that crisis was followed by the sovereign debt crisis, the discussion on the LLR in the euro area regained momentum, albeit with a different take.

Several authors—for example, Buiter and Rahbari (2012a, 2012b), De Grauwe (2012), and Wyplosz (2012)—call for a LLR in the euro area, not only for the banking sector but also for sovereigns, whereby the LLR should stand ready to buy the government bonds of euro area countries hit by the crisis. Arguably, an important step in this direction was the pledge of the ECB President to do 'whatever it takes to save the euro' by announcing the Outright Monetary Transaction programme in the summer of 2012. This decision was also subject to a legal dispute (and extensive legal commentary: see, e.g., the special

[3] See, for example, *German Law Journal* (2013), Special Issue, the ESM before the Courts, 14 (1).

issue of the *German Law Journal* 2014) brought by some German economists and policy-makers before the German constitutional court, which subsequently interrogated the European Court of Justice on certain legal aspects of the case.

Finally, as in the previous literature on EMU, there were 'trinities' in Banking Union. In his seminal work, Schoenmaker points out the 'financial trilemma' (2011, 2013) in international finance—namely, the interplay of financial stability, international banking, and national financial policies. He argues that any two of the three objectives can be combined—given the rise of globally systemically important cross-border banks—but not all three: one has to give. Schoenmaker focuses upon global bank governance, but he dedicates a few paragraphs in his conclusion to the design of European Banking Union as a regional example of supranational banking governance.

Pisani-Ferry (2012) highlights the 'impossible trinity' within EMU—that is, three features that could not all simultaneously hold. First, there was the prohibition on direct monetary financing of the debts of member states, which prevented the ECB's direct purchases of sovereign debt. Second, there was no collective responsibility for public debt or common borrowing capacity, which exposed member states in fiscal difficulty to considerable market pressure (and market volatility). Third, the interdependence between sovereigns and banks in each member state resulted in the 'vicious loop' noted above (see also Gros 2012b). Just as Monetary Union offered a solution to the original Mundell 'unholy trinity', Banking Union could provide the solution to both the Pisani-Ferry 'impossible trinity' and Schoenmaker's 'financial trilemma'.

Some elements of Banking Union directly involve the 'allocation of costs of significant magnitude' and thus have distributional implications (Elliott 2012: 2). A handful of academic studies explore these implications and their political dynamics underpinning Banking Union. Underhill (2012: 139) argues that the main battle lines on Banking Union are between creditor and debtor member states in the euro area and that the implementation of Banking Union is 'a proxy for conflicts over resource transfer'. As in the debate over the operation of the ERM, creditor countries are countries that have a sustained surplus in their balance of payments and a positive net external position. Debtor countries are countries that run persistent deficits in their balance of payments and have a net external debt (Dyson 2010, 2014). The two groups of countries articulate different narratives of the cause of and solutions to the sovereign debt crisis. Particularly controversial are the issues of how the burden of adjustment should be borne among participating member states and how costs deriving from Banking Union should be shared, which in turn raises concerns about the risk of moral hazard, as elaborated below (see 'The Analytical Framework of the Book' below).

Overall, the literature on Banking Union is mainly focused on economic and legal analyses of specific components. With the exception of the handful of works reviewed earlier in the chapter, the literature is largely devoid of important political and political economy considerations. Three main points can be teased out of the existing literature on Banking Union, and these are further explored in our study. The first point is the functionalist pressure for the establishment of Banking Union, in that the Banking Union was intended by its proponents to be a solution to the 'vicious loop' and the 'impossible trinity' in the euro area. The second point concerns the different (often competing) interests of the member states, which help to explain why the solutions adopted were often sub-optimal from an economic point of view. In several cases (e.g., the ESM and the SRF) they were also sub-optimal from a legal point of view, meaning that the legal instruments used were somewhat atypical in the EU legal order and were therefore criticized by lawyers. The third point is the division between the member states directly hit by the doom loop created by the sovereign debt crisis (and which therefore were in great need of confidence-boosting measures), and the member states with relatively stable public finances and banking sectors (and which therefore were more reluctant to accept the potential costs associated with support and resolution mechanisms). These groups of countries had different bargaining powers, which account for the design of Banking Union that was eventually adopted.

The Analytical Framework of the Book

Building on the literature on EMU and Banking Union, our study is driven by a two-step explanation. First, we explain the functional drive towards Banking Union by using the concept of the 'financial trilemma'. We then explain the design of Banking Union by elucidating the preferences of national policy-makers on its main components through a political economy analysis of the configuration of national banking systems and moral hazard concerns.

The first step of our explanation builds on and develops further Schoenmaker's 'financial trilemma' (2011, 2013) in international banking—namely, the interplay of financial stability, international banking, and national financial policies. We argue that in the EU—to be precise, in EMU—the single currency made the 'financial trilemma' particularly acute. On the one hand, the single currency reinforced financial (banking) integration in the euro area. On the other, the single currency undermined national financial policies because the function of LLR could no longer be performed at the national level. Moreover, national resolution powers were constrained by fiscal rules in the euro area.

Consequently, the safeguard of financial stability was outside the control of the national authorities and could only be achieved at the euro area level. For these reasons, euro area member states agreed (in some cases with great reluctance) to move to Banking Union. The interrelated international financial crisis that erupted in 2007 and then the euro area sovereign debt crisis that broke out in 2010 highlighted the difficulties arising from the sharpening of the 'financial trilemma' within EMU, as argued in Chapter 4. The sovereign debt crisis was also necessary to overcome the entrenched opposition in a range of euro area member states reluctant to transfer prudential supervision and resolution from the national to the supranational level. Prior to 2012, home-country control dominated, and financial support for failing banks came almost entirely from national fiscal authorities—proving Mervyn King's adage that banks were 'international in life but national in death' (*Financial Times*, 30 March 2009). The collapse or threatened collapse of a range of cross-border European banks in the context of the two crises and the threat to other banking systems reinforced the logic of moving beyond bilateral or ad hoc arrangements. The sovereign debt–bank loop in the euro area periphery countries further undermined their ability to rescue or resolve failing banks.

For these reasons, euro area member state governments decided to explore the move to Banking Union and, more specifically, to create the SSM and the SRM. Banking Union was to replace the third element of Schoenmaker's trilemma, namely national financial policies. National financial policies include regulation, which, even prior to Banking Union, was largely set at the EU level; supervision, which for large systemically important banks was to be performed by the SSM in Banking Union; and resolution, which was to be performed by the SRM in Banking Union, accompanied by the use of the ESM as a common fiscal backstop and the creation of a CDGS.

While Schoenmaker presents an economic analysis to explain the existence of the trilemma, our book examines national preference formation with regard to Banking Union by focusing on national banking systems. In the context of our analysis, the presence of large banks with a significant cross-border presence and, more generally, banking system internationalization increased the interest of national policy-makers in Banking Union. Exposure to other euro area member states, and notably those on the periphery, reinforced national policy-makers' awareness of and sensitivity to the problems created by cross-border banking involving unstable or potentially unstable banking systems and economies. The fragmentation of the EU financial markets—specifically, the rapid drop in cross-border banking in the EU—in the context of the financial and sovereign debt crises undermined financial stability in all member states, and in particular in the EU/euro area periphery. Clearly, this fragmentation also ran contrary to market integration expectations.

Our understanding of pertinent internationalization is thus the 'EU internationalization' of national banking systems. In the EU (and especially the euro area) context, the logic of the 'financial trilemma' encouraged support for supranational supervision at the EU level rather than globally—the focus of Schoenmaker's work. We focus on both EU and euro area exposure because, as confirmed in interviews, euro area countries sought the participation of *all* EU member states in Banking Union both because of Single Market concerns and because of the high level of cross-border banking throughout the EU—and not just among euro area member states.

The second step of our analysis explains the preferences of national policy-makers on the main components of Banking Union by building on and developing further the political economy literature on the configuration of national banking systems and moral hazard. Recent work analyses the significant changes to national banking systems over the past two decades.[4] Hardie and Howarth (2013; see also Hardie et al. 2013) develop the concept of 'market-based banking' by focusing on banks' business models, highlighting the fact that over the last decade large European banks have funded themselves, to varying degrees, in the wholesale market (market-based liabilities), and have invested, to varying degrees, in non-traditional banking activities (market-based assets). The contributors to Hardie and Howarth's edited volume (2013; see also Quaglia and Royo 2015) use this approach in order to explain the playing out of the international financial crisis and the sovereign debt crisis across a variety of countries. Other authors (e.g., Epstein 2014; Spendzharova 2014) examine how the configuration of national financial systems shaped national preferences on EU post-crisis financial reforms.

In order to explain the preferences of national policy-makers on Banking Union, the main feature of national banking systems that we consider is the degree and form of internationalization. We develop Schoenmaker's understanding of cross-border banking, which he uses to explain the contribution to international financial instability that large cross-border banks can make. However, Schoenmaker's econometric analysis and his focus upon very large, globally important cross-border banks provides only a limited picture of internationalization that fails to provide an effective guide to the preferences of national policy-makers on the details of Banking Union, which would have a direct impact upon all euro area headquartered banks, including the smallest. In Chapter 3 we develop the concept of 'domestic reach of internationalization' to account for some specific national preferences on Banking Union components.

The concept of moral hazard is generally applied with reference to banks—the argument being that banks are more likely to engage in riskier activities in

[4] Until recently, the comparative political economy work of reference on national financial systems was John Zysman's *Governments, Markets and Growth: Financial Systems and the Politics of Industrial Change* (1983), which distinguished between credit-based and capital market-based financial systems (see also Allen and Gale 2000; Deeg 1999; Deeg 2010).

the knowledge that they will be bailed out in the context of crisis (Campbell et al. 2009; Mayes 2004; Mayes, Halme, and Liuksila 2001; Pisani-Ferry 2013). However, moral hazard also applies to countries, not only to their banks, in that countries are more likely to run unsustainable fiscal policies if they know that they will be bailed out through external financial support (Eichengreen 2000; Issing 2003; letter to *Financial Times*, 30 November 2011).

In the context of the sovereign debt crisis and euro area financial assistance to ailing countries, there were two forms of moral hazard. First, there was the moral hazard afflicting euro area periphery member states, which for a decade or so took full advantage of low interest rates and capital inflows as a result of EMU, whereby lenders believed that the government bonds of these countries offered a 'risk free rate'. Euro area financial assistance to these countries, unless subject to strict limits and conditionality, could provide an incentive for future reckless fiscal behaviour. Second, there was the moral hazard afflicting the lenders, including banks in the core euro area member states, which in the run-up to the international financial crisis did not factor into their lending behaviour the ability of euro area periphery governments to repay the loans they received. When the international financial crisis broke out in 2008 and was followed by the sovereign debt crisis, German and French banks and other owners of euro area periphery sovereign and corporate debt were bailed out, allowing them to avoid the consequences of their pre-crisis risky behaviour (Lane 2012; *The Economist*, 29 September 2012).

In the context of Banking Union, a potential moral hazard for both sovereigns and banks was created by EU-level support, whereby the main points of contention were the sharing of resolution costs, especially through the establishment of the SRF, the creation of a CDGS, and, ultimately, the provision of a common fiscal backstop, even though a number of academic economists also made recommendations on the design of Banking Union with the explicit aim of reducing the problem of moral hazard (e.g., Valiante 2014). Varying national government concern about moral hazard—greater in the euro area 'core' and marginal in the periphery—mainly depended on the 'manageability' of real and potential bank losses, which in turn depended on the health of national banking systems and the state of public finances.

Indeed, the argument of moral hazard featured prominently in the German debate (Dyson 2013, 2014). Even though the term, as such, was not regularly used by most German policy-makers, Finance Minister Wolfgang Schäuble used it both to justify the transfer of supervisory power over banks receiving aid from the ESM (*New York Times*, 18 November 2011) and to oppose the creation of the CDGS (*Financial Times*, 8 December 2015). More generally, the fear of moral hazard was implicit in talk of fiscal transfers. It is telling that the Bundesbank President, Jens Weidmann, drew a parallel between ECB

President Mario Draghi and Mephisto in Goethe's 'Faust' (*The Economist*, 29 September 2012), although he did not say so explicitly. In Goethe's work, the devil (Mephisto) advises the Emperor to print money to pay for the public debt: 'Such paper, in the place of actual gold, is practical: we know just what we hold... But wise men will, when they have studied it, place infinite trust in what is infinite.'[5]

Although this is not a book on the negotiations on Banking Union as such, this study also considers the bargaining dynamics underpinning these negotiations and links them to political economy factors that determined in large part the bargaining power of euro area member states. Notably, member states had an asymmetric distribution of bargaining power determined by the size of the national economy and banking system, the relative stability of the national banking system, and the state of public finances. Countries that were directly hit by the sovereign debt crisis, or were likely future targets, were in the position of 'demandeurs': they needed Banking Union in order to deal with or avert the crisis and its dire consequences; hence, they had relatively limited bargaining power. Countries that were not directly hit by the sovereign debt crisis and were therefore relatively less exposed to it—first and foremost Germany, which was also, by a significant margin, the largest economy in the EU with the second-largest banking sector after the UK—were better positioned to resist the requests of the 'demandeurs' and impose their design for Banking Union. Hence, there was an asymmetry.

Germany was the pivotal country, the 'win set' (see Putnam 1988) of which determined what was acceptable (or not) in the negotiations on Banking Union. However, Germany had 'constrained veto power' (Bulmer and Paterson 2013) because German banks were heavily exposed (i.e., they had invested substantially) in the EU/euro periphery. Moreover, Germany had a stake in the survival of the euro area, which was at risk of losing members and even falling apart because of the sovereign debt crisis. Indeed, the prospect of euro area collapse was worrisome for all its members, Germany included. Hence, German policy-makers were willing to proceed—albeit with some reluctance—with Banking Union.

Countries were not 'unitary actors' in the negotiations on Banking Union because they often had different (even competing) domestic political economy preferences that had to be reconciled (Moravcsik 1993: 30–1). In other words, different domestic economic interest groups were likely to be affected in different ways by Banking Union; they therefore lobbied domestically as well as at the EU level in order to pursue their preferences. This was particularly the case in Germany, where the national position was pulled in different

[5] Mephistopheles, from Faust Part Two, by Johann Wolfgang von Goethe; cited in the *Financial Times*, 23 September 2012.

directions by the representative associations of each of the three pillars of the German banking system. The big commercial banks wanted Banking Union and wanted it to apply to all banks in Germany and the euro area, while the domestically focused cooperative and savings banks did not want Banking Union to apply to them. Domestic divisions weakened German reluctance to Banking Union, contributing to Germany's negotiating position as a 'constrained veto player'.

Overall, this study makes two main theoretical contributions, which are outlined here and developed further in the empirical chapters. First, it explains why the 'financial trilemma' was particularly acute in the euro area and how it played out in the sovereign debt crisis. Second, this study investigates the political economy of Banking Union in the six EU member states with the largest economies by explaining how the configuration of national financial systems, and varying concerns about moral hazard, influenced national views on the 'financial trilemma' and the preferences of national policy-makers on the main components of Banking Union.

Conclusion

There are clear parallels between the establishment of EMU and Banking Union. EMU was sought by France and weak currency countries to redress the asymmetry of the operation of the ERM and to gain a say in a single monetary policy with a seat at the ECB, rather than having to follow the lead of the German Bundesbank. Similarly, Banking Union was sought by France and euro periphery countries as a way to deal with the banking and sovereign debt crises. French banks were particularly exposed to difficulties in Southern Europe given their large holdings of euro periphery sovereign and corporate debt. With a very large banking sector of its own and a rising public debt burden, the 'manageability' of potential bank losses in France was also a concern. France was a likely subsequent target in the playing out of the crisis.

Germany reluctantly agreed to Banking Union—just as it had reluctantly agreed to EMU—and sought to set in place measures to limit the moral hazard posed by EMU first and Banking Union later. German policy-makers imposed much of the design for Banking Union—and specifically on the SSM, SRM, and limited fiscal backstop—as they had done in the case of the ECB design, the no bail-out rules, and no monetary financing rules in EMU. The result was an asymmetric and incomplete Banking Union, which paralleled the asymmetric and incomplete EMU. Moreover, the issue of how to deal with euro area macroeconomic imbalances, which were worsened with the elimination of the exchange rate as an instrument of adjustment, was left largely unresolved in EMU. In EMU, the former current account imbalances among euro area member states were transformed into imbalances in the Trans-European Automated Real-Time Gross Settlement Express Transfer System (TARGET 2) payments system between national central banks and into imbalances between banking systems, as explained in the following chapters. The concern for these imbalances formed part of the logic underpinning the establishment of the EFSF, the ESM, and the Macroeconomic Imbalance Procedure.

3

The Financial Trilemma and the Vicious Circle of Banking and Sovereign Debt Crises

This chapter examines the two interconnected crises—the international financial crisis (2007–9) and the euro area's sovereign debt crisis (from 2010)—which set the background to the intergovernmental negotiations on Banking Union, and which largely explain its timing. The chapter begins by outlining the framework for financial stability in the EU that existed prior to the international financial crisis. It then reviews the main causes of the crisis that began in late 2007 and reached its peak in the autumn of 2008. The chapter explains the 'differentiated' impact of this crisis across the EU, which mostly had to do with the configuration of national financial systems across Europe. Several governments intervened to rescue their ailing banks, but not all of them had sufficient fiscal margin of manoeuvre to do so. The chapter also discusses the reform of the framework for financial stability in the EU in the aftermath of the international financial crisis.

Next, this chapter outlines the unfolding of the sovereign debt crisis that began in Greece in early 2010, explaining how and why it subsequently extended to much of the rest of the euro area periphery, specifically Ireland, Portugal, and Spain. The crisis hit Italy in the summer of 2011, though the Italian government managed to avoid having to resort to external financial assistance. The chapter then examines the three main immediate economic causes of the euro area's sovereign debt crisis, which were; the need to prop up domestic ailing banks following the international financial crisis, especially in Ireland and later in Spain; a 'domestic' fiscal crisis, especially in Greece, Portugal, and Italy, three countries with persistent pre-crisis fiscal deficit and debt problems; and a balance of payments crisis, which was caused by pre-crisis current account deficits and capital inflows, followed by sudden capital outflows during the crisis in the euro area periphery. The penultimate section of the chapter interprets the sovereign debt crisis as an institutional crisis, caused by the asymmetric framework of EMU, as established in the

TEU. This section also discusses the lack of political leadership in the EU and the collective action problems arising in the management of the euro area crisis. Often, domestic political economy interests prevailed at the expense of effective collective euro area solutions.

This chapter argues that the sovereign debt crisis created a vicious circle between the instability of the banking sector—which had to be bailed out in the majority of euro area countries—and the fragility of public finances, which were becoming unsustainable in some countries. In Greece, the crisis took the form of a 'traditional' fiscal crisis, caused by persistent fiscal imbalances, mounting public deficits, and large public debt, mostly held abroad. The potential insolvency of the Greek government threatened the stability of the country's banks, which held large amounts of sovereign debt. Moreover, the credit rating of banks was linked to the rating of their sovereign. In other countries, such as Spain and Ireland, the bailing out of national banks threatened the sustainability of public finance and the solvency of the state.

The crisis brought to the fore the reality that EMU had made the financial trilemma more acute and ultimately untenable. The Financial Services Action Plan (FSAP) and the introduction of the euro substantially increased financial integration in the EU—especially cross-border banking in the euro area—but supervision, support, and resolution remained at the national level. The international financial crisis was an external shock to euro area financial stability, but the member states no longer had all the instruments to deal effectively with crisis at the national level, nor had these instruments been set up at the EU/euro area level. The establishment of EMU constrained both national support (bail-out) and resolution powers because of the budgetary limits imposed by the SGP. Moreover, the introduction of the euro eliminated the possibility of monetary financing of sovereign debt (to be discussed in Chapter 8). Finally, national supervision of large EU cross-border banks suffered from severe limitations.

The Pre-crisis Framework for Financial Stability in the European Union

'Financial stability' involves crisis prevention and crisis management. 'Crisis prevention' comprises financial (prudential) regulation, financial supervision, and cooperation between supervisors, which is also paramount in crisis management. Prior to the international financial crisis and the euro area sovereign debt crisis, financial regulation in the EU was largely set at the EU level, whereby EU laws set the framework for financial legislation in the member states; financial supervision was carried out almost entirely at the national level; and crisis management was to take place at the national level and euro area level. These points are elaborated in turn.

Prior to the above-mentioned crises, EU financial regulation was mostly based on directives, which left some room to manoeuvre (national discretions) in the process of national implementation across the member states. EU banking legislation (e.g., the CRD) and securities markets law (e.g., the four 'Lamfalussy directives') were often based on a minimum common denominator, resulting from convoluted compromises and trade-offs during the negotiation process (see Quaglia 2010a, b). Furthermore, in some cases, such as the CRD, ample use was made of 'national discretions' in the domestic transposition of EU rules, as evidenced in Chapter 9. This 'regulatory collage' made uniform supervision across EU member states more difficult. For example, in a letter sent to the Economic and Financial Affairs Council (ECOFIN) at the start of the international financial crisis, the Italian Treasury Minister, Tommaso Padoa-Schioppa, noted that the lack of a unified 'rulebook' in the EU was an obstacle to intra-EU cooperation, especially in times of crisis (Padoa-Schioppa 2007).

In the EU, financial supervision was mainly carried out at the national level by the central bank (whenever it was responsible for banking supervision) or the banking supervisory authority, if separated from the central bank, and the supervisors of other financial activities (e.g., securities trading). However, there were EU committees of national supervisors in which their activities were (or were supposed to be) coordinated.

In the banking sector, the Banking Supervision Committee of the European System of Central Banks was set up in 1999 with a secretariat at the ECB, and comprised banking supervisors from all EU member states. It assisted the ECB in drafting banking legislation and supported the Eurosystem in the conduct of its tasks in the field of prudential supervision of credit institutions and financial stability. The Committee of European Banking Supervisors (CEBS) was established in 2004, following the recommendations of the Committee of Wise Men, chaired by Alexander Lamfalussy. The CEBS was part of the so-called Lamfalussy framework, which was based on a complex multi-level system of EU rule-making and enhanced cooperation between national supervisory authorities, underpinned by the so-called Lamfalussy committees.

As far as regulation was concerned, the 'first level' consisted of the traditional Community method, whereby the Commission drafted legislation after consulting the 'level 3' 'advisory committees' of national supervisors. The Commission's proposal was then co-decided by ECOFIN and the European Parliament (EP), laying out common EU rules and principles, in the form of either directives or regulations. These general rules were supplemented by 'technical' regulations and implementing measures produced through 'comitology', the 'level 2' 'regulatory committees' in which the Commission's proposals were voted upon and Qualify Majority Voting (QMV) applied. These committees also provided advice to the Commission on draft level 1 legislation, based on the input provided by level 3 committees. Each level 2 committee had one voting national representative per member state and one technical expert nominated by the relevant ministries. The Commission service chaired and provided the secretariat (see Quaglia 2008).

At level 3, the advisory committees were to ensure the consistent implementation of the measures agreed, by coordinating the execution of national supervision and advising the Commission on the drafting of level 2 measures. The level 2 committees could request advice from the level 3 committees. In level 3 committees, each member state had one vote allocated to the supervisory authority. The Commission had observer status. Both national central banks, with and without supervisory responsibility, and the ECB took part in the level 3 banking committee, the CEBS, but only the supervisory authorities possessed a vote. The level 4 consisted of national implementation, with an important monitoring role for the Commission.

'Crisis management' concerns the cooperation between financial supervisors, central banks, and national governments (treasuries) at the national level and across borders, on the basis of bilateral and multilateral memoranda of understanding (MOUs) and supervisory coordination and exchange of information in relevant fora. Crisis management takes place at the systemic level, which mainly involves the function of liquidity provision (traditional LLR) and at the level of specific institutions. In the euro area these functions were shared between the ECB (national central banks), as explained in Chapter 8.

In the EU prior to the crises, there were a variety of MOUs designed to promote supervisory cooperation in crisis management. These MOUs, unlike EU legislation, were not legally binding and concerned only the signing parties. To begin with, following the recommendations of the EU Economic and Financial Committee (EFC) in 2001, an MOU on high-level principles of cooperation between the banking supervisors and central banks in crisis management situations was adopted in March 2003, under the auspices of the Banking Supervision Committee.[1] In September 2003, a simulation exercise involving central banks and banking supervisors was carried out in order to test the provisions of the MOU adopted (ECB 2007a). In addition, in January 2001, an MOU on the cooperation between banking supervisors and central banks in their capacity as payment systems overseers was signed. Although this agreement did not specifically focus on crisis management, it contained provisions dealing with the exchange of information in the event of liquidity or solvency problems (ECB 2007a).

[1] The EFC is a committee of the EU Council of Ministers consisting of representatives from national finance ministries and from the ECB. National central banks and the Commission send observers.

As a follow-up to the priorities set by the EFC in 2004, an MOU on cooperation between the banking supervisors, the central banks, and the finance ministries in financial crisis situations was signed in May 2005 (*Financial Times*, 15 May 2005). This MOU also included arrangements for the development of contingency plans for the management of crisis situations, along with stress testing and simulation exercises. A simulation exercise was carried out in April 2006, involving the ECB, national central banks, national banking supervisors, and finance ministries, in order to assess whether they could effectively work together to contain a financial crisis (*Financial Times*, 9 April 2006).

Other instruments to promote cross-border supervisory cooperation were the colleges of supervisors. The CEBS supported the development of colleges of supervisors of cross-border banks in the EU. Furthermore, the CRD III (2006), which implemented Basel II (2004) in the EU, specifically set rules dealing with cooperation among supervisors of cross-border banks operating in the EU. It established rules for determining which supervisor, also known as the 'lead/consolidating supervisor', was to exercise consolidated supervision over a cross-border bank, and was also to lead the cooperation within the college. The colleges were to promote harmonization of supervisory approaches, and to coordinate major supervisory decisions and on-site inspections. The colleges included supervisors from all EU member states where credit institutions had subsidiaries, and supervisors were given the option to waive such participation. However, the colleges of supervisors lacked a mandatory mediation process if the supervisors could not agree (Alford 2010).

The Causes of the International Financial Crisis and its Effects in the European Union

The pre-crisis framework for financial stability in the EU was severely tested by the international financial crisis. The beginning of the crisis can be dated back to the collapse of the US sub-prime mortgage market in early 2007 as homeowners who had been granted loans in spite of their poor credit ratings struggled to make repayments in the face of higher interest rates and falling property prices (Rajan 2012). Afterwards, problems quickly spread to the United States (US) banking sector and then to the international financial system at large because these toxic assets had been securitized by banks, largely pushed off bank balance sheets, and then sold worldwide, principally to other banks (Blundell-Wignall 2012).

The international financial crisis reached its peak in the autumn of 2008 when the US investment bank Lehman Brothers was not rescued by the US authorities and filed for bankruptcy. This episode sent shock waves through the international financial system because it made clear that US authorities were willing to let (even large) banks and financial institutions fail. Moreover, it was unclear to what extent other financial institutions were exposed to the Lehman Brothers' failure, notably through their purchase of complex, and often repackaged, securitized products. Interbank markets froze, and governments in Europe and the US had to intervene to rescue their banks through state capital injections, public guarantees on loans and deposits, and liquidity provisions.[2]

Much has been written about the causes of the crisis (e.g., Rajan 2010; Reinhart and Rogoff 2009). Overall, they can be summarized as excessive international macroeconomic imbalances, a relatively loose monetary policy—especially in the US—and unfit for purpose financial regulation. International macroeconomic imbalances had been building up over the decade preceding the crisis (Obstfeld 2012). China, in particular, had an astonishing export performance in trade, coupled with substantial capital exports, due to the considerable excess savings in the domestic market (Knight and Wang 2011). Chinese capital outflows resulted in abundant cheap credit in the recipient countries, first and foremost the US and the EU (which Bernanke (2005) referred to as the 'global saving glut'). Low real interest rates also encouraged the quest for high yields, often associated with financially risky activities (Caballero, Farhi, and Gourinchas 2008; IMF 2005). Several scholars also point to the 'great complacency' as an important cause of the crisis—that is, relatively loose monetary policy in the US and the EU during the previous decade which favoured the formation of bubbles and worsened macroeconomic imbalances (see Cobham 2012; Mishkin 2011).

Inadequate 'light-touch' financial regulation is widely considered to be another main cause of the international crisis (De Larosière et al. 2009; FSA 2009; Group of Thirty 2009). The (sub-prime) mortgage market in the US, where the crisis originated, was poorly regulated, resulting in predatory loans which had little chance of being repaid. Through securitization, the risk on these loans was spread across the financial system, including banks (Rajan 2010). There was also the growth of a 'shadow' unregulated banking sector linked to regulated banks, notably structured investment vehicles and asset-backed commercial paper vehicles created by banks in order to move assets off their balance sheet, allowing banks to expand their assets and still meet capital rules (Hardie and Howarth 2013). A number of other financial services, such as over-the-counter derivatives, rating agencies, and hedge funds, were mostly subject to industry self-regulation (Brunnermaier et al. 2009; De Larosière et al. 2009; Group of Thirty 2009). Finally, complex models that underestimated

[2] For the EU response at this stage of the crisis, see Quaglia et al. (2009); for a comparison and explanation of different European government responses, see Woll (2014).

risk led to 'irrational exuberance' (Greenspan 1996; see also Schiller 2005), creating the wrong 'incentive structures' and encouraging moral hazard.

In the EU, a number of British and Irish banks were among those most affected by the first stage of the international financial crisis, principally because of their funding models, which relied on massive securitization of lending, but also because of their huge holdings of mortgage and other asset-backed securities sold by US banks (Hardie and Maxfield 2013). The British government responded by partially nationalizing two of the country's largest banks, purchasing significant shares of the then world's largest bank (by assets) Royal Bank of Scotland (RBS) (81 per cent), forcing the merger of the collapsing Halifax Bank of Scotland and the stable Lloyds-TSB, and taking over a 43.4 per cent share of the merged entity.

In the run-up to the crisis, Irish banks had substantially expanded their balance sheets by (often very) short-term borrowing in wholesale markets to finance a domestic real-estate boom (Lane 2012). When interbank markets froze after the collapse of Lehman Brothers in September 2008, Irish banks lost their access to their main source of (external) funding. In such a scenario, the Irish government provided a blanket guarantee of all bank liabilities and assumed responsibility for all the toxic assets of the largest national banks, which were transferred to a government-created bad bank. Irish government expenditure paying off bank creditors amounted to the largest actual expenditure in support of the banking sector as a percentage of national wealth of any national bail-out programme (268.5 per cent of gross domestic product [GDP]) (Woll 2014). The assets were purchased through the issue of government debt, resulting in a massive increase in the Irish public deficit and debt load, sowing the seeds of the fiscal crisis that resulted in Ireland becoming the second country to request external EU and International Monetary Fund (IMF) financial assistance, following Greece (Hardie and Howarth 2013).

Measured relative to GDP, the Netherlands had by far the greatest EU member state exposure to asset-back securities (although the impact on the country was mitigated by the highly fortuitous sale of ABN Amro to RBS), followed by Belgium and Germany (Hardie and Howarth 2013). In the Netherlands, pre-crisis banks also relied significantly on market-based sources of financing. Germany was also hit hard by the international financial crisis: total German bank write-downs were only exceeded by those of British banks. Four German banks—including the country's third largest—effectively collapsed, and only massive federal and regional government intervention saved a number of banks. The main losses were suffered by the public Landesbanks, and (less) by large banks. The Landesbank losses were in areas far from regionally based lending: through off-balance-sheet vehicles, the Landesbanks had heavily invested in the (toxic) US mortgage market and were therefore more exposed to market movements than any other EU-headquartered publicly owned banks (Hardie and Howarth 2009, 2013).

Total French bank losses were lower than those in the UK and Germany. At the same time, France was far worse hit than the financial systems of Southern Europe, at least in the initial stages of the crisis (Howarth 2013). The main losses were suffered by the big internationalized banks, first and foremost BNP Paribas and Société Générale. French mutual banks made losses across a range of activities, with problems at Natixis particularly acute, but such losses were lower because of their lower financialization and higher diversification, especially greater involvement in retail banking (Howarth 2013). In both France and Germany, the governments responded by extending their ownership in several banks and by providing credit guarantees and loans to banks.

By contrast, banks in Greece, Italy, Portugal, and Spain weathered the first part of the international financial crisis rather well and experienced no major losses. These banks were relatively sheltered from the most intense forces of international financial contagion in 2008–9 because they had not invested in the complex securitized asset packages that later proved to be 'toxic'. The largest banks in these countries had a more traditional business model and the large majority of their assets comprised customer loans. As for liabilities, they had a broad and stable funding base, mainly from retail customers, with the exception of Spanish banks and, to a more limited extent, Italian banks (Pagoulatos and Quaglia 2013; Quaglia and Royo 2015).

In late 2009, major financial problems began for many of the Spanish savings banks (*cajas*). The collapse of the real-estate market eventually led to a traditional banking crisis. Bad mortgages and loans to construction companies, which had fuelled a property bubble in Spain, accounted for the huge losses for Spanish *cajas* (Royo 2013a, b). However, the exposure of the 'Big Three' Spanish banks (BBVA, Santander, and La Caixa, the Catalonia-headquartered *caja*) to the Spanish real-estate sector was more limited. Portuguese banks also experienced problems because of their links with Spanish savings banks (Royo 2011).

Whereas in Ireland and Spain the banking crisis became a fiscal crisis, in Greece and Italy the fiscal crisis ran the risk of becoming a banking crisis. Greek and Italian banks, which had coped well with the international financial crisis, carried a heavy toll as a result of the sovereign debt crisis, being badly affected through declining credit ratings on their sovereign debt holdings.[3] Greek banks held a large amount of Greek government debt, which became a major burden following the depreciation of their government securities portfolio in 2010 (Pagoulatos and Quaglia 2013). From the spring of that year, Greek banks followed the government in successive downgradings by credit rating agencies. Greek banks were hit hard by the country risk and

[3] 'Country risk' is the risk related to investing in or lending to a country that might eventually be unable to service and repay its debt.

collapsed sovereign creditworthiness, leading to the depreciation of large asset portfolios of Greek government bonds, the collapse of bank equity prices, and the inability to raise funds on the interbank market. By early 2010, Greek banks were almost completely dependent on ECB credit (Pagoulatos and Quaglia 2013). In the first months of 2011, Italian banks were also hit by the sovereign debt crisis. Italy's two largest banks lost nearly 30 per cent of their market value between April and June 2011. Intesa and Unicredit held a total of €228 billion of depreciating government debt as of April 2011 (*Wall Street Journal*, 12 July 2012). Moreover, as the conditions of the Italian economy deteriorated, Italian banks were hit by large non-performing loans (see Figure 8 in Chapter 4).

The deterioration of the economic situation in the euro periphery and plummeting ratings assigned to both sovereign debt issued by euro periphery governments and bank debt also threatened the stability of banking systems throughout the EU. Although banks headquartered in northern EU member states moved to decrease their holdings of euro periphery debt (see Table 5 in Chapter 4), exposure remained significant in 2012 (see Figure 4 and Tables 4 and 6 in Chapter 4).

To conclude, the international financial crisis hit the banking systems of certain European countries (notably the UK, Germany, and Ireland) more forcefully than others (notably Italy and Greece). This mostly had to do with the configuration of national financial systems—to be precise, the extent to which banks held market-based assets and liabilities (Hardie and Howarth 2013). By and large, a large number of market-based assets increased the losses suffered by banks, whereas a large number of market-based liabilities restricted the funding that banks were able to provide to the real economy.

The national banking systems worst hit by the international financial crisis were those whose banks had a large number of market-based assets and liabilities. Some countries engaged actively in the securitization of assets, notably the UK, Ireland, and the Netherlands, followed by Germany and Spain. A number of banks purchased huge quantities of securitized assets—notably in Germany, the UK, the Netherlands, and Ireland. Several governments (including the British, French, and German) intervened to rescue their ailing banks, but not all of them had sufficient funding available to do so, as in the case of Ireland and Spain. Hence, the banking crisis became a fiscal crisis in these countries, and they had to resort to external financial assistance.

The Post-crisis Reform of the European Union Framework for Financial Stability

The international financial crisis triggered the reform of the EU framework for financial stability. The crisis revealed the weaknesses of existing macro-prudential oversight in the EU and the inadequacy of nationally based supervisory models in overseeing integrated financial markets with cross-border operators (FSB 2008; Kudrna 2012; Pauly 2008). The crisis exposed shortcomings in the consistent application of Community law (the lack of a European rulebook), as well as insufficient cooperation between supervisors in exchanging information and in crisis management (de Larosière Group 2009). In this respect, Italian Treasury Minister Padoa-Schioppa (2007) noted:

> in crisis situations, European supervisors can be expected to act based on a narrow national perspective and to pool crucial information only to a minimum extent... The reality we must face is that in spite of progress in recent years, the system is still unable to effectively respond to the challenges of a globally integrated market. Common principles have been developed, but the convergence of day by day practice has lagged behind.... In strengthening the supervisory structure, two main goals should be pursued: (i) adopting a single European rulebook... [and] (ii) an integrated supervision over cross-border market players.

As a response to the outbreak of the crisis, in September 2007 the EFC produced a report that outlined 'common principles for cross-border crisis management' and 'burden sharing'. These (rather vague) principles were subsequently endorsed by ECOFIN in October 2007, and in the spring of 2008 they were incorporated in the existing MOU signed in 2005. In May 2008, ECOFIN endorsed the introduction of a European dimension into the mandate of national supervisors and the introduction of QMV and 'comply or explain' procedures in the Lamfalussy committees of supervisors. ECOFIN also agreed on the strengthening of the role of colleges of supervisors, to be extended to all cross-border European financial groups.

In 2009, a group of high-level practitioners and financial experts, chaired by the former Governor of the Bank of France, produced a report on the issue, which was named after the chair of the group. Building on the De Larosière Report, in September 2009 the Commission put forward a series of legislative proposals for the reform of the micro- and macro-prudential framework for financial supervision in the EU. The Commission proposals were eventually agreed by ECOFIN and EP in the autumn of 2010 and were implemented in early 2011 (see Buckley and Howarth 2011; Hennessy 2014; Kudnra 2012; Spendzharova 2012).

The main institutional innovations of the post-crisis reforms were the establishment of the European Systemic Risk Board (ESRB) to be in charge of monitoring macro-prudential risk, its chair to be elected by and from the members of the General Council of the ECB; and the transformation of the so-called level 3 Lamfalussy committees, discussed earlier in this chapter, into independent authorities with legal personality, an increased budget, and enhanced powers. The new European Supervisory Authorities (ESAs)—namely the European Banking Authority (EBA), the European Insurance and Occupational Pension Authority, and the European Securities Markets Authority—were charged with the tasks of coordinating the application of supervisory standards and promoting stronger cooperation among national supervisors (Hennessy 2014). The authorities were given the power to mediate between supervisory authorities in case of disagreements.

In the negotiations of these institutional reforms, disagreements broke out in ECOFIN and between ECOFIN and the EP concerning the powers of the newly created bodies. In ECOFIN, there were (mainly British) concerns about giving the new authorities powers over national regulators and the possibility of supervising individual financial cross-border institutions (*European Voice*, 4 March 2009; 6 April 2009). Moreover, the UK government was reluctant to grant decision-making powers to EU-level bodies, especially when public funds to tackle banking crises came from national budgets (*Financial Times*, 20 March 2009; Buckley and Howarth 2011). To this effect, Gordon Brown, the British Prime Minister, secured a guarantee that the new supervisory system would not include powers to force national governments to bail out banks. The UK also stressed that the EU's supervisory architecture should fit in with global arrangements and should support the development of 'open, global markets' (Darling 2009). That said, a number of member states, particularly those with large financial centres (namely the UK, France, and Germany) favoured the limited reform approach and were hesitant about transferring substantive power to the EU level (Buckley and Howarth 2010). This led to a significant reduction in the scope of the Commission proposals during the negotiations in ECOFIN.

By contrast, the EP argued that the Commission's proposals did not go far enough and was adamant that the powers of the ESAs should be safeguarded. Hence, the EP called for the strengthening of the financial and human resources available to the ESAs. It also called for the presidency of the ESRB to be given to the President of the ECB, so as to augment the authority of this newly created body. Members of the EP (MEPs) inserted provisions to enable the ESRB to communicate rapidly and clearly. They defended the powers of ESAs to make decisions that were directly applicable to individual financial institutions in cases of manifest breach or non-application of law, and where there was disagreement among national authorities. The EP was keen for the ESAs to be able temporarily to prohibit or restrict harmful financial activities or products already covered by specific financial legislation or in emergency situations (*Financial Times*, 14 July 2010). On all these issues, the EP was successful in getting what it wanted. The question of which authority (ECOFIN, the EP, or the Commission) was to have the power to call an emergency in the EU's banking sector was an issue of great contention. However, in the end the Council—and, hence, national governments—retained the sole power to declare a crisis.

The Unfolding of the Sovereign Debt Crisis in the Euro Area Periphery

The reform of the framework for financial stability in the EU in the wake of the international financial crisis did not prevent the sovereign debt crisis in the euro area. The first country to experience the sovereign debt crisis and to request external financial assistance was Greece (see Featherstone 2011; Jones 2013; Zahariadis 2012). After the general election in October 2009, the newly elected Greek government of George Papandreou revealed a deficit of 12.7 per cent of GDP, against a 6 per cent level officially estimated by the previous Conservative government. In November 2010, Eurostat—the EU Commission's statistical agency—revised the Greek 2009 deficit to 15.4 per cent GDP. This large deficit prompted substantial market speculation against Greek sovereign debt: the spreads of Greek bonds vis-à-vis German bunds reached record levels. Greek public bonds were downgraded to junk bond status by the main credit rating agencies in spring 2010 (Pagoulatos and Quaglia 2013). Greece eventually requested external financial help in April 2010, following which the EU agreed on emergency financial support for Greece, financed by member state bilateral loans given the EU treaty provision banning EU bail-outs to member states (Art. 125 Treaty on the Functioning of the European Union [TFEU]) (Buti and Carnot 2012; Marzinotto, Pisani-Ferry, and Sapir 2010).

As market tensions persisted and threatened to extend to other countries in the periphery of the euro area, in May 2010 the European Council decided to establish two funds to provide financial assistance to ailing countries in the EU: the €60 billion EFSF—run by the European Commission with funds from the EU budget—and the larger €440 billion EFSF (they are discussed in Chapter 8). Subsequently, the €110 billion EU/ECB/IMF Emergency Financing Mechanism attached to a rigorous three-year conditionality programme (including an austerity package) was granted to Greece. However, the Greek crisis was far from over, as the country needed additional financial help, and several renegotiations of its loans took place over the following years.

The Greek crisis and bail-out were only the first chapter in the euro area sovereign debt crisis. The next victim was Ireland (Whelan 2011), where public debt and deficit had skyrocketed as a result of the government's decision to rescue its ailing and over-expanded banking sector (Woll 2014). Yet, the Irish government lacked the financial resources to guarantee the liabilities of a banking sector that held assets at roughly eight times national GDP in 2010. Consequently, in November 2010 Ireland accepted conditional financial support from the two new EU funds established six months earlier, as well as from the IMF. The overall support package (including a bilateral loan of £3.25 billion from the UK) was approximately €67.5 billion, and was designed to support the banking system as well as to help fund government expenditure.

Like Greece, Portugal denied that it would need external financial aid until market conditions strongly deteriorated (see Rodrigues and Reis 2012). Prime Minister Socrates requested external financial aid in May 2011 and an assistance package of €78 billion was agreed—consisting of €26 billion each from the EFSM, the EFSF, and the IMF—with attached austerity measures. The main problem in Portugal was as much fiscal policy as excessive private sector consumption, financed by banks, including branches and subsidiaries of Spanish banks in Portugal (Gros 2012c). Portuguese banks experienced heavy losses when their customers (both households and firms) were unable to service their loans once the economy went into recession. The Portuguese state had to intervene to prop up the banks, as had happened in Ireland and Spain, resulting in a rapid rise in government debt.

The fourth country to request external financial assistance was Spain. Spanish banks had weathered the first stage of the international financial crisis rather well, but, as a consequence of the deteriorating economic conditions, the *cajas* suffered heavy losses because mortgage holders and property developers were unable to service their loans. Banks badly needed recapitalization. However, the dire fiscal situation of the Spanish government meant that it was not in a position to provide financial support to ailing banks (Royo 2013a, b, c; Gavilán, Jimeno, and Rojas 2011). In December 2012, the Spanish government formally requested of the EU the disbursement of about €39.5 billion of ESM funds (see Chapter 8).

Like Greece, Italy was in a weak fiscal position, with a public debt in excess of 120 per cent GDP. The main concern in Italy was the sustainability of the public debt, given the country's low economic growth since joining EMU (Jones 2012). As the spread on Italian government bonds increased in 2010, so too did the risk of debt unsustainability as due debt had to be rolled over at higher rates. With Italian and Spanish bond yields rising rapidly, the ECB intervened in bond markets in August 2011. Four months later, it established the Long-Term Refinancing Operation (LTRO), which issued three-year loans to banks at low rates. Reportedly, Italian and Spanish banks were the main beneficiaries of these ECB measures (*The Guardian*, 8 August 2011; *Bloomberg*, 8 August 2012). These banks reinvested the loans in national sovereign debt, which helped to bring down Italian and Spanish sovereign debt yields but aggravated the sovereign debt–bank doom loop.

In February 2012, following the agreement reached with the other euro area member states on a second bail-out package in the Eurogroup (Eurogroup 2012), Greece declared a default on its sovereign debt, whereby private holders of Greek government bonds suffered a substantial 'haircut' (approximately 75 per cent). This was a fatal blow for Cyprus, which had initially been unaffected by the sovereign crisis, mainly due to its low public debt (approximately 50 per cent of GDP and small budget surplus in 2008). However, Cypriot banks, which had invested heavily in Greek sovereign debt, suffered losses of approximately 25 per cent of the country's GDP and required government support (Zenios 2015). After successive downgradings from rating agencies, Cypriot banks and the Cyprus government lost access to international financial markets (*Financial Times*, 16 April 2012). Cyprus suffered from the same destabilizing feedback loop between bank and sovereign risk as in the other euro periphery countries (Jobst and Gray 2013).

In June 2012, the Cyprus government applied to the 'troika' (the IMF, the European Commission, and the ECB) for assistance, but negotiations on terms dragged on. Almost a year later, in March 2013, the ECB threatened to end its Emergency Liquidity Assistance (ELA) to Cypriot banks unless the Cyprus government agreed to the conditions for financial assistance proposed (Jones 2013; *Financial Times*, 6 November 2014; *The Guardian*, 19 March 2013). Subsequently, the Eurogroup, the Commission, the IMF, and the ECB reached an agreement with the Cyprus government on a €10 billion bail-out assistance for the national government and a €5.8 billion bail-in for troubled Cypriot banks, subject to conditionality. Capital controls had to be imposed to stop massive capital outflows.

The international financial crisis first and the euro area sovereign debt crisis later caused the fragmentation of the single financial market in the EU, which in turn affected the ability of the ECB to operate an effective monetary policy (ECB 2012a). Several measures demonstrate the increasing fragmentation of the EU's financial market: a significant increase in the differentiation of average unsecured interbank lending rates across the euro area member states; the divergence of euro area member state lending rates; a decline in unsecured transactions undertaken with non-domestic counterparties in the euro area from 2007, both in real terms and relative secured transactions; and the increased dispersion in credit default swap premiums across the euro area member states for sovereign and bank debt (ECB 2012a: 23).

The EU banking market fragmented in 2008 on a range of measures. The establishment and activity (measured in assets) of foreign branches and subsidiaries dropped marginally between 2008 and 2012 (ECB 2012a: 27). However, the cross-border merger and acquisition activity of banks—another indicator of market integration—declined sharply from 2008 and remained low in 2012. The share of loans granted to monetary financial institutions (MFIs) by MFIs of other euro area countries stabilized for two years after a drop from 2008, but then began to decline again in 2011. Although the level of cross-border interbank loans in the EU remained relatively high (at around 35 per cent of the total at the end of 2011), this was nonetheless a significant decline from the 45 per cent peak in 2007. The dispersion of bank interest rates applied to new loans to non-financial companies (NFCs) rose considerably from the low of 2007 (ECB 2012a: 29).

The cross-border bond holdings of euro area MFIs (as a percentage of the total) declined markedly from the middle of the 2000s, with no indication of stabilization prior to 2012. In 2005, of the government and corporate bonds held by MFIs, over 40 per cent were cross-border. By 2011, this figure had dropped to 23 per cent (see Figure 1). Similarly, the share of cross-border collateral used by euro area MFIs had dropped from over 50 per cent of the total to approximately 33 per cent (see Figure 2). The euro area periphery and the EU periphery (Central and Eastern European countries [CEECs]) were most affected by this retreat to domestic debt, given the declining confidence of non-periphery banks in the value of sovereign and corporate debt issued in the periphery (see also Table 5 in Chapter 4).

In the euro area periphery, a destabilizing sovereign debt–domestic bank loop was created (BIS 2011). Higher periphery government spending and rising debt burden increased sovereign risk (Merler and Pisani-Ferri 2012) and threatened to disrupt the collateral function of sovereign debt, with a resultant damaging effect on bank funding conditions (BIS 2011). From 2008,

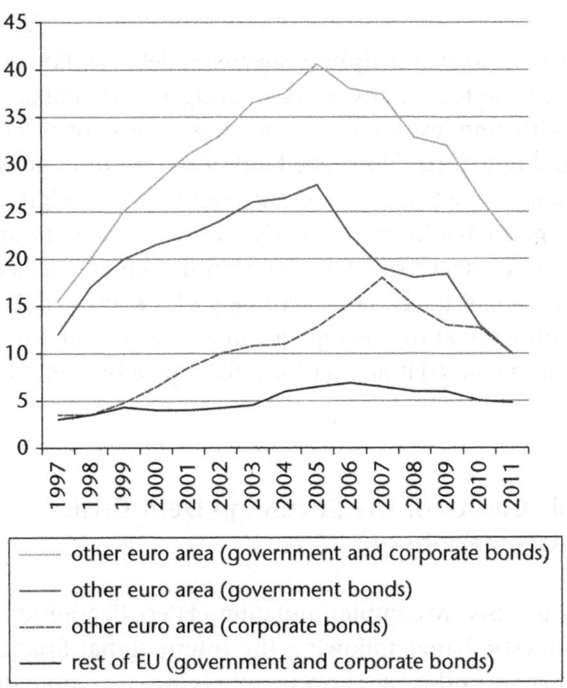

Figure 1. Cross-border bond holdings of European financial institutions (percentage of total) (end-June figures)
Source: ECB (2012a: 22).

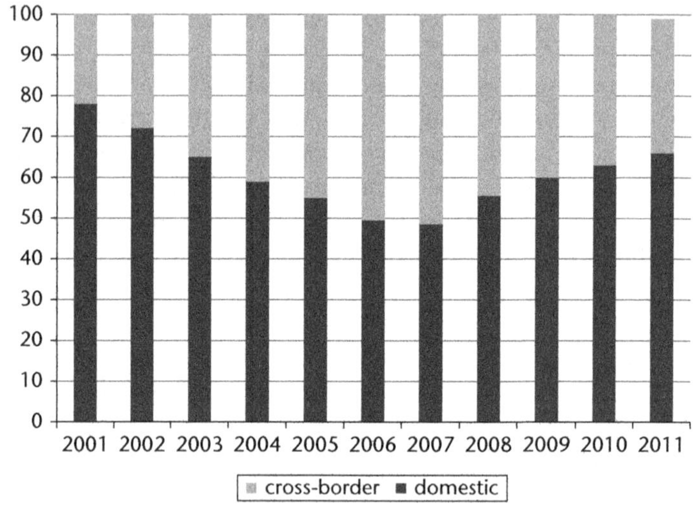

Figure 2. Share of domestic and cross-border collateral used in Eurosystem operations (percentage)
Source: ECB (2012a: S10).

the percentage of euro area periphery sovereign debt held by domestic banks increased markedly as foreign investors—fearing unsustainable euro periphery debt burdens—became less willing to purchase this debt or keen to discard it. Thus, increasingly-at-risk domestic banks came to hold growing amounts of downgraded sovereign debt, while the ability of sovereigns to bail out or wind down domestic banks in an orderly manner (to avoid a systemic crisis) diminished as public debt loads rose (see Howarth and Quaglia 2013a). There was a downward spiral in the euro periphery of a rising public debt burden, rising yields, and credit rating downgrades on sovereign debt, a retreat of foreign investors, and an increased holding of sovereign debt by domestic banks.

The Economic Causes of the Sovereign Debt Crisis in the Euro Area Periphery

The causes of the crisis are complex and interrelated. In addition to the cost of bailing out domestic banks following the international financial crisis, the sovereign debt crisis in the euro area periphery was a combination of a fiscal crisis and a balance of payments crisis. These components of the crisis, however, had different combinations in different countries. Greece and, to some extent, Italy experienced a 'traditional' fiscal crisis, worsened by the fact that in Greece the public debt was mostly short term and held abroad. Prior to the crisis, the public debt in Greece and Italy was well above 100 per cent of GDP. Greece also had a higher public deficit compared with Italy, which most of the time posted a (small) primary surplus (budget balance net of interest payments on debt).[4] Portugal had a public debt of about 70 per cent of GDP prior to the crisis, higher than Ireland and Spain, but lower than Greece and Italy. However, it had a high private debt.

Spain and Ireland did not have a high public debt prior to the crisis: about 40 per cent of GDP in Spain, and less than 20 per cent in Ireland. Their public accounts were close to balance or in surplus. Their deficit and debt levels shot up after the international financial crisis, mainly because of government financial support to ailing banks. However, private debt was also high in Spain, Ireland, and Portugal. In 2009, private debt was respectively 224 per cent of GDP for Italy and 219 for Greece, but 268 for Spain, 273 for Ireland and 314 for Portugal, compared with a euro area average 249 per cent.

An interesting question is why Italy did not suffer a fully fledged sovereign debt crisis and did not resort to external financial assistance, despite the staggering figures of its public debt. Italy had managed a public debt of over 100 per cent of GDP over the three decades prior to the crisis. On the positive side, the level of private debt in Italy was comparatively low. Moreover, most of the Italian public debt was long term and held domestically, hence it was less subject to market sentiments (Jones 2012). On the negative side, the Italian government failed to take advantage of low interest rates following the entry of the country into Stage Three of EMU in 1999—a move that could have substantially reduced the outstanding public debt (Bini Smaghi 2013).

The main problem in the Italian case was not so much the high level of public debt, especially when accounting for the relatively low level of private debt and the fact that public debt was mostly held domestically. Rather, it was the low growth rate that raised serious issues regarding the sustainability of public debt (Jones 2012). Italy had suffered from low economic growth for more than a decade: it experienced 0.54 per cent annual average real GDP growth between 2000 and 2010, compared with 1.37 per cent for the euro area. Thus, when the spread on Italian sovereign bonds began to rise in 2011, the sustainability of Italian public debt was called into question.

The second component of the sovereign debt crisis was the balance of payments crisis (Knedlik and Von Schweinitz 2012; Lane 2012; Schmitz and Von Hagen 2012), and this is linked to one of the institutional explanations—that is, the absence of a mechanism to deal with macroeconomic imbalances in EMU, discussed in the following section. In the euro area, economic imbalances

[4] In Greece, the excess consumption was financed by the government and, as a consequence, most of the foreign debt was owed by the government (Bini Smaghi 2013).

built up over the decade prior to the crisis as massive capital flows moved from core euro area countries (first and foremost Germany) to Southern euro area countries (Gros 2012c; Higgins and Klitgaard 2011). The capital-exporting countries invested their surplus savings abroad, and a large share of these cross-border flows was intermediated through the global banking system and other highly regulated intermediaries (e.g., insurance companies and pension funds). These intermediaries had a strong bias towards investing in the euro area.

Capital outflows were mainly directed towards the capital-importing periphery of the euro area (Schmizt and Von Hagen 2012)—making the financial trilemma explained in the previous chapter more acute in the euro area. However, the inflow of foreign capital served different goals. In Spain, like in Ireland, foreign capital was used to sustain massive construction booms, while in Greece and Portugal it served to fund consumption (Gros 2012c). By contrast, Italy experienced lower capital inflows and did not experience a pronounced credit boom: most of the capital inflows in Italy were purchases of sovereign debt.

As Bini Smaghi puts it (2008), external imbalances are the reflection of internal imbalances. The expansion of domestic demand, financed by capital inflows, undermined Southern euro area countries' competitiveness. The loss of competitiveness was thus a symptom, rather than a primary cause, of imbalances (Gros 2012c). All the periphery countries hit by the sovereign debt crisis had a persistent current account deficit over the previous decade, coupled with significant private capital inflows from 2002 to 2009. Unlike Italy, which had moderate external liabilities, Greece, Ireland, Portugal, and Spain had large external liabilities (Sinn 2014). In ten years, the external debt of Greece, Portugal, and Spain rose from around 30 per cent of GDP to 100 per cent. Ireland went from a surplus to a net debt of more than 100 per cent of GDP.[5]

Among the periphery countries, Italy had the smallest current account deficit and net foreign debt. Unlike the other periphery countries, Italy had the second-largest manufacturing and industrial base in Europe, after Germany, and was one of the biggest export-oriented economies in the euro area. 'Made in Italy' was a valuable brand around the world. Furthermore, Italian banks, unlike those in Spain and Ireland, did not channel capital inflows into a property bubble. Most Italian bank lending was to manufacturing and service sectors, which avoided the formation of a property or

[5] See Trading Economics (<http://www.tradingeconomics.com>) for figures for the five euro periphery countries, accessed on 3 August 2015. See Wolfgang Munchau, 'The EU will regret terminating a banking union', *Financial Times*, 1 July 2013.

consumer bubble and allowed investment in these sectors (unlike, e.g., in Spain and Greece) (Pagoulatos and Quaglia 2013; Quaglia and Royo 2015).

In all periphery countries hit by the sovereign debt crisis, current account imbalances were mainly funded through portfolio debt securities and bank loans, rather than through foreign direct investment. As Merler and Pisani-Ferry (2012: 12) note, 'such a financing structure, biased towards banks' intermediation, rendered the deficit countries very exposed to the unwinding of capital inflows'. Indeed, at the inception of the international financial crisis, private cross-border flows reverted suddenly and a massive withdrawal of foreign private resources from the euro area periphery took place.

These capital outflows were reflected by the Eurosystem central banks' position in TARGET 2 (the Eurosystem's interbank payments system). Until 2007, TARGET 2 positions were close to balance. When the international financial crisis began in 2007, and even more so when the sovereign debt crisis broke out in 2010, imbalances emerged within TARGET 2, whereby the German central bank was the largest creditor, and the Greek, Spanish, Irish, and Portuguese central banks were net creditors (Bindseil and König 2012; Sinn and Wollmershäuser 2012). The Bank of Italy, which was previously a creditor, became a major net debtor in TARGET 2 in late 2011 (Quaglia and Royo 2015).

All the periphery countries hit by the balance of payments crisis suffered from a loss of competitiveness over the decade after 1999. Between the introduction of the euro and 2008, salaries grew faster than productivity in all the euro area periphery, and unit labour costs in the manufacturing sector—the strongest indicator of economic competitiveness—increased more rapidly than the euro area average (Sinn 2014; see also Armingeon and Baccaro 2012; Knedlik and Von Schweinitz 2012). By contrast, since joining EMU, productivity in Germany increased by an average of 3 per cent per year while wages grew by only about 1 per cent per year—thus reducing unit labour costs relative to all the other euro area member states. Between 1999 and 2008, the competiveness relative to Germany in terms of average unit labour costs fell more than 40 per cent in Spain, 30 per cent in Italy, and 20 per cent in Ireland and Portugal (Bini Smaghi 2013; see also World Economic Forum's annual competitiveness ranking 2012).

To sum up, the sovereign debt crisis was a combination of several interrelated crises, namely the international financial crisis, especially its repercussions in Ireland and later in Spain; the fiscal crisis, especially in 'fiscally profligate' countries such as Greece, Portugal, and Italy, which had persistent fiscal imbalances in the decade prior to the crisis; and the balance of payments crisis in all the 'debtor' countries, which was caused by high current account deficits coupled with capital inflows prior to the crisis, followed by sudden capital outflows during the crisis. In all these countries, the main policy response was based on austerity policies, mostly imposed from outside. In the case of Greece, Ireland, and Portugal, austerity was imposed by the 'Troika' (composed of the ECB, the European Commission, and the IMF) as a condition for financial assistance. In the case of Spain and Italy, it was 'voluntarily' adopted in an effort (mostly ineffective) to reassure financial markets (Armingeon and Baccaro 2012).

The Institutional and Political Causes of the Sovereign Debt Crisis in the Euro Area

The sovereign debt crisis in the euro area was also an institutional crisis that highlighted three flaws in the institutional design of EMU: the asymmetry created through a full monetary union without a full economic (fiscal) union; the absence of a mechanism to prevent and deal with macroeconomic imbalances; and the asymmetry created through monetary integration without financial (especially banking) supervision which mostly remained at the national level.

When EMU was agreed in 1992, and even more when the third and final stages of EMU began, several authors pointed out the asymmetric nature of EMU, whereby monetary union was not accompanied by a full economic (fiscal) union (Dyson 2000; Verdun 1996). During the negotiations leading to the Maastricht Treaty (Dyson and Featherstone 1999), when the blueprint for EMU was agreed, some member states, first and foremost Germany, opposed fiscal (or transfer) union for political and economic reasons. Politically, fiscal union was seen as a step too far, impinging upon a core area of national sovereignty. Economically, member states with sound fiscal positions, led by Germany, were concerned by the potential moral hazard that a fiscal union would bring about, and that they would end up financing countries that lacked sufficient fiscal discipline (for an overview of this debate, see Dyson and Quaglia 2010).

The EMU framework lacked effective arrangements to counter divergent budgetary policies and more broadly divergent economic policies. Budgetary discipline was basically entrusted through the SGP (see Heipertz and Verdun 2012) to an intergovernmental body, whereas the member states had an incentive towards forbearance (i.e., not to impose sanctions on each other), limiting the credibility of common budgetary rules (Micossi 2012). Moreover, excessive confidence was placed on the disciplining effects of financial markets. When the Maastricht Treaty was negotiated and the no bail-out rule included, the expectation was that financial markets would be able to differentiate between different member state borrowers and would therefore impose fiscal discipline in EMU (Bini Smaghi 2013; Committee for the Study of Economic and Monetary Union 1989).

This was not the case: until the crisis broke out, the markets treated the euro area as a single entity without appreciating the specific economic conditions of the member states. Basically, financial markets underpriced private and sovereign credit risks in the implicit belief that all debts were equal (ECB 2012a; Micossi 2012). Another aspect that had been ignored in the establishment of EMU was the possibility that a country struggling with its public finances could lose access to financial markets. With full capital mobility and a single currency (hence, no exchange rate risk), this was not conceived as a real possibility. Therefore, no mechanism to assist countries experiencing financial distress (to be precise, liquidity shortage) was envisaged (Micossi 2012).

EMU was not an OCA (McKinnon 1963; Mundell 1961), and no institutional mechanism (e.g., fiscal transfers, automatic stabilizers) had been established to deal with asymmetric shocks (Eichengreen 1987). Euro area member state economies had not converged sufficiently to surrender the exchange rate as a politically and economically expedient mechanism to deal with different and diverging degrees of competitiveness. In EMU, the greater competiveness of the German economy resulted in massive real exchange depreciation for Germany vis-à-vis other euro area countries and the rest of the world, with enormous benefits for its exporting industry (Gros 2012c), as explained in the previous section. Prior to the creation of EMU, the Deutsche mark would undergo periodic revaluations to compensate for Germany's increased competitiveness.[6] The only way to restore competitiveness in EMU was painful (and somewhat ineffective: see Armingeon and Baccaro 2012) internal devaluation, mainly based on wage compression.

The second shortcoming of the institutional framework of EMU was the absence of a mechanism to deal with macroeconomic imbalances. When EMU was designed, it was believed that current account imbalances were not important because they would be akin to imbalances between different regions in a country and could be easily funded through full capital mobility (Bini Smaghi 2013). However, in a monetary union, balance of payments imbalances mainly manifest themselves as disequilibria in the banking sector—to be precise, between national banking systems. Prior to the crisis, countries in the periphery of the euro area experienced persistent current account deficits, funded by capital inflows from surplus countries (Gros

[6] The literature on the EMS/ERM is extensive. See especially Buiter, Corsetti, and Pesenti (1998), De Grauwe and Papademos (1990), Fratianni and Von Hagen (1992), Giavazzi and Giovannini (1989), Giavazzi, Micossi, and Miller (1988), and Gros and Thygesen (1998).

2012c). These current account deficits were caused by a loss of competiveness from the start of EMU's Stage Three in 1999 (Sinn 2014). In turn, capital inflows from surplus countries promoted the formation of domestic bubbles in deficit countries.

As Micossi (2012: 2) puts it, 'the explosion of credit from German banks to the "periphery" of the [euro area] was the financial counterpart to the accumulation of massive trade and payment imbalances within the [euro area]'. In debtor countries, excessive debt accumulation by the private (financial and non-financial) sector, and by the public sector (notably in Greece and Italy) and house price bubbles, were direct consequences of the single monetary policy and were financed by 'core' country banks. Capital inflows into the euro area periphery countries were directed towards sectors not exposed to international competition, such as the public sector (Greece and Italy) and real estate (Spain and Ireland). When sudden and substantive capital outflows took place during the international financial crisis, this created a de facto balance of payments crisis in the debtor countries, as explained in the previous section.

The other asymmetry brought into relief by the crisis was the imbalance that existed between a single monetary policy (conducted by the ECB for the euro area) and financial supervision and crisis management (conducted almost entirely by individual member states). In the negotiations on EMU, member states discussed but could not agree upon whether the ECB should be assigned supervisory responsibilities (Dyson and Featherstone 1999). These intergovernmental discussions tied into a broader debate in the economic literature on whether or not the monetary policy function of a central bank should be separated from prudential supervision (see, e.g., Goodhart 1999; Goodhart and Eric 2000). There were also ongoing debates as to which authorities should be responsible for macro-stability (that is, the stability of the system) and crisis management, and for micro-stability (that is, the solvency of individual financial entities) and consumer protection—matters of concern highlighted in several reports issued in the wake of the financial crisis, including the De Larosière Report (2009) and the Group of Thirty Report (2009). Banking Union was a means to address this asymmetry.

The sovereign debt crisis was also a political crisis: it was worsened by the lack of political leadership in the EU, and the disagreement among member state governments as to the main causes of the crisis and thus possible solutions. When the international monetary regime of Bretton Woods collapsed, Kindleberger (1973) argued that the international system needed a (benevolent) hegemon to provide the public good of stability, a role played in the past by the US. With regard to the EU/euro area, some commentators argued that Germany should take on the role of hegemon (Paterson 2011). However, Germany has been reluctant to assume the role of hegemon (Mabbett and

Schelkle 2015). This reluctance reflects the country's (limited) domestic capacities and domestic political constraints, as well as a long-standing concern about moral hazard. In the absence of a benevolent hegemon, Marsh (2013) claims that the euro has become a currency for which no one is responsible. Indeed, the delayed and piecemeal response of the EU/euro area to the sovereign debt crisis highlighted both the lack of political leadership and the revival of national interests (Marsh 2013).

During the unfolding of the sovereign debt crisis but also in the debate on Banking Union, which was a way of dealing with the crisis by breaking the vicious link between the banks and their sovereign, the main line of division was between euro area countries directly hit by the crisis—namely Greece, Ireland, Portugal, Spain, and Italy—and countries that were not directly affected by the crisis—namely Germany, Austria, the Netherlands, and Finland—with France in between. The first group of countries had balance of payments deficits, weak fiscal positions, and eventually needed external financial support, with the exception of Italy (which did, however, benefit from ECB interventions). The second group of countries had balance of payments surpluses and broadly sound fiscal positions, and were concerned about the risk of moral hazard in providing EU or euro area financial assistance during the crisis. As the former Italian Prime Minister and Finance Minister Mario Monti quipped, 'for Germany, economics is a branch of moral philosophy' (*The Economist*, 29 September 2012).

The sovereign debt crisis in the euro area involved two sets of moral hazards concerning, respectively, lenders and borrowers (Mackintosh 2015). On the one hand, there was the irresponsible behaviour of banks in so-called creditor states in the run-up to the 2008 crisis, which took no account of the borrowers' ability to repay the (cheap) loans they received (e.g., Greece), and which caused credit bubbles (e.g., Portugal) and real-estate bubbles (e.g., Spain and Ireland) in the euro area periphery. The EU's (piecemeal) intervention in the early stages of the sovereign debt crisis 'bought' time for international investors, including banks in core countries, to disinvest from the periphery, thereby worsening the crisis. On the other hand, there was the irresponsible behaviour of the euro area periphery, which for a decade took advantage of cheap credit and lenders who believed that bonds of periphery countries offered a 'risk free rate'. Unconditional EU/euro area financial support and/or debt restructuring would have provided the euro periphery hit by the crisis with an incentive to engage in hazardous financial conduct in the future (Mackintosh 2015).

However, there was also a 'hazard', though perhaps not a 'moral' one, in doing nothing, which could threaten the very survival of the euro, or in imposing debt restructuring, which could trigger chain reactions in the markets and contagion (Mink and De Haan 2013), transforming 'a local event into a systemic crisis' (Bini Smaghi 2013: 66). First, contagion could come from the collection of insurance purchased to protect against the effects of a restructuring (credit default swaps). Financial institutions that sold these securities would find themselves in difficulty. Second, market participants would question the ability of other euro area periphery countries in financial distress to repay their debt. Capital outflows to these countries would stop, driving up interest rates and further threatening debt sustainability. Indeed, whenever fears about the restructuring of Greek debt surfaced, interest rates on government bonds in all the periphery countries increased. Third, domestic banks that held large quantities of government bonds would find themselves suddenly undercapitalized as a result of debt restructuring (Bini Smaghi 2013).

Conclusion

This chapter has examined the pre- and post-crisis framework for financial stability in the EU, the causes of the international financial crisis and the sovereign debt crisis, and the EU/euro area response to it. As a response to the first crisis, the EU partly reformed its framework for financial stability. The EU response to the sovereign debt crisis initially focused on austerity measures, meaning tightened fiscal policy. However, it subsequently became clear to a range of observers that large deficits and ballooning debt loads were more a symptom of the crisis than the main cause of it, with the exception of Greece (see, e.g., Bini Smaghi 2013). In 2007, both Ireland and Spain had fiscal surpluses. Fiscal deficits in Italy and Portugal were far lower than in Greece. When the international financial crisis occurred, capital movements plummeted. Investors re-evaluated the credit risk of their investments and reduced their exposure to the most indebted countries (Bini Smaghi 2013). These capital outflows had recessionary effects, led to the deterioration of public finances, and caused a balance of payments crisis. The main underlying problem was the excessive and persistent balance of payments deficits in countries in the periphery of the euro area from the beginning of EMU, and partly as a result of it. Hence, a policy response focused on the tightening of fiscal policy was not enough to solve the crisis.

Policy-makers in various countries had different (often opposite) views about the causes of and hence the solutions to the sovereign debt crisis, which helps to explain why the crisis was so difficult to resolve. The EU/euro area response was often delayed by internal disagreements and (re)negotiations (Armingeon and Baccaro 2012; Lapavitsas 2012; Lynn 2010; Marsh 2013). This response was piecemeal and reactive, which allowed the crisis to fester. After several tentative solutions, the euro area member state governments took the bold decision to establish Banking Union to sever the link between the banking crisis and the sovereign debt crisis in the euro area periphery. These two interrelated crises also highlighted the financial trilemma at the core of EMU.

Only since 2010 have the moral hazards—of both 'stability' and 'growth' free-riding (Rommerskirchen 2014)—that plagued EMU from its earliest years been transformed into an existential threat to the survival of the single currency. Crisis was also necessary to overcome the entrenched opposition in a range of euro area member states reluctant with regard to the transfer of prudential supervision, support, resolution, and deposit guarantee functions from the national to the supranational level. Prior to 2012, improved supervision of banks with a strong presence in other EU member states was arranged largely on an ad hoc basis, through bilateral agreements between national supervisory authorities. Home-country control dominated, and financial support for failing banks came almost entirely from national fiscal authorities—proving Mervin King's adage that banks are 'international in life but national in death' (*Financial Times*, 30 March 2009). The collapse or threatened collapse of a range of cross-border European banks in the context of the two crises and the threat to a number of banking systems reinforced the logic of moving beyond such unilateral and ad hoc arrangements.

Banking Union was presented by euro area member state governments and the European Commission as a series of mechanisms which would—collectively—stabilize and build confidence in national banking systems exposed directly to the sovereign debt crisis by breaking the link between rising sovereign debt in the euro area periphery member states and domestic banks, which had come to hold an increasing amount of this debt. Some domestic banks—for example the Spanish *cajas*—had been badly hit by the international financial crisis, economic depression, and the collapse of domestic real-estate prices. Hence, they needed financial support that their governments found difficult to provide, especially in the context of a rapidly rising public debt burden.

Some member state authorities and the European Commission saw Banking Union as a mechanism to provide external (euro area) direct financial support to ailing banks, while subjecting banks to euro area supervision. More generally, Banking Union was presented by a range of supporters as instrumental to address financial market fragmentation in the EU, especially in the euro area. Following almost a decade of financial integration in EMU, the crises threatened the complete reversal of previous gains, demonstrating that the financial trilemma was no longer tenable in the context of the euro area. Banking Union was presented by the four EU presidents as a necessary deepening of EMU. Indeed, the verb officially—and hyperbolically—used was to 'complete' EMU, suggesting that these elements—rarely discussed in European policy-making circles prior to 2012—were the sine qua non of 'full' EMU (European Council 2012b).

4

European Banking Systems in Times of Crisis

Introduction

This chapter examines the configuration of the six largest national banking systems in the EU (those of Germany, France, the Netherlands, Italy, Spain, and the UK) by considering several sets of potentially relevant measures. The presence of very large cross-border banks in all six countries made the financial trilemma particularly acute in the euro area, explaining the functional drive towards Banking Union, first and foremost supranational bank supervision. However, the importance of very large cross-border banks in explaining the interest of our six countries in Banking Union and their preferences on the specific elements of Banking Union varied.

Five other factors had a significant impact upon national preferences: banking-system-wide internationalization patterns, specifically EU and euro area periphery exposure; the presence and organization of alternative banks; bank capital and liquidity; and the 'health' of the banking system. Moreover, the 'manageability' of real and potential bank losses was linked mainly to the 'health' of the national banking system, its relative size, and the state of public finances. 'Manageability' shaped the concerns of national policy-makers with regard to moral hazard, which in turn shaped national preferences on Banking Union, its elements, and their specific design. Given Germany's pivotal role in the debate on Banking Union, particular attention is devoted to the German banking system.

The first of these five features is the level of banking system internationalization. From the trilemma, we hypothesize that the greater the internationalization, the greater the interest of national policy-makers in Banking Union. We have selected the largest euro area national banking systems, which are also the least internationalized in the EU (on a range of measures), and thus this feature becomes a potentially less helpful guide in explaining national preferences with regard to our five euro area case studies. A second feature is national bank holdings of EU, and notably euro periphery, sovereign debt. We hypothesize that the greater the exposure of the national banking system and economy to the EU and euro periphery and potential default, the greater the interest in Banking Union. More specifically, the greater the exposure, the greater the interest in financial support mechanisms—the ESM to support recovery, and the SRM, SRF, and a common DGS to support resolution—as a means to bolster confidence in international financial markets as to the stability of both banking systems and sovereigns.

Third, the size and the organization of the alternative banking sector were potentially relevant factors. Alternative banks had a significant presence in five of the six country cases. We hypothesize that the more centralized the alternative banking sector (through semi-consolidated groups or joint liability schemes with central financial institutions), the greater the interest in Banking Union. This factor—concerning the 'reach' of internationalization into the banking system—is of particular importance in explaining national preferences on the size threshold for banks to be subject to direct ECB supervision.

Fourth, the capital and liquidity positions of banks and system-wide patterns in bank capital and liquidity are potentially important measures of the robustness of the banking system—notably to withstand crises. We hypothesize that the lower the capital and liquidity position of the national banking system and the higher the risk weight of bank capital, the greater the interest of national policy-makers in Banking Union. Capital position also becomes potentially relevant on a number of specific issues given that bank capital, and specifically risk weight capital, determined contributions to the SRF and potential contributions to the DGS. Capital and liquidity positions shaped national preferences on the Single Rulebook—the principal foci of which were capital and liquidity requirements.

Fifth, the health of the banking sector can be measured by a diversity of indices in addition to bank capital, including non-performing loans, return on equity, and return on asset ratios. We hypothesize that the better the health of the banking sector, the less the interest of national policy-makers in Banking Union and the creation of generous support mechanisms.

A sixth feature is directly related to the sovereign debt–bank doom loop and potentially helps to explain national concern for moral hazard created by euro-area-level financial support mechanisms for banks. This feature is the 'manageability' of national banking system real and potential losses. This 'manageability' can be measured (approximately) by a combination of factors, including the health of the banking sector, bail-out costs, actual bank losses (write-downs), losses to national GDP, bail-outs as a ratio of government spending, exposure to EU (and specifically euro area) periphery debt, the relative size of the banking sector, and the government debt burden. The lower the 'manageability' of real and potential bank losses, the greater the interest in Banking Union and, specifically, the mutualization of bank risk. The greater the 'manageability', the greater the concern regarding moral hazard.

The next section outlines these six factors and their specific measures. This is followed by a brief overview of the six national banking systems, in which the most relevant features of each are highlighted. Finally, we present our preliminary findings with regard to the six hypotheses and national interest in Banking Union. These findings will be further explored in the following chapters focused on national preferences on the four main elements of Banking Union and the Single Rulebook for banking.

Measuring Banking System Internationalization

In order to explain the preferences of national policy-makers on Banking Union, we develop Schoenmaker's understanding of bank internationalization, which he uses to explain the contribution to international financial instability that such large cross-border entities can make. His principal measurement for cross-border banking is the assets held by individual large banks outside the home country which, however, provides only a limited picture of the internationalization of national banking systems and is of limited guidance with reference to national preferences on Banking Union (see Table 1). Assets held outside the home country by large banks are only one element of bank internationalization which might motivate national policy-makers to reinforce international cooperation in bank supervision and even move to supranational supervision. The internationalization of bank funding is also relevant. We consider five sets of measures of banking system internationalization: the total assets held outside the home country; the domestic reach of internationalization; the exposure of home banks to the EU and euro area periphery; the degree and origin of foreign bank penetration; and the relative dependence of banks upon short-term bank funding.

1. The *total assets held outside the home country* of all nationally headquartered banks. Figure 3 distinguishes between the internationalization of national banking system assets and the internationalization of the assets of the two or three largest banks, distinguishing between assets held in other euro area countries and those held in the rest of the world. Table 2—covering all EU member states—breaks down the figures further, distinguishing between assets held in the EU and specifically the euro area. This demonstrates that for five of the six countries, internationalization—while important—was limited, not reaching more than 30 per cent of total assets. Only in the UK did the figure

Table 1. Internationalization of large banks, end 2011 (percentage of total bank assets; rounded figures)

	EU	Rest of World
France		
BNP Paribas	34	17
Société Générale	12	9
Crédit Agricole	11	8
CACIB	30	41
BPCE	14	15
Natixis	21	22
Crédit Mutuel	10	4
Germany		
Deutsche Bank	32	34
Commerzbank	17	32
Landesbank BW	20	8
Landesbank Bayerische	12	11
DZ Bank	21	6
Italy		
Unicredit	56	2
Intesa Sanpaolo	14	4
Netherlands		
ING Bank	30	30
ABN	12	8
Rabobank	9	17
Spain		
Santander	41	32
BBVA	9	35
Caixa Bank	2	0
UK		
HSBC	11	54
RBS	8	30
Barclays	27	39
Lloyds Banking Group	7	3
Standard Chartered	4	81

Source: From Schoenmaker and Peek (2014).

reach 40 per cent for the entire banking system. The level of internationalized assets for most other EU member states (Table 2) is even lower.

The thirty largest European banks—in their large majority publicly in favour of all or most elements of Banking Union (as demonstrated in their responses to Commission consultations and other documentation)—had influence over national preferences. However, the largest European banks did not dictate these preferences. In Germany, the limited influence of the two largest banks in shaping national policy on Banking Union is clear. Deutsche Bank and Commerzbank were both strongly in favour of Banking Union and both very critical of German policy-makers reticence (see, e.g., Speyer 2013).

The relative weight of large banks with a strong European/international presence in the national banking system is a relevant consideration

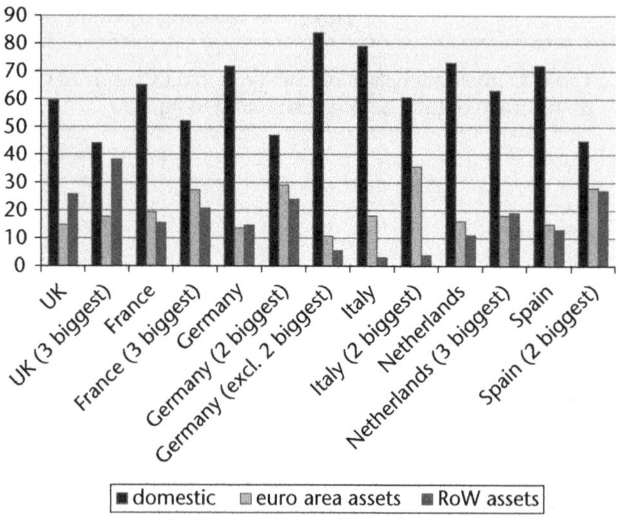

Figure 3. Bank internationalization (percentage of total bank assets, 2007–11 average)

Sources: Bank of England, Banque de France, Bundesbank statistical databases. Registration documents for RBS, Barclays, HSBC, BNP Paribas, Crédit Agricole, and Société Générale.

Notes: The three largest Germany-headquartered banks (measured by assets) became two with the forced merger of Dresdner and Commerzbank.

Table 2. Internationalization of EU-27 banking systems 2010–13 (percentage of total assets held outside home member state, average, rounded)

	Domestic	RoW	EU	Euro area
Euro area				
Austria	79	6	15	8
Belgium	83	6	11	8
Cyprus	89	3	4	4
Estonia	99	0	1	0
Finland	94	1	5	1
France	75	13	13	11
Germany	72	15	14	11
Greece	91	0	9	2
Ireland	84	10	6	2
Italy	79	3	18	3
Malta	83	5	12	9
Netherlands	73	11	16	12
Portugal	81	6	13	13
Slovakia	99	0	1	1
Slovenia	93	0	7	7
Spain	72	13	15	8
Non-euro				
Bulgaria	96	1	3	2
Czech Republic	97	0	3	3
Denmark	85	2	13	5
Hungary	96	0	4	3
Latvia	98	1	1	0
Lithuania	96	0	4	3
Poland	94	0	6	5
Romania	97	1	2	2
Sweden	84	7	9	5
UK	60	26	15	13

Source: National central bank data.

(see Figure 6). Smaller banks tend to be less international, with the exception of some specialized institutions. In five of the six country cases examined in this volume, alternative (public, savings, and cooperative) banks held a large share of total bank assets—from 21 per cent in Italy to 43 per cent of the total in Germany—and were responsible for an even larger share of retail banking, reaching up to 50 per cent in Germany. These banks—smaller institutions, for the most part—were even less likely to have an international focus given the explicit social- and local-oriented nature of their activities. Countries with the least concentrated banking systems with large numbers of smaller banks—notably Germany, but also Italy to a lesser extent—might be expected to oppose supranational banking supervision or at least limit it to the largest banks, which is why we consider the 'reach' of internationalization as a separate criteria.

2. *The domestic reach of internationalization.* If internationalization was limited to a small number of large institutions, while a large number of smaller banks were more domestically focused, less support from national policy-makers for supranational supervision would be expected. These smaller banks were both commercial and alternative banks.[1] In all our countries except for the UK, there were a large number of alternative (public, savings, and cooperative) banks. These banks historically had an important social function and most continued to have a strong connection to a locality. This local connection had a clear political, if not politicized, dimension—most obviously in Germany, where local politicians continued to serve on the governing boards of savings banks (Ayadi et al. 2009; Bülbül, Schmidt, and Schüwer 2013; Simpson 2013), which continued to benefit from implicit guarantees of local government support. In Germany and Spain, alternative banks continued to be the main lenders to small and medium-sized enterprises (SMEs), while alternative banks in Italy and France were major lenders to SMEs, with their share of lending far exceeding their percentage of total national bank assets.

We consider the extent to which small and parochial alternative banks were affected by internationalization. The relevant difference here is due to the structure of the alternative bank sector. In four of the five countries which had a large number of small alternative banks, these banks operated joint liability schemes which meant that if one institution collapsed, other banks

[1] The term 'alternative' banks is used because these entities—mostly cooperative and savings banks—normally did not issue equity and were not principally, or only, profit-oriented. Cooperative banks by definition are controlled by their depositors, who become members with a single vote regardless of their level of investment. Cooperatives pursue the interests of their members rather than profit maximization per se. The cooperative banking sector in all EU member states had diversified over the previous few decades and had come to include a number of larger central financial institutions created to provide services to and for members of the smaller banks. Some of these larger institutions issued shares and operated similarly to commercial banks. Ayadi et al. (2009) discuss the challenge of defining a savings bank—created under public law, locally rooted with a clear social function—which had also created central financial institutions.

would come to its rescue. The precise details of these schemes varied. In Germany, France, and the Netherlands, small alternative banks (cooperatives or savings banks, or both) created central financial institutions in the context of partial or far-reaching consolidation in the 1980s and 1990s. These central financial institutions engaged in a larger range of commercial and investment banking activities than their much smaller associated banks. They all engaged in significant international activities and, in a number of cases, were among the most internationalized of large EU banks. The structure of these part-consolidated banking groups and the internationalization of their central financial institutions is outlined in Table 3.

Table 3. The institutional position of alternative banks and the internationalization of their central financial institutions

Country	Alternative bank assets as a percentage of total bank assets (end 2011)	Institutional position	EU exposure of central financial institution and linked investment banks
France	43	Consolidated, very limited autonomy of members. Savings banks and cooperative banks federated into large entities. Very few independent alternative banks.	Moderate to moderately high. Crédit Mutuel 10 per cent. Crédit Agricole 11 per cent. BPCE high 14 per cent (29 per cent international). CACIB 30 per cent (71 per cent international). Natixis 21 per cent (43 per cent international).
Germany	43	Autonomous entities in joint liability and supervisory schemes. Central financial institutions created but without joint liability with smaller entities.	DZ Bank at 21 per cent (but no joint liability with cooperatives). Landesbanks range from 8 to 20 per cent (but no joint liability with savings banks).
Italy	21	Regional banks.	Low
Netherlands	31	Centralized and Semi-consolidated. 129 small Cooperative Rabobank banks (at end 2012) under a Central Rabobank with joint liability.	Coöperatieve Centrale Raiffeisen-Boerenleenbank (Rabobank) high at 18 per cent (38 per cent international).
Spain	38	Regional savings banks. Bankia created from seven regional banks in December 2010.	Low
UK	0.5	Cooperative banks consolidated.	Low

This list of alternative banks includes only cooperatives and savings banks; it does not include a range of public and semi-public banks (e.g., Post Office and municipal banks).

Source: National central bank data. Bank registration documents and annual reports.

In France and the Netherlands, joint liability schemes created a financial commitment by a large number of very small and parochial banks to internationalized and systemically important institutions, the collapse of which would impose massive costs upon the smaller entities. This was very different from the situation in Germany, where more than 400 small savings banks and over 1,000 cooperative banks maintain a looser relationship with and financial commitment to central financial institutions. Crucially, the joint liability schemes run by the savings banks and by the cooperative banks covered only the smaller banks themselves and not their central financial institutions. The Italian cooperative banks and the Spanish savings banks did not operate joint liability schemes—although the Italian cooperatives operated their own ex-post-funded DGS (see Chapter 7). The institutional position of alternative banks, and notably the organization of joint liability schemes, is an important explanatory variable with regard to national preferences on the threshold for direct ECB supervision (Chapter 5), on the creation of a SRM (Chapter 6), and on the creation of a Common Guarantee Scheme (Chapter 7).

3. *The exposure of home banks to the EU and euro area periphery* (Table 4). This measure is of particular relevance to our claims of the distortion of internationalization patterns in the context of EMU, which made the financial trilemma ultimately untenable. The operation of the euro area prior to the international financial crisis resulted in converging sovereign debt yields and bank interest rates, thanks to market perceptions that euro area countries in difficulty would be bailed out despite EU treaty provisions to the contrary. This in turn resulted in distorted EU/euro area bank internationalization. The EU and notably euro periphery debt and other asset holdings of EU (and in particular euro area) banks increased markedly as a percentage of total assets and, specifically, foreign holdings in the period from 1999 to 2007. However, the absence of supranational supervision and resolution from 2007 meant that this distorted internationalization contributed to financial instability.

The perception of likely bail-out in the euro area was thus crucial to internationalization patterns and financial instability both prior to the sovereign debt crisis and after its outbreak in late 2009. Notably, banks in 'creditor' member states (i.e. countries that had a balance of payments surplus), stocked up on EU and euro periphery assets (including sovereign and private sector debt) prior to the outbreak of the international financial crisis (see Chapter 3). With the onset of the international financial crisis, those banks moved to decrease their exposure in the EU periphery, a development that proceeded apace with the outbreak of the sovereign debt crisis. Nonetheless, the exposure of several creditor member states—notably France and Germany—to euro periphery assets remained significant in 2011 and 2012

Table 4. Banking system exposure to EU and euro periphery (end 2011)

	Percentage of bank assets held in EU periphery (Southern Europe and CEECs)	Bank assets held in EU periphery as a percentage of GDP	Exposure to at-risk countries (euro periphery) as percentage of bank risk-weighted assets	Exposure to at-risk countries (euro periphery) sovereign debt as percentage of Core Tier 1
France	8.2	30.2	21.9	28
Germany	7.4	23.0	25.9	45
Italy*	3.0 (88)*	6.3 (183.0)	8.6	6 (167)*
Netherlands	4.8	21.2	13.6	4
Spain*	3.7 (85)*	10.9 (250.8)	15.2	9 (161)*
UK	3.6	15.9	7.8	3

Sources for EU consolidated foreign claims of reporting banks—immediate borrower basis: Bank for International Settlements (BIS), ECB statistical warehouse, EBA, EU Capital Exercise. The euro periphery includes Italy, Spain, Greece, Portugal, and Ireland.

Consolidated foreign claims of reporting banks—immediate borrower basis EU in from ECB (2013) *Banking Structures Report.* 'EU out' includes assets held in the EU of all national banks (including subsidiaries of foreign banks).

* The figures in brackets include assets held in the domestic market.

at the start of discussions on Banking Union (see Table 4). We hypothesize that high euro area exposure increased interest in proposals to supranationalize banking supervision, both as a mechanism to stabilize euro periphery banking systems and economies, and to stabilize home banks in creditor countries with significant exposure to the periphery.

Bank holdings of specifically euro area periphery sovereign debt in total and relative terms might be seen as a good indicator of German, French, and Dutch interest in Banking Union (e.g., *Reuters*, 26 July 2010; *Wall Street Journal*, 17 February 2010). Euro area (especially euro periphery) debt holdings of banks relate to both internationalization and euro area LLR concerns. The rapidity of disinvestment from the euro area periphery and retreat to the core is also of relevance to our study. By 2012, most euro area and other EU-headquartered banks had significantly cut their exposure to euro periphery sovereign debt (Table 5). Thus, while the threat of contagion of sovereign debt default remained, banks and governments were far less exposed by the start of discussions on Banking Union than they had been at the start of the sovereign debt crisis—although Figure 4 and Table 6 demonstrate the significance of ongoing exposure. Euro area-headquartered banks (outside the periphery) were almost 50 per cent less exposed in mid-2012 than they had been at the start of the sovereign debt crisis. Table 5 thus demonstrates—over the two years prior to the June 2012 Banking Union announcement—the implications of the financial trilemma in the context of the sovereign debt crisis for both European financial market integration and, notably, for the stability of the euro periphery member states.

Table 5. Bank sovereign debt holdings (March 2010–June 2012)

	Greece	Italy	Portugal	Spain	Ireland	Germany and France
Non-euro periphery euro area banks						
March 2010	24,509	75,600	7,767	13,417	2,477	142,389
December 2010	24,886	97,729	8,513	25,761	3,254	262,052
September 2011	20,231	72,521	7,360	18,771	2,814	233,920
December 2011	14,889	44,250	4,614	13,034	2,463	191,505
June 2012	1,595	47,445	2,886	12,099	2,024	205,736
Non-euro area EU banks						
March 2010	4,874	12,077	2,808	6,544	6,610	105,082
December 2010	2,897	27,335	2,911	12,643	1,706	110,923
September 2011	1,538	23,814	1,902	7,869	993	120,679
December 2011	2,466	18,231	1,691	5,989	1,044	108,725
June 2012	77	15,285	1,662	5,525	917	109,244
Euro periphery banks						
March 2010	60,570	154,635	14,144	148,627	6,201	33,862
December 2010	57,665	171,196	18,848	163,162	11,352	28,867
September 2011	2,747	164,082	19,021	147,459	10,775	29,480
December 2011	2,585	153,923	15,467	115,594	10,487	33,568
June 2012	146	189,508	20,544	127,847	11,938	29,410

Source: Acharya and Steffen (2014: 40), modified by the authors.

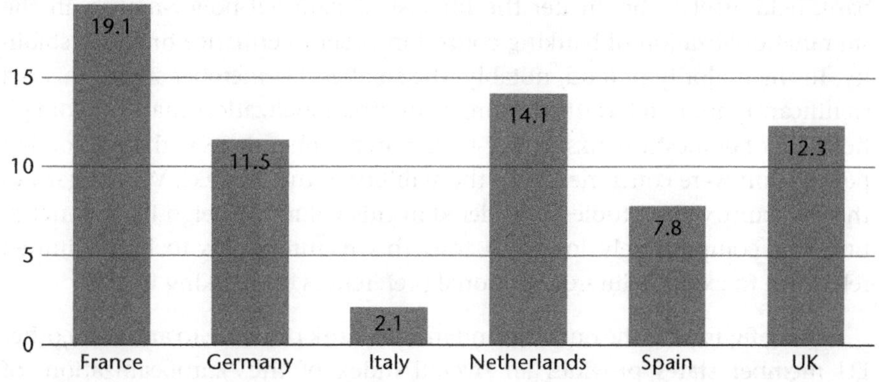

Figure 4. National bank exposure to euro periphery sovereign debt (end 2011, percentage of GDP)
Source: BIS.

Table 6. Bank exposure to euro periphery sovereign debt (as a percentage of bank Core Tier 1 capital, end-2011 figures)

	Greece	Ireland	Portugal	Spain	Italy	Total
France	4	1	2	3	18	28
Germany	5	1	3	14	22	45
Italy	2	0	0	4	161	167
Netherlands	0	0	1	2	1	4
Spain	0	0	3	152	5	160
UK	0	0	1	1	0	2

Source: Organization for Economic Co-operation and Development (OECD).

Table 7. EU and Rest of World (RoW) exposure of national banking systems (assets as a percentage of total bank assets*) (end 2012)

	EU in	EU out*	EU total (in + out)	RoW in	RoW out*	RoW total (in + out)
France	10	15	25	0.5	13	13.5
Germany	12	7	19	1	15	16
Italy	13	18	31	0.5	3	3.5
Netherlands	10	10.5	20.5	2	11	13
Spain	9	15	24	0	13	13
UK	17	15	32	28.5	26	54.5

Sources for EU in: national central bank data bases.

Sources for EU consolidated foreign claims of reporting banks (immediate borrower basis): BIS, ECB statistical warehouse, EBA, EU Capital Exercise.

Source for consolidated foreign claims of reporting banks (immediate borrower basis) from ECB (2013) *Banking Structures Report*.

EU / RoW out includes assets held in the EU / RoW of all banks (including subsidiaries of foreign banks).

* Figures rounded to the nearest 0.5.

4. *The degree and origin of foreign bank penetration.* We hypothesize that the higher the level of foreign bank penetration in a national banking system (notably through branches, but also through subsidiaries and other foreign bank held assets), the greater the interest of national policy-makers in the supranationalization of banking control in order to enhance financial stability. In the majority of (and, notably, the smaller) EU member states, this is a significantly more relevant measure of internationalization than the foreign holdings of domestic banks. Policy-makers in member states with high foreign penetration were concerned as to the stability of these banks. With regard to the six country case studies considered in this volume, foreign bank penetration was comparatively low, and thus this feature seems to be of limited relevance to explain different national preferences on Banking Union.

Adding figures for the outward and inward bank presence to and from other EU member states provides an overall index of the 'Europeanization' of national banking systems which is somewhat more revealing (Table 7). Germany is the least 'Europeanized', which suggests less interest in Banking Union, while Italy is the most 'Europeanized', suggesting greater interest.

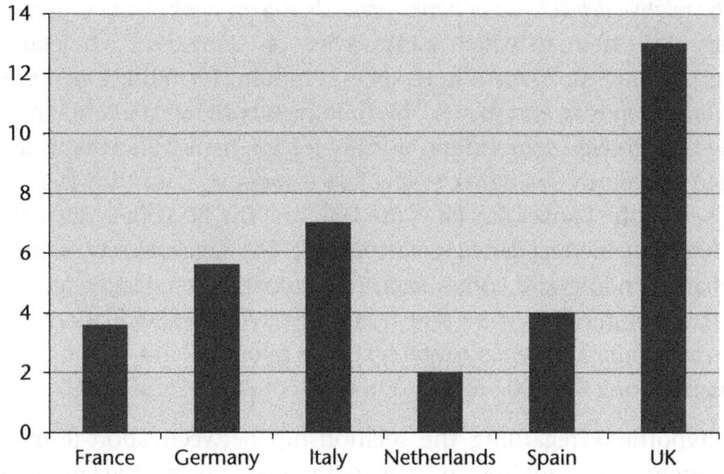

Figure 5. Foreign bank lending to NFCs and households (percentage of total; end 2011)

Source: National Central Banks. Foreign banks include both EU- and non-EU-headquartered banks.

The retail presence of foreign banks (and the origin of these banks) is of potential importance—specifically, lending to NFCs and lending to households. We hypothesize that policy-makers in member states with higher foreign bank retail presence would have been more sensitive to the need for supranational banking supervision/control, given the potential of transfer of deposits from domestically headquartered banks to the branches of foreign banks, which might appear better supervised and more financially sound (Darvas and Wolff 2013). Subsidiaries of banks headquartered in larger and/or wealthier member states might also benefit from the perception of greater stability and likelihood of bail-out.

A clear political interest in Banking Union is thus created for policy-makers in member states with strong foreign retail presence. This was notably the case for most of the smaller EU member states, the member states in Central and Eastern Europe, and, specifically, those outside the euro area, where the dominance of foreign banks—in terms of both total bank assets and retail banking—reached over 90 per cent, as in the Baltic States and Romania (Darvas and Wolff 2013). However, the foreign bank (retail) presence in the five euro area member states considered in our study was very low (Figure 5); only the UK had a significant foreign bank retail presence. Therefore, this dimension of internationalization, while likely of great importance for a number of EU member states in terms of encouraging their interest in Banking Union, was less relevant for the member states with the largest banking sectors.

5. *The relative dependence of banks upon short-term bank funding*. This measure considers the extent to which banks relied on short-term wholesale market funding, in comparison with other sources of funding including long-term wholesale funding, deposits, and shares. This funding is both less stable and more likely to come from foreign sources, and notably foreign banks. Short-term funding is measured differently by different credible sources of data (the ECB, national central banks, the Banker database, the IMF, and the BIS) but is normally measured at less than one year or two years (the ECB). The large majority of this funding is interbank funding and comes from foreign banks (see Hardie and Howarth 2013). This funding is less stable and more prone to market fluctuations and, even, the freezing of markets when (notably) banks refuse to lend to one another—as in extremis during the 2007–9 period in much of Europe and the US.

The hypothesis regarding the relationship between short-term funding and preferences on Banking Union is that policy-makers of EU member states where banks relied more on short-term funding were, ceteris paribus, more likely to support supranational banking supervision/control in order to boost confidence in interbank lending. Accordingly, the greater the percentage of short-term funding that came from banks and financial institutions headquartered in other EU and, specifically, euro area member states, the greater the interest in supranational banking supervision in the EU/euro area context. Table 8 shows the extent to which bank funding in the six country cases is through short-term debt issues (less than two years). French banks were the most reliant upon short-term funding, and over 28 per cent of total debt issued by French banks was short term. German banks were the least reliant upon short-term funding. Therefore, it is expected that French policy-makers were particularly sensitive to instability in interbank/wholesale markets in the euro area and would support supranational efforts to stabilize these markets. It is expected that Germany would be less preoccupied by instability in interbank/wholesale markets.

Table 8. Bank reliance on short-term* debt issues (end 2011)

	Short-term debt issues / total liabilities (percentage)	Short-term debt issues / total debt issues (percentage)	Short-term debt issues / euro area debt issues (percentage)
France	4.2	28.3	29.3
Germany	0.4	2.4	2.6
Italy	1.0	4.4	4.5
Netherlands	1.9	8.3	9.5
Spain	0.8	6.9	6.9
UK	2.1	15.4	22.3

Sources: National central banks; ECB Statistical Data Warehouse; Debt Securities Issued, Liabilities, MFI Balance Sheets, Monetary Statistics, Monetary and Financial Statistics.
* Less than two years.

Additional Banking System Features of Potential Significance

In addition to the five above-mentioned features of internationalization, a range of other features might have shaped the preferences of national policy-makers on supranational banking supervision/control. The first is the concentration of banking systems—whereby less concentrated systems, ceteris paribus, tend to be less internationalized, while greater concentration suggests greater internationalization (see Figure 6). We take the Herfindahl index used by the ECB to measure concentration. The fit is far from perfect—a few large banks were more domestic in their focus (e.g., Lloyds-TSB), while a number of smaller banks were more internationally oriented. However, there is a strong correlation between bank size (measured in terms of assets) and bank internationalization. The relative importance of these big banks in national systems should also be considered because this would have affected their relative influence over the preferences of national policy-makers.

We hypothesize that policy-makers in member states with more concentrated banking systems were more likely to support Banking Union. Dutch and German preferences corresponded more closely to expectations, while concentration levels are a less clear guide for other national preferences. Concentration levels are more helpful in explaining national preferences on the specific element of Banking Unions: specifically, banking sector concentration

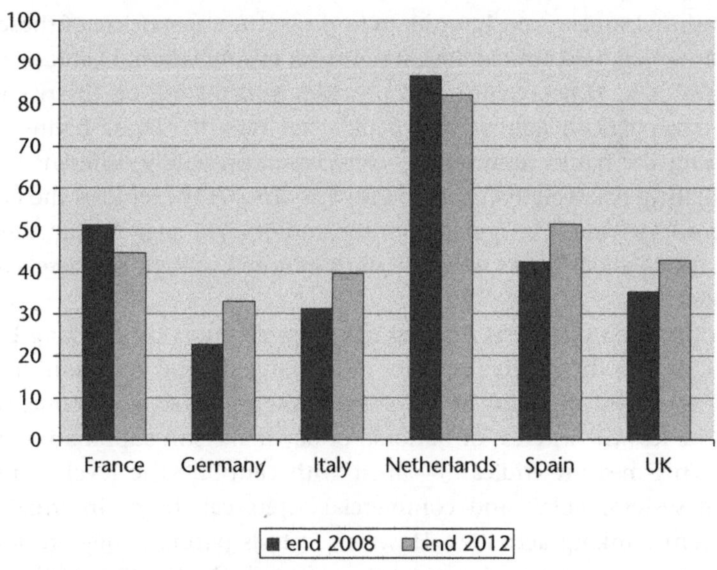

Figure 6. Banking system concentration* (end 2008 and end 2012)

Source: ECB (2013) *Banking Structures Report*; Bank of England.

*Herfindhal index: the share of the largest five banking institutions (individual institutions, not consolidated groups) as a percentage of total assets.

Table 9. Ratio of risk-weighted assets to total assets of large EU-headquartered banks (end 2011, highest figures for the thirty largest banks)

Bank	Country	Ratio
Deutsche Bank	Germany	17.6
Crédit Agricole	France	19.4
Barclays	UK	25.0
Société Générale	France	29.6
BNP Paribas	France	31.2
Commerzbank	Germany	35.8
Lloyds	UK	36.3
Santander	Spain	45.2
Unicredit	Italy	49.7
Intesa Sanpaolo	Italy	50.9
BBVA	Spain	55.3

Source: Bank balance sheets.

(and average bank size) had implications with regard to national preferences on the design of bank contributions to the SRF (see Chapter 6) and the common DGS (see Chapter 7).

The risk weight of bank assets and thus activities is the second additional feature of potential interest. The hypothesis to be tested here is that the policy-makers in member states with banking systems engaged in activities with a higher risk weight, notably investment banking, were more likely to support supranational supervision in order to improve the supervision of these assets, which are often held abroad. Risk weights for entire national banking systems are unavailable. However, the EBA provides information on the risk weights for the largest EU-headquartered banks (see Table 9). These figures—which came from the banks themselves—were based on wildly different measures of calculating risk weights in the banks and (in 2011) excluded the effects of netting out derivatives. Figures from the end of 2011 suggest that the largest Italian and Spanish banks were the most exposed to high-risk assets and the least safe.

The opposite hypothesis relating risk to preferences on Banking Union is that the greater the relative reliance of banking systems on traditional retail activities—notably, lending to NFCs and households—as a percentage of total assets, the less the interest of national policy-makers in supranational supervision. This measure indicates—albeit with caution—the level of risk in a banking system. Retail and commercial assets can be as international as investment banking activities. However, ceteris paribus, they are less risky (and are ascribed a lower risk weight)—although the location of these assets remains an important contributing factor to their risk weight. Figure 7 summarizes the extent to which national banks were focused upon lending to NFCs and households. This lending formed a larger percentage of the more

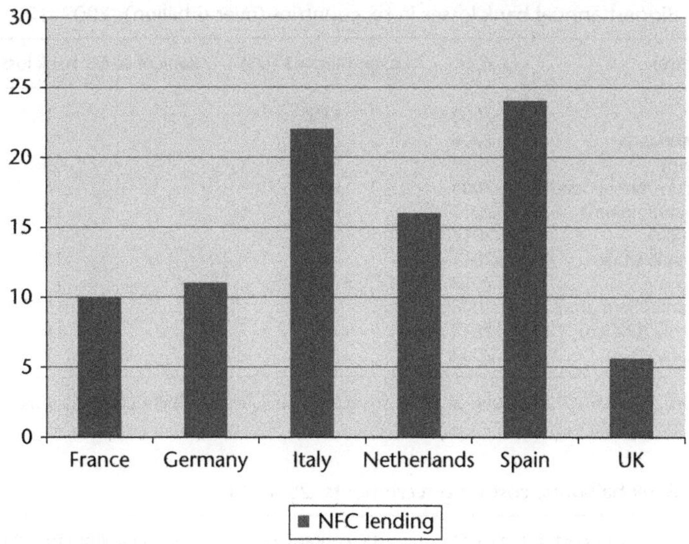

Figure 7. Bank lending to NFCs (percentage of total assets, end 2011)

Source: ECB data warehouse.

Notes: figures for the five euro area member states are for all euro area lending; figures for the UK are for domestic lending only.

traditional Italian and Spanish banking systems and the least of the British banking system, where banks were more engaged in investment banking activities.

Measuring the Health of the Banking System

The health of the banking system can be examined by way of a collection of measures. We explain below why the health of the banking system is also relevant to varying national policy-makers' preoccupation with moral hazard. There are several relevant measures here: published (official) bank losses, government support for banks, bank capital and liquidity position, return on assets and equity, and non-performing loans. Bank losses during and over the years following the international financial crisis (Table 10) and the level of government support (Table 11) potentially increased the interest of national policy-makers in transferring banking supervision/control to the supranational level, in response to the perceived inadequacy of national regulatory and supervision frameworks (or even regulatory and supervisory forbearance) prior to the international and then sovereign debt crises. However, as large bank losses in the UK and Germany suggest, interest in revised

Table 10. Biggest annual bank losses in six countries (over 6 billion), 2007–12

Bank (Country)	Year	Losses billion $ (US)	Rank of all EU bank losses to 2013
RBS (UK)	2008	43.2	1
Fortis (Netherlands)	2008	28.0	2
Bankia (Spain)	2012	19.2	3
Fortis (Belgium/Netherlands)	2008	18.5	4
Dexia (France/Belgium)	2011	11.6	10
Unicredit (Italy)	2011	9.2	11
Intesa Sanpaolo (Italy)	2011	8.2	12
RBS (UK)	2012	7.3	13
Commerzbank (Germany)	2008	6.6	15
Crédit Agricole (France)	2012	6.5	16
KfW (Germany)	2007	6.2	17

Source: Reuters, 1 March 2013, available at <http://blog.thomsonreuters.com/index.php/biggest-banking-losses-in-europe-graphic-of-the-day>.

Table 11. Bank bail-outs, cost for governments, 2008–11

	Net cost in € billion*	Percentage of GDP	Bank recapitalization in € billion (rounded)
France	–2.4	–0.10	20
Germany	16.56	0.70	51
Italy	–0.13	–0.00	3
Netherlands	3.44	0.60	17
Spain	–1.45	–0.10	11
UK	25.03	1.00	89

Source: Eurostat. Costs and revenue to public budgets only.

* Negative figures show gains for the government.

bank supervision did not necessarily encourage national policy-makers to focus on supranational supervision but rather on domestic institutional reform to improve supervision.

The losses of banks in the immediate aftermath of the financial crisis corresponded largely to levels of 'market-based banking' in at least four of the six countries (Hardie and Howarth 2013). Losses in Italy and Spain, however, largely reflected the impact of more traditional bank crises (see Chapter 3). While the correlation between bank losses and government support (in total and relative to GDP) and national policy-makers' interest in Banking Union is likely to be limited, this consideration has been raised by a range of policy-makers interviewed and other observers in all six national contexts, it has been closely associated with supervisory forbearance in some national contexts (notably Spain), and it merits further examination (Lehmann and Nyberg 2014).

We also consider a range of standard (non-crisis-related) measures to determine the health of banks (and thus the banking system) in the context of the sovereign debt crisis and how health progressed from 2011 to 2013 (IMF

Financial Stability Indicators). The health of banks is of relevance to our study in several ways. First, the weaker financial situation of banks in a country may have increased national policy-makers' interest in modifying both national bank regulation and supervisory frameworks so as to boost international confidence in national banking systems, but also to force through change in the domestic banking system that might otherwise be politically difficult.

Second, the weaker financial situation of specific national banking systems—notably Spain and Italy—may have encouraged other member states to seek to extend EU-level banking supervision. Third, the weaker financial situation in these countries also increased the concern of other national policy-makers with regard to controls in Banking Union to prevent moral hazard for both sovereigns and banks. Specifically, some member states (notably Germany and the Netherlands) sought to prevent Banking Union support and resolution mechanisms from applying to the so-called legacy problems of banks—that is, those problems pre-dating the operation of the SSM starting in November 2014. Such concerns prompted, above all, interest in a mandatory Comprehensive Assessment for the larger euro area banks that were to be subject to direct ECB supervision.

Thus, the health of the national banking system had a direct impact on the interest of national policy-makers in Banking Union and on the specifics of its design. The figures for return on equity and assets, and non-performing loans demonstrate most clearly the difficult situation facing Italian and Spanish banks in the context of the sovereign debt crisis (see Table 12 and Figure 8). In contrast, for the French, German, British, and Dutch banking systems, the difficult years of the financial crisis seem to have passed by 2011.

The figures for non-performing bank loans also demonstrate the uneven impact of the financial and then sovereign debt crises upon the real economy in the six countries. As expected, non-performing loans rose highest in the two countries worst hit by the sovereign debt crisis: Italy and Spain. The figures for the other four countries remained either broadly stable over previous years or increased only marginally.

Table 12. Return on equity and return on assets (banks in six countries)

	Return on equity percentage (2011)	2012	2013	Return on assets percentage (pre-tax) (2011)	2012	2013
France	8.25	5.99	8.44	0.39	0.31	0.49
Germany	13.05	10.82	7.53	0.53	0.45	0.36
Italy	−12.99	−0.92	−11.51	−0.87	−0.06	−0.77
Netherlands	9.59	7.38	6.21	0.42	0.33	0.29
Spain	1.46	−21.04	5.38	0.09	−1.39	0.38
UK	6.11	3.38	4.22	0.29	0.17	0.22

Source: IMF Financial Stability Indicators, IMF elibrary, available at <http://data.imf.org/?sk=f15905b8-c65e-4aff-abc8-41c925a3aad7&sId=1390030109571&ss=1390030323199>.

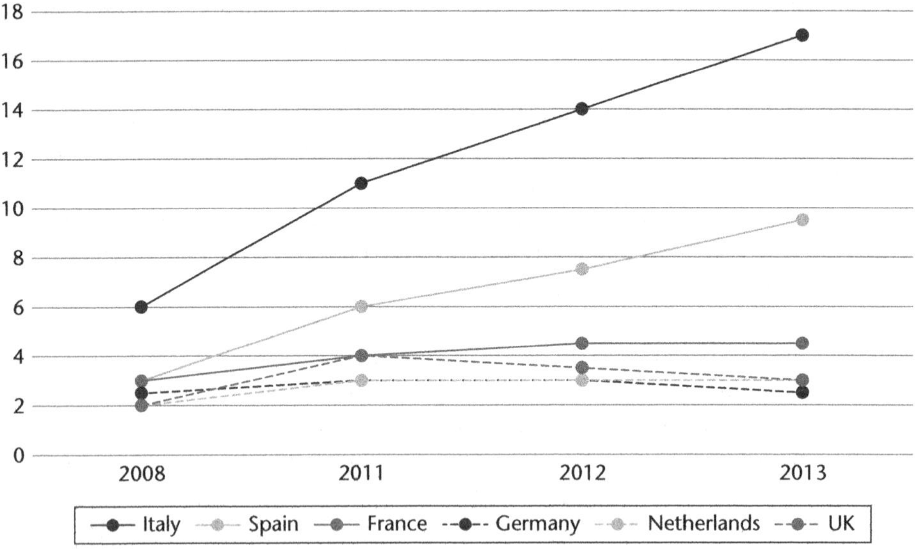

Figure 8. Non-performing loans (percentage of total; 2008–13)

Source: World Bank Global Financial Development, <http://databank.worldbank.org/data/>, accessed on 12 December 2015; and IMF Financial Stability Indicators, <http://data.imf.org/?sk=f15905b8-c65e-4aff-abc8-41c925a3aad7&sId=1390030109571&ss=1390030323199>, accessed on 12 December 2015.

Note: Figures are rounded to the nearest 0.5.

Headline bank capital figures are less indicative of bank (banking system) health. Systems containing a large number of otherwise perfectly sound alternative banks which do not issue equity might appear to be significantly undercapitalized. The ban on hybrids and the double counting of insurance subsidiaries in Basel III (adopted in December 2010) would have a potentially significant impact upon the capital ratios of many EU-headquartered banks. However, the proposed revision to the CRD (CRD IV)— eventually adopted in June 2013—promised to water down the application of Basel III in the EU (see Howarth and Quaglia 2013b). Thus, official capital figures were inflated.

Some British banks, recapitalized by the national government, and Spanish banks, recapitalized by the ESM, appear more robust than they actually were (Table 13). If we consider the deleveraging of banks from the end of 2008 (Figure 9), it appears that British banks went the furthest in raising their capital ratio by shrinking their balance sheet (see Cosimano and Hakura 2011), while Spanish banks expanded their balance sheets notably by taking on sovereign debt. EBA stress tests provide a relatively good indication of relative capital levels, demonstrating in both 2010 and 2012 that Italian banks had the furthest to go to (in either deleveraging or capital-raising) to meet Basel III/EU capital requirements (Table 13). Tables 14 and 15 show the

Table 13. Bank capital and liquidity positions, 2011–13

	Tier 1 bank capital to risk-weighted assets (2011)*	2012	2013	Liquid assets to total assets (liquid coverage ratio) (2011)**	2012	2013
France	4.75	5.20	5.82	41.83	39.21	39.11
Germany	4.36	4.73	5.45	39.60	39.70	45.04
Italy	5.45	5.39	5.40	12.28	14.61	16.63
Netherlands	4.28	4.69	4.78	24.84	24.31	23.60
Spain	5.92	5.76	6.79	N/A	N/A	N/A
UK	5.10	5.51	6.35	20.47	22.51	22.70

Source: IMF 'Financial Stability Indicators', IMF elibrary, available at <http://data.imf.org/?sk=f15905b8-c65e-4aff-abc8-41c925a3aad7&sId=1390030109571&ss=1390030323199>.

* Target figures of 6 per cent of risk-weighted assets (from 1 January 2015) and 8.5 per cent with capital conservation buffer (from 1 January 2019) under Basel III and the CRD IV.

** Target figures of 60 per cent (from 1 January 2015) rising to 100 per cent (from 1 January 2019) under Basel III and the CRD IV.

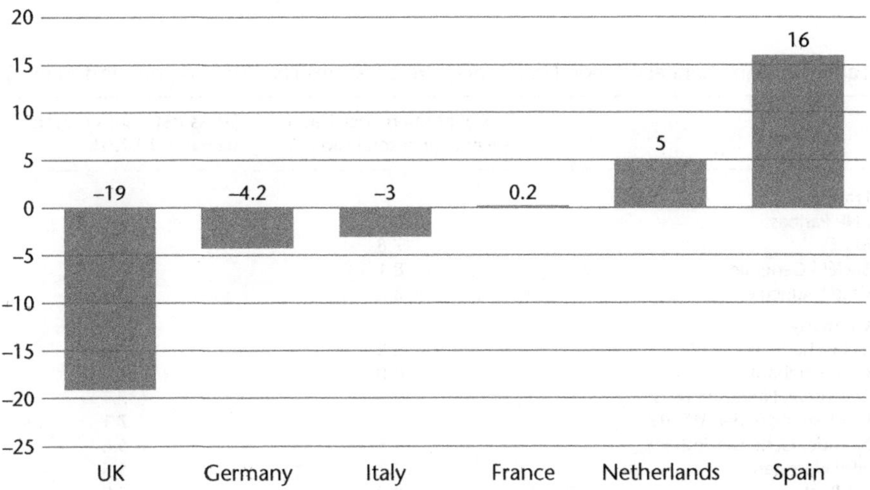

Figure 9. Deleveraging: national bank asset trends (change, percentage; end 2008 to end 2011)

Source: Bloomberg, Financial Statements, Deloitte Insight, available at <http://www2.deloitte.com/content/dam/Deloitte/uk/Documents/financial-services/deloitte-uk-fs-european-bank-deleveraging.pdf>.

particularly difficult position facing all Italian banks, Spanish savings banks, and the German Landesbanks. On liquidity, the low figures for Italian banks raised some concerns, alleviated by liquidity provision from the ECB (IMF 2013c). The lower the Liquid Asset Ratio (the ratio of liquid assets to total assets), the lower the ability of a bank to pay off its creditors (notably short-term debt obligations) and the nearer the bank to insolvency.

Table 14. Banking system capital ratios under the adverse scenario, 2010, 2012

	2010	2012
Germany	9.4	6.8
France	8.4	7.5
Italy	7.4	6.5 (7.3)*
Netherlands	10.6	9.4
Spain	7.4	6.5 (7.3)*
UK	10.1	7.6
Total EU	**8.9**	**7.4 (7.7)***

Source: EBA (2011) 'European Banking Authority 2011 EU-Wide Stress Test Aggregate Report', 15 July, p. 8, available at <https://www.eba.europa.eu/documents/10180/15935/EBA_ST_2011_Summary_Report_v6.pdf/54a9ec8e-3a44-449f-9a5f-e820cc2c2f0a>.

NB: Basel III target of 8.5 per cent, including mandatory capital conservation buffer.

*With capital-raising up to 30 April 2011 in brackets.

Table 15. Bank Capital Position (Tier 1) and stress tests results (2011) (largest institutions)

	Capital position (Tier 1 as a percentage of total capital)	Stress test results (adverse scenario, 12.12)*
France		
BNP Paribas	9.2	7.9
BPCE	7.8	6.8
Société Générale	8.1	6.6
Credit Agricole	8.2	8.5
Germany		
Deutsche Bank	8.8	6.5
Commerzbank	10.0	6.4
Bayerische Landesbank	9.3	7.1
Landesbank Baden-Württ.	8.2	7.1
Norddeutsche Landesbank	4.6	5.6
HSH Nordbank	10.7	5.5
DZ Bank	8.2	6.9
Italy		
Unicredit	7.8	6.7
Intesa Sao Paolo	7.9	8.9
Banca Monte dei Paschi	5.8	6.3
Unione Di Banche Italiane	7.0	7.4
Banco Popolare	5.8	5.7
Netherlands		
ING	9.6	8.7
Rabobank	12.6	10.8
ABN Amro Bank	9.9	9.2
SNS Bank	8.4	7.0
Spain		
BBVA	8.0	9.2
Santander	7.1	8.4
BFA Bankia	6.9	5.4
Catalunya Caixa	6.4	4.8

UK		
HSBC	10.5	8.5
Lloyds	10.2	7.7
Barclays	10.0	7.3
RBS	9.7	6.3

Source: EBA (2011) 'European Banking Authority 2011 EU-Wide Stress Test Aggregate Report', 15 July, available at <https://www.eba.europa.eu/documents/10180/15935/EBA_ST_2011_Summary_Report_v6.pdf/54a9ec8e-3a44-449f-9a5f-e820cc2c2f0a>.

Note: Recall, target figure of 8.5 per cent Tier 1 (including countercyclical buffer).

* Including mitigating capital-raising as of 30 April 2011.

We argue that the emphasis placed upon moral hazard concerns by national policy-makers depended in large part upon the 'manageability' of real and potential bank losses. The measurement of 'manageability' can at best be approximate. Two rough indicators of 'manageability' are the credit ratings for and the yield on sovereign debt, although these are determined specifically by how sustainable credit rating agencies and financial market operators perceive sovereign debt more generally. The current health of the banking system (several measures) is an important factor. However, two other factors are crucial: the relative size of the national banking sector relative to GDP, and national debt load (Figures 10 and 11). We also consider the size to GDP of the largest banks in the six case study countries (Table 16), a measure that is of central importance with regard to banks that are considered 'too big to fail'.

Despite the large size of the banking sector relative to GDP and a rapidly rising public debt load in the aftermath of the international financial crisis, the UK's 'manageability' was improved by the autonomy of national monetary policy, and the ability of the Bank of England to monetize sovereign debt and provide cheap funding to banks through quantitative easing. In the euro area, the ECB de facto undertook both debt monetization and quantitative easing, despite treaty prohibitions on the former. However, the state of national public finances, and the health and size of the bank sector still determined how international financial market operators perceived 'manageability'—thus provoking a significant rise in bond yields for both Spain and Italy in the summer of 2011.

Among our five euro area case study countries, Italy and Spain had the lowest 'manageability' due to large public debt loads (notably Italy; see Figure 10) and large and unhealthy banking sectors (although the Italian was considerably smaller than the Spanish). The Netherlands was heavily exposed, as demonstrated by its very large bank sector and two 'too big to fail' banks. France had a large and rapidly growing public debt to GDP ratio (Figure 10), the largest banking sector to GDP ratio, and at least two 'too big to fail' banks.

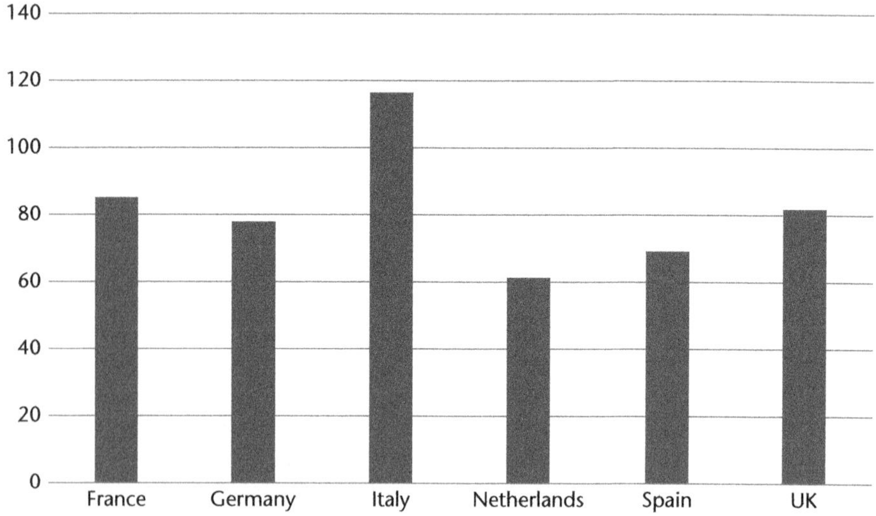

Figure 10. Public debt load (percentage of GDP; end 2011)
Source: OECD.

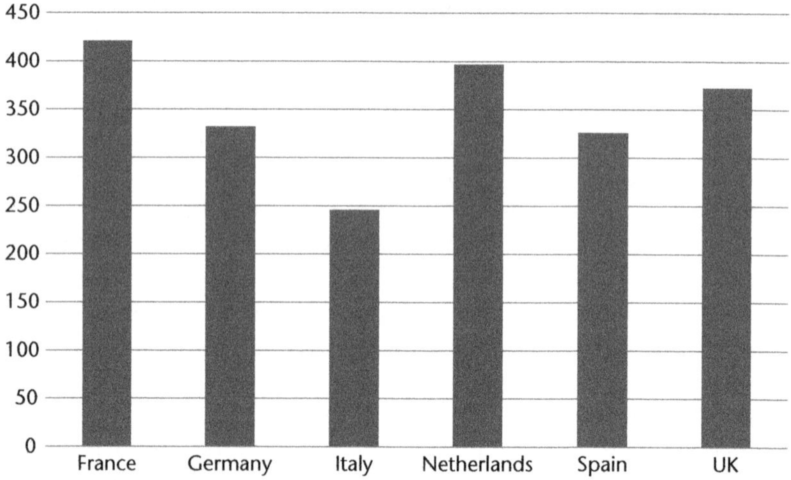

Figure 11. Banking sector size (percentage of GDP; end 2011)
Source: ECB (2013).

However, the relative health of its banking sector boosted confidence in the 'manageability' of bank debt. Germany appears to have had the most manageable banking sector, with the second-lowest public debt load among the five euro area member states (Figure 10), the smallest banking sector relative to GDP figures, and only one bank that could be classified as potentially 'too big to fail'.

Table 16. Large bank size to GDP (end-2011 figures)

Bank	Home country	Total assets (euros)	Assets to national GDP (percentage)	Total assets to EU GDP (percentage)
Deutsche Bank	Germany	2,164,103	84.8	17.4
HSBC	UK	1,967,796	119.8	15.8
BNP Paribas	France	1,965,283	99.8	15.8
Barclays	UK	1,871,469	113.9	15.0
Royal Bank of Scotland	UK	1,803,649	109.8	14.5
Crédit Agricole	France	1,723,608	87.5	13.8
Santander	Spain	1,251,525	118.2	10.1
Société Générale	France	1,181,372	60.0	9.5
Lloyds Banking Group	UK	1,161,698	70.7	9.3
ING	Netherlands	961,165	161.5	7.7
Unicredit	Italy	926,769	59.4	7.4
BPCE	France	795,728	40.4	6.4
Rabobank Group	Netherlands	731,665	122.9	5.9
Commerzbank	Germany	661,763	25.9	5.3

Source: HLEG (2012), modified by authors.

Six National Banking Systems

Germany: Defending the 'Local Champions'

The German banking system was a central pillar of the country's Coordinated Market Economy (CME), providing 'patient capital' through both cross-shareholding of the large commercial banks (which had declined significantly by the late 2000s) and 'relational banking' (Deeg, 2010; Hackethal 2004; Hackenthal and Schmidt 2005). The German CME has been characterized by the following features: heavy NFC (notably SME) reliance on bank credit; the under-development of equity and corporate debt markets; a strong institutional link between NFCs and banks (notably through formal bank representation on company boards); and a long-term relationship of trust between the Mittelstand (SMEs) and their 'Hausbank' as a lender with a special responsibility. 'Relational banking' thus reflected and reinforced the crucial position of small retail-focused alternative banks in the German system.

The German banking system was both the least concentrated in Europe (see Figure 6) and one of the least internationalized (see Figure 3), with only 25 per cent of bank assets held outside the country in 2012. There were three distinct pillars, each subject to specific regulation and supervision: commercial, savings and Landesbanks, and cooperative banks. Although Germany was home to one very big, highly internationalized commercial bank (Deutsche Bank) and a second very big commercial bank with a significant European presence (Commerzbank), there was a diverse range of other banks, including 5 remaining Landesbanks owned by regional (Land) governments, slightly more than 420 public law savings banks (Sparkassen), and 1,200 small cooperative banks (Volksbanken and Raiffeisen) which provided the bulk of funding to, and maintained close relations with, SMEs. Almost one-third of the euro area's banks were German. These banks were what we label as Germany's 'local champions'.

Savings banks were locally or regionally based entities with a vested interest in the local economy and a strong presence in local community life. In late 2012, the largest savings bank had a balance sheet of approximately €40 billion, about one-fiftieth that of Deutsche Bank, and more than 100 had less than €1 billion in assets (*Financial Times*, 2 December 2012). The bulk of German savings banks enjoyed a lower cost of capital compared with their commercial rivals because they relied disproportionately on high levels of funding through local-government-held long-term debt (a form of hybrid capital referred to as 'silent participations', which the EU's CRD IV allowed as Tier 1) and were under no obligation to make pay-outs to their local municipalities (*Financial Times*, 2 December 2012).

Furthermore, the savings banks (and the regional Landesbanks) benefited from the German regulatory practice that considered loans among them to be risk free—which meant that no capital had to be held against such exposures. Savings bank directors appeared to be unanimous in their view that home regulators better understood their characteristics and way of doing business (Simpson 2013; *Financial Times*, 2 December 2012). The savings banks were not required to file combined accounts as a single financial group, and accounts were first overseen by auditors from within the savings bank group, not external auditors. There was also strong economic logic to retaining a tolerant supervisory framework: with negligible reliance on short-term wholesale market funding, the savings and cooperative banks repeatedly demonstrated their ability to maintain lending when commercial banks were more reticent (Hardie and Howarth 2013).

Critics of the sector argued that the savings banks presented themselves as small and systematically less relevant, but then benefited from being part of a large, closely linked network and collectively one of the largest financial groups in the world with more assets (€1 trillion) than Deutsche Bank, a collective 38 per cent share of German bank lending, and almost 37 per cent deposits (Bundesbank, various dates; *Financial Times*, 2 December 2012;

Simpson 2013). Savings banks were also bound up, through ownership stakes, loans, and mutual guarantees, with the regional Landesbanks, which were in turn backed by regional (Land) governments—officially, until the elimination of new government guarantees on their borrowing from July 2005 (Grossman 2006), and unofficially since then. Land governments also funded the Landesbanks through 'silent participations'.

The publicly owned Landesbanks were badly hit by the international financial crisis (see Chapter 3). The five that survived the crisis—NordLB, HSH Nordbank, Helaba, BayernLB, and LB Baden-Württemberg (with the possible exceptions of HSH Nordbank, which suffered massive losses in 2013, and Helaba, which German policy-makers repeatedly shielded from EBA stress tests)—were by the end of 2012 in a much stronger capital position than they were at the onset of the crisis in 2007 and on track even to meet Basel III rules by 2019 (*Financial Times*, 20 June 2013). Notably, the remaining Landesbanks reduced their foreign exposure, writing down billions in toxic assets and retreating from lending in Central and Eastern Europe (their principal exposure elsewhere in the EU). The Landesbanks also increased their capital holdings, following the lead of NordLB, which arranged to have a €15 billion portfolio of assets part-guaranteed by its two state owners—the Länder governments of Lower Saxony and Saxony Anhalt (*Financial Times*, 25 July 2012). This move echoed the British government's Asset Protection Scheme and allowed the Landesbanks to significantly improve their capital ratios. In 2012, the Landesbanks provided a quarter of lending to the German corporate sector and Landesbank profits reached their highest level since 2006.

The measures of bank internationalization discussed above suggest limited interest of German policy-makers in Banking Union despite German participation in the single currency. Foreign assets were a small percentage of total assets and were concentrated in a very small number of banks. Only half of all German foreign assets were in the EU (54 per cent, versus 46 per cent in the rest of the world) (BIS data, authors' calculations). Only a third (33 per cent) of German foreign assets were in the euro area and only a small percentage of total German assets were in the euro area (9 per cent in 2012). German exposure to the EU and euro periphery was, however, comparatively high by several measures (see Table 4), and only behind France as a percentage of total assets, but exposure also decreased rapidly from 2009. German bank holdings of euro periphery sovereign debt—most at risk of default—were comparatively very high as a percentage of Core Tier 1 capital, but this figure better demonstrates the limited Core Tier 1 capital held by German banks. As a percentage of GDP, their holdings of euro periphery sovereign debt were far below French and Dutch levels, and even below the British level (see Figure 4). On the liabilities side of the balance, German banks were even less internationalized. Reliance on short-term wholesale market funding was very limited and only concerned a small number of commercial banks (Table 8). The savings and Landesbanks (and most commercial banks) relied on stable, long-term, largely domestically held wholesale market funding (*Pfandbriefe*) and silent participations, while the cooperatives relied principally on deposits to fund bank lending.

The domestic reach of internationalization was also very limited, given the institutional organization of German savings and cooperative banks. The cooperative banks included two central financial institutions (DZ Bank and WGZ Bank) and a number of specialized service providers (e.g., a large building society (Bausparkasse Schwäbisch-Hall) and an asset management company (Union Investment)) operating nationwide. DZ Bank operated as a commercial bank and was considerably engaged in cross-border activities (about 20 per cent in the EU and 27 per cent internationally). However, the cooperatives' joint liability scheme did not cover these larger institutions and, with the exception of DZ Bank, their focus was overwhelmingly domestic (Fonteyne 2007).

Savings banks had joint liability schemes (Haftungsverbund) with other small, domestically oriented entities, which were financially stable—none had to be bailed out by governments over the last fifty years or so. In certain regions, the savings banks had ties to regional Landesbanks, some of which were internationally active, such as LB Baden-Württemberg. However, as with the cooperatives, there were no joint liability schemes that linked the savings banks to Landesbanks. The design of joint liability schemes was an important factor shaping national preferences on the threshold of ECB supervision (see Chapter 5). Alone in Europe, German cooperatives and savings banks formally maintained the regional principle, which blocked competition among cooperatives and savings banks, respectively, thus maintaining local fiefdoms (Ayadi et al. 2009; Bülbül, Schmidt, and Schüwer 2013).

German caution with regard to Banking Union stemmed in part from the relative importance of German public sector, savings, and cooperative banks in the country's banking system. German policies on all the elements of Banking Union—including some of the regulatory developments to stabilize banking in the aftermath of the financial crisis—demonstrated half-hearted interest, with frequent German back-tracking on general commitments. If Germany accepted some form of Banking Union, this was for reasons less connected to the interests of the German banking system per se. German policies on the design of Banking Union were shaped to a large extent by moral hazard concerns—which stemmed in large part from the comparatively good health of the German banking system and the comparatively favourable German budgetary position. However, the configuration of the German banking system also contributed to the contours of national policy on the different elements of Banking Union. The existence of ex ante funded joint liability schemes created by the savings and cooperative banks ensured considerable German reluctance regarding both the SRM and the CDGS.

France: Defending the 'National Champions'

The French banking system was somewhat more concentrated than the British (Figure 6) and was known for five very large banks. The French retail market was even more concentrated, with over 90 per cent of bank lending provided by the biggest five banks at the end of 2012 (Howarth 2013; IMF 2011c; 2012d). These banks all had a significant presence elsewhere in the EU, although Schoenmaker describes only one as a major regional bank (BNP Paribas) and one as a 'semi-international' bank (the large alternative group, Banques Populaires et Caisses d'Epargne (BPCE)) (Table 1). At the same time, the largest French banks relied far more on domestic retail banking than the largest British banks (over 50 per cent for the largest three banks). The retail presence of the three large French commercial banks (BNP Paribas, Société Générale, and Crédit Agricole) in other EU member states (and, notably, other euro area member states) was also far greater than that of British and German banks. However, overall, the French banking system was considerably more nationally focused than the British, with domestic assets at a similar level to the German, Dutch, and Spanish banking systems.

France had a large number of small savings and cooperative banks that were grouped into one of three large centralized semi-consolidated groups, in which the small banks advertised as distinct entities at the local and regional level but had only limited autonomy from the mother bank. The central institutions and, in the case of the part-listed Crédit Agricole and BPCE, specially created investment banks (Crédit Agricole Corporate and Investment Banks (CACIB) and Natixis) were highly internationalized. The international financial crisis resulted in significant losses from credit securities purchased by both these investment banks and the central institutions (Howarth 2013; Xiao 2009). Crédit Mutuel was less internationalized but still held a significant percentage of its assets (14 per cent) outside France.

At the end of 2012, roughly 50 per cent of French bank foreign exposure was in the EU and 41 per cent in the euro area (BIS data). With 38 per cent of French bank assets held abroad in 2012, this meant that 19 per cent of the total were in the EU and 16 per cent in the euro area specifically. With a banking sector approximately 420 per cent of GDP, French banks and the French economy therefore had significant exposure to the euro area (67 per cent of GDP). French banking system exposure to the euro periphery was the highest in the world in relative terms and 60 per cent higher than German bank exposure in 2012 (BIS data). Exposure to the euro periphery reached 6.8 per cent of total assets (or 28.6

per cent of French GDP). At the end of 2012, approximately a fifth (19 per cent) of French bank assets held abroad were held in the euro periphery. The comparatively high exposure meant that, more than for other non-periphery euro area member states, we would expect French interest in Banking Union.

Despite the relative importance of retail banking (50 per cent of total assets at the end of 2012) and a large deposit base, French banks relied heavily upon short-term funding on wholesale markets (especially interbank lending). Total funding on wholesale and money markets reached 29 per cent of total funding at the end of 2012, considerably more than any other European banking system (Bank of France data). Short-term funding of less than two years stood at 14 per cent of total funding or 42 per cent of GDP (ECB data, Table 8). The international financial crisis demonstrated the dangers of such funding, and French bank reliance had declined somewhat since 2008. Furthermore, unlike short-term funding of British and Dutch banks (much of which came from the US-based banks), French short-term funding came largely from other banks headquartered in the EU (BIS data). This fact further reinforced French interest in EU- (or euro area) level measures to boost the stability of other European national banking systems.

The Netherlands: A Surprisingly Parochial System

Despite the image of the Netherlands as one of the most open trading economies on the planet, the Dutch banking system of the first two decades of the twenty-first century had a similar level of internationalization (assets) as the German, Spanish, and French banking systems. The internationalization of the biggest systemically important Dutch banks was only 10 per cent higher than average national figures—well below the levels for the largest German and Spanish banks. Dutch banks were chastened by the financial crisis, and one of the biggest, ABN AMRO, sold off major internationally focused operations. In 2012, the Netherlands was home to two of the world's thirty largest banks (by asset size) (ING and Rabobank) and a third very large bank that had previously been one of the world's largest (ABN). All the small and locally focused Dutch cooperative banks (Raffeisen) formed part of a semi-consolidated group and participated in a joint liability scheme with a 'mother bank' (Rabobank) with a very strong international presence. Dutch savings banks had merged decades earlier and operated as a standard commercial retail bank.

The biggest Dutch banks may have been major European and international players, but the bulk of their assets (over 60 per cent on average) were held domestically. Even the largest French banks, which were known for both a strong domestic and international presence, held only about 50 per cent of the assets domestically. The conservative, domestically focused

Rabobank, and the chastened ABN AMRO, held the large majority of their assets domestically (74 per cent and 80 per cent, respectively). Only ING was a truly international bank, with 60 per cent of assets outside the home-country market, evenly spread across the EU and the rest of the world. Thus, in comparative terms, the largest Dutch banks were domestically focused, with the important exception of ING. Not a single Dutch bank enters into the top ten in terms of its ratio of risk-weighted assets to total assets (Table 9). Of foreign assets, 56 per cent were EU based and 41 per cent were in the euro area. Foreign bank presence in the Netherlands was also comparatively very low, dropping from a high of 17 per cent prior to the international financial crisis to 9 per cent in 2012. Dutch bank holdings of euro periphery debt were cut rapidly in the period from the outbreak of the sovereign debt crisis. By the end of 2013, 3.4 per cent of assets were still in the euro periphery (sovereign debt and euro area corporate debt) and 13.5 per cent of GDP (BIS data).

In terms of funding, Dutch banks were highly internationalized in comparative terms. Indicating a gap in retail funding, the loan-to-deposit ratio of ING Bank, Rabobank, ABN AMRO, and SNS Bank ranged between 122 per cent and 162 per cent at the end of 2011, and the bulk of the shortfall was covered by short-term debt issuance, well above the level of nearly all of the other top 30 European banks.[2] At the end of 2010, 38 per cent of Dutch bank funding came from wholesale markets and 8.5 per cent was short term (less than two years). Thus, short-term funding (most exposed to freeze-ups in the short-term markets) amounted to over 33 per cent of Dutch GDP (ECB and Netherlands Central Bank data). In particular, the three largest Dutch banks had heavy structural reliance on wholesale and non-domestic funding sources to finance a significant portion of their core domestic lending. While British bank short-term funding shrank in the years following the crisis, Dutch short-term funding dropped less rapidly and less significantly. Much Dutch (like British) short-term interbank funding was from US banks and in dollars (BIS). This reliance rendered banks vulnerable to potential sudden changes in market confidence.

With the exception of bank funding, then, the limited internationalization of the Dutch banking system suggests limited interest in supranational cooperation. Yet Dutch policy-makers were strongly in favour of Banking Union. In structural terms, the large size of the Dutch banking system in relation to the national economy (at over 400 per cent, this is one of the largest in the EU), the relative size of the three 'too big to fail' Dutch

[2] 'Moody's downgrades Dutch banking groups; most outlooks now stable', Global Credit Research, 15 June 2012, available at <https://www.moodys.com/research/Moodys-downgrades-Dutch-banking-groups-most-outlooks-now-stable–PR_248387>.

banks, and significant bank losses during the financial crisis—Fortis suffered the second highest losses of any EU-headquartered bank (Table 10)—point to Dutch interest in the reinforcement of European supervision/control.

The Italian Banking System and its 'Half-Hearted' Consolidation

The Italian banking system was closer to the German than to the French or British systems and was characterized by both a very small number of systemically important banks, frequently with a strong presence elsewhere in Europe, as well as many small cooperative and regional banks. The pace of consolidation of the Italian banking system accelerated following the establishment of EMU in 1999 and the FSAP in 1999. Yet, at the end of 2008, the five biggest banks in Italy held only 31 per cent of total assets, with only the German banking system less concentrated (ECB 2013). By the end of 2012, this figure had risen to almost 40 per cent.

On the asset side of the balance sheet, Italian banks had lower levels of foreign holdings as a whole (just over 20 per cent), but foreign holdings were more likely to be held in the EU (65 per cent of the total) than outside the EU (Schoenmaker and Peek 2014). Of foreign holdings, 57 per cent were within the euro area (BIS figures, authors' calculations). The biggest Italian bank, Unicredit, was a major European player, with approximately 56 per cent of its total assets held in other EU member states and 2 per cent held internationally. The second-largest Italian bank (Intesa Sanpaolo) was far more domestic in focus, with only 14 per cent in the EU and 4 per cent internationally.

Foreign penetration into Italy was low but increased significantly during the first half of the 2000s with the arrival of, principally, French banks. Foreign penetration, however, stagnated at around 13 per cent over the years following the start of the financial crisis. On the liabilities side of the balance sheet, almost a quarter of bank funding came from wholesale markets (23 per cent in 2012). However, most of this was through longer maturity debt issues. Only just over 3 per cent of total Italian bank funding came from shorter maturity debt (less than two years) and only a tiny amount from interbank lending.

Apart from the five largest groups, Italian banks operated almost entirely in the domestic market, where a large number of small entities, including cooperative banks, specialized in local financing. In Italy, legally, there were three types of bank: limited liability companies, savings banks, and cooperative banks. As in France, the previously state-owned Italian banking system was privatized in the 1990s, when savings banks were transformed into limited liability companies (Ciocca 2005) and listed on the stock market (Giordano 2007; Panetta 2004), which allowed private banks to acquire holdings in, or merge with, Italian savings banks (Carletti, Hakenes, and Schnabel 2005). The regional principle was also abolished. Hence, there was a consolidation of the banking sector through mergers and acquisitions, which led to the formation of large banking groups bringing together commercial banks, savings banks, and, in some cases, cooperative banks (Deeg 2005). Thus, Italian savings banks diverged significantly from German savings banks, in both their institutional design and their operation.

Cooperative banks remained an important element of the Italian banking system, accounting for approximately 30 per cent of both loans and deposits of the Italian banking system (Gutiérrez 2008). There were two types of cooperative: mutual banks (formerly rural and artisans' banks) and peoples' banks (*banche popolari*). Italian mutuals had non-tradable shares, and were subject to the so-called principle of prevalence, requiring more than 50 per cent of assets to be detained by members, and the principle of mutuality, whereby the activities were mainly biased in favour of associates and included supporting the cultural and economic development of the local community (Barra, Destefanis, and Lubrano Lavadera 2011). The regional principle was maintained. These banks had an important role in the financing of households, artisans, and small businesses. Peoples' banks were not subject to geographical restrictions. They tended to be much larger than mutuals and included in their number Italy's fourth and fifth largest banks. Bülbül, Schmidt, and Schüwer (2013) note that the peoples' banks were 'almost "normal" banks' that had drifted 'away from their former cooperative and local roots'. However, few of their operations were international.

Despite significant losses suffered by the country's two largest banks in 2011 at the height of the sovereign debt crisis, the Italian banking system was generally considered to be relatively stable, and far more so than other euro periphery banking systems. Italian banks had not been hit significantly by the international financial crisis, and the government provided little in the way of financial support. At less than 250 per cent of GDP in 2011, the Italian banking system was one of the smallest in relative terms in Western Europe and thus, with the exception of Unicredit, failure was potentially more manageable. However, as shown in Tables 12, 13, and 14 and Figure 8, the Italian banking sector was far from healthy and was affected by the country's anaemic economic growth. Of the six banking systems examined here, Italian banks had the highest rate of non-performing loans and consistently the worst position for return on equity and assets. But even these poor results were likely the result of overly generous analysis of bank balance sheets.

In 2014, the ECB's Comprehensive Assessment of euro area banks found that Italian banks had weak capital positions and were among the most exposed to a future crisis, with nine failing—considerably more than any other member state. Italian banks were responsible for a quarter of the total over-valued assets, just less than 1 per cent of their risk-weighted assets. Once capital injections in early 2014 were taken into account, four Italian banks still faced shortfalls, including the country's third-largest and fourth-largest institutions: the Monte dei Paschi di Siena (MPS) and Banco Popolare. MPS, which needed to cover a shortfall of €2.1 billion, was the largest failure of the Comprehensive Assessment (*The Economist*, 26 October 2014; *Financial Times*, 26 October 2014).

Italian banks were hit particularly hard by the harmonized definition of non-performing loans, which suggested that the previously used Italian definition was too lax. In 2014, Italian bank bad loans reached a total of €160 billion—more than double their level in 2010—and they were expected to rise to nearly €1200 billion in 2015 (*Reuters*, 3 December 2014). About 17 per cent of Italian bank loans—€333 billion—were non-performing, according to the IMF (Jassaud and Kang 2015; see also *New York Times*, 13 February 2015). The Italian authorities responded to the Comprehensive Assessment by considering the possibility of setting up a bad bank—that is, a vehicle designed to absorb some of the non-performing loans of the banking sector—as established previously in Spain (the SAREB) (*New York Times*, 13 February 2015). Banks hoped that the establishment of a bad bank would allow them to sell their bad loans at higher prices (*New York Times*, 13 February 2015).

The Spanish Banking System: Destabilized by a Traditional Crisis

In 2011, Spain was near the EU average for bank assets relative to GDP (326 per cent), which was nonetheless a high figure by international standards. The Spanish banking system was dominated by two very large undercapitalized internationally present banks and a number of regional savings banks (*cajas*) (Royo 2013a, b, c). The Spanish banking system was similarly parochial compared with the other four large euro area banking systems (Figure 1), and far more than the EU average. However, the two biggest Spanish banks, Santander and BBVA, were among the largest in Europe and held a large proportion of assets outside the country. BBVA could be described as a semi-international bank, with 44 per cent of assets outside the country and the bulk of these outside the EU (35 per cent in the rest of the world versus 9 per cent in the EU). Santander was one of the most internationalized banks headquartered in the EU, holding 41 per cent of its assets in other EU member states and 32 per cent outside the EU. However, excluding these two highly internationalized banks, international asset figures for the Spanish banking system were very low. Of Spanish assets held abroad, 59 per cent were held outside the EU and 84 per cent were held outside the euro area (BIS figures, authors' own calculations). Spain was, with the Netherlands, one of the least open banking systems, with only 9 per cent of Spanish bank assets held by the branches and subsidiaries of foreign banks at the end of 2012.

In terms of liabilities, Spanish banks benefited from a broad and stable funding base, dominated by deposits from retail customers. Wholesale interbank funding was comparatively low, reaching only approximately 13 per cent of total funding between 2010 and 2013, and more stable longer maturity debt securities covered over 8 per cent. Short-term wholesale funding (less than two years) was very limited (less than 5 per cent of total liabilities between 2010 and 2013—far lower than Germany, France, the Netherlands, and the UK, and one of the lowest in the euro area [about 18 per cent of GDP in 2013]). Spanish banks and the Spanish economy were thus only marginally affected by difficulties in short-term wholesale markets post-2010 that created difficulties for a range of EU-headquartered banks—despite concerns raised by the Bank of Spain.[3] The significant funding gap prior to the financial crisis had dropped dramatically because of the collapse of lending by Spanish banks from 2008.

Thus, an application of Schoenmaker's triangle of incompatibility in itself suggests limited Spanish interest in supranational banking supervision in the euro area—at least beyond the two largest banks. The euro area member state with the greatest immediate interest in constructing Banking Union was a country with very limited interest structurally. The interest of Spanish policymakers was the result of a desperate situation—with the looming default of a range of Spanish banks (notably the *cajas*) and the sovereign—exacerbated by the sovereign debt–bank doom loop. Spanish banks held very high levels of domestic government debt in their total government debt portfolios (well over 80 per cent in 2012) (Bank of Spain data), and this figure rose substantially from 2010.

On a range of data, the Spanish banking system was among the weakest in the EU. On non-performing loans, only Italy exceeded Spain (see Figure 8). On return on equity and return on assets, Spain recorded the lowest figures of our six country cases (Table 12). BBVA and Santander had the highest ratio of risk-weighted assets to total assets (Table 9). In 2012, Bankia—the institution produced from the merger of a number of failing *cajas*—had the highest bank losses, and the third highest since the outbreak of the international financial crisis (Table 10). The capital position of Spanish banks appears comparatively strong in the aggregate (Table 13). However, this reflects the comparatively strong position of the country's two largest banks and disguises the weak position of the *cajas*.

The poor state of the Spanish banking sector was due largely to the difficulties facing the country's savings banks (*cajas*). Prior to 2010, these banks were widely considered to be successful by a range of measures. Bülbül et al. (2013)

[3] 'Dublin bail-out spooks investors in Spain,' *Financial Times*, 27–28 November, 2010.

and Manghetti (2011) called them a model of successful savings banks, with profit levels similar to two giant Spanish commercial banks. In 2011, the *cajas* held 35 per cent of total banks assets, down from a high of 39 per cent in 2006 (European Savings Banks Group 2013), and they held around 50 per cent of Spanish deposits.

From the 1970s, the *cajas* had been privatized and merged, while the regional principal was ended, allowing their expansion throughout Spain and their transformation into universal banks. With one of the highest number of branches-to-population ratios in the EU, the *cajas* turned to high-risk commercial real-estate investments in order to maintain their high profit margins (IMF 2012b). Despite these changes, the *cajas* continued to maintain a range of social functions for which they were created, notably the promotion of savings among poorer socio-economic groups to prevent their exclusion from the financial system; the provision of charitable or social-cultural services to the community; and regional development (IMF 2012b). Savings banks did not engage in pure profit maximization, and dedicated a significant portion of their provisions (in most cases over 20 per cent) to social causes (Royo 2013a).

Owing to their legal form, savings banks could not be taken over by banks from another category. Since *cajas* did not have any share capital, their ability to raise external equity capital was limited. In the absence of shareholders, control exercised over *cajas* was not coupled by legal ownership of shares, and therefore their corporate governance differed considerably from that of commercial banks (IMF 2012b). *Cajas* had strong links with the regions in which they operated because political parties and unions participated in the banks' governing bodies (Cuñat and Garicano 2009; Garicano 2012). *Cajas* were regulated by both the national government in charge of basic norms and by the regional governments (autonomous communities) in charge of application and development of the rules established by the central government. The supervisory powers of the Bank of Spain were de facto thwarted by political interference (Bülbül, Schmidt, and Schüwer 2013; Cuñat and Garicano 2009; Garicano 2012).

The abrupt end of the Spanish real-estate boom hit the *cajas* particularly hard and non-performing loans rose dramatically. They were rescued with public funds and/or were forced to merge with other *cajas*—the total number of savings banks had dropped from 45 to 11 by 2012. Most infamously, Bankia was a new bank formed by the central government through the forced merger of several failing savings banks from the Madrid metropolitan area. When the Spanish government received euro area financial assistance from the ESM in 2012 (see Chapter 8), it pledged to restructure its financial sector. The reforms enacted afterwards strengthened the regulatory regime for the few remaining savings banks, strengthened their governance, and barred them from undertaking business beyond their home region.

The International Champions of the British Banking System

The British banking system was only moderately concentrated in terms of total bank assets (Figure 6), which reflects the important presence of foreign bank subsidiaries and branches in the City. However, the British retail banking market was highly concentrated as few of these foreign bank subsidiaries and branches engaged in retail banking—Santander being the most significant. In the 2000s, the bulk of lending to domestic NFCs and households (consistently over 80 per cent) was provided by the largest six banks (Bank of England data). Yet, at the same time, domestic lending formed only a small part of most of these banks' assets (Figure 7). The British banking system was by far the most internationalized of the six largest EU member states, with the highest percentage of assets held in other EU member states and the euro area, as well as outside the EU. This pattern of internationalization—with British banks holding a comparatively large percentage of assets outside the EU—contributes to explaining the limited interest in specifically European solutions to coordination problems in bank supervision and resolution. The UK's exposure to the rest of the world was greater than exposure to the EU/euro area, of which the UK was not a member.

The British banking system was home to three 'international champions', which were among the world's ten largest banks in terms of asset size throughout most of the 2000s. Hong Kong and Shanghai Bank of Commerce (HSBC), RBS, and Barclays were highly internationalized and well-capitalized institutions with limited reliance on the domestic real economy (Tables 1 and 15). All three held a majority of their assets internationally, and a large majority of these international assets beyond Europe (Figure 3). As for liabilities, British banks relied more than most upon short-term (normally interbank) funding prior to the outbreak of the international financial crisis. However, by 2012, all British-based banks had massively cut their reliance upon this funding source, with total levels dropping well below French bank levels. During the international financial crisis, the British authorities required two of the banks (RBS and Lloyds-HBOS) to accept state funding (with share purchase reaching 78 per cent for the former and 18 per cent for the latter), but intervention in bank management was minimal and 'nationalization' was officially presented as being limited in duration (Woll and Grossman 2014).

Conclusion

This chapter examines several measures of internationalization and other distinctive features of national banking systems in order to tease out expectations about national preferences on Banking Union—both general interest in supranational control over banks and preferences on the specific elements of Banking Union. The 'manageability' of real and potential bank losses—resulting from the state of health of the national banking system, its relative size, and the state of public finances—shaped the concerns of national policy-makers regarding moral hazard. These concerns in turn shaped national preferences on the specific elements of Banking Union. The following chapters will assess the extent to which the banking system features analysed in this chapter can account for the preferences of our six country cases on the specific elements of Banking Union.

We apply the banking system features outlined above to draw general expectations as to national preferences on Banking Union. These features are categorized into six groups: internationalization patterns (and euro periphery debt holdings); the size and design of the alternative banking sector; bank capital and liquidity positions; the health of the banking system; and the 'manageability' of real and potential bank losses. In terms of general interest in Banking Union—that is, supranational control specifically in the EU—we see that Schoenmaker's financial trilemma, focused as it is on large cross-border banks, only provides limited guidance as to national preferences.

We would expect significant interest in all six countries, given the presence of very large internationalized 'too big to fail' banks. Indeed, all these large banks expressed their support for Banking Union—including the largest British banks, even though they did not campaign for UK membership. The relative size of these large banks in the national banking system (as a percentage of total assets) made national policy-makers more or less favourable to Banking Union, as demonstrated most clearly in the case of the Netherlands (higher) and Germany (lower). Thus, concentration levels mattered for at least two of our country cases. While the concentration level is lower in France, the presence of four very large banks with a significant cross-border presence encouraged French interest in Banking Union.

Internationalization and concentration patterns are, however, a less helpful guide to Italian and Spanish preferences on Banking Union. The presence of three of the EU's largest, highly internationalized 'too big to fail' banks in these two countries clearly provoked national interest. However, the fragility of the national banking sector was principally elsewhere (notably the *cajas* in Spain). Clearly, relative levels of euro periphery debt holdings—obviously highest in the euro periphery itself—sparked interest in Banking Union. Germany had the largest alternative banking sector of the five euro area case countries. But all the other country cases had significant alternative banking sectors as well, with the exception of the UK.

The design of the alternative banking sector—specifically the link between small parochial entities and larger internationalized financial institutions—determined the reach of internationalization into the banking system and contributed to national policy-makers' interest in Banking Union. As will be discussed further in successive chapters, the design of the alternative banking system shaped national preferences on all the elements of Banking Union, most obviously the threshold of direct ECB supervision. Overall, the limited interest of German policy-makers was shaped in large part by the design of the country's alternative banking sector and the limited reach of internationalization. The opposite can be noted with regard to the interest of French and Dutch policy-makers.

Capital position does not provide a good indication of interest in Banking Union—especially given that banking systems with a larger presence of alternatives tended to have less Core Tier 1 and Tier 1 capital. However, we would expect the importance of capital position in shaping national preferences on the Single Rulebook and, specifically, the importance of systemic risk-weight patterns in shaping national preferences on rules determining bank contributions to the SRF and the common DGS.

We would expect the weak health of the banking system to promote interest in Banking Union. Similarly, we would expect the weaker 'manageability' of real and potential bank losses to increase interest in Banking Union. 'Manageability' was highest in Germany, followed by the Netherlands, and thus the concern for moral hazard was highest in these two countries. 'Manageability' was lowest in Spain and Italy. Policy-makers in these two countries were strong proponents of Banking Union and the need to 'pool' bank risk. France was in between the two euro periphery and the two 'core' member states. However, with significant bank exposure to the periphery—notably Italy—French policy-makers played down moral hazard concerns.

Taking into consideration the six main features outlined above, the health of the banking system, and the 'manageability' of real and potential bank losses, we draw the following expectations regarding national preferences on Banking Union. We would expect Germany to have had the least interest in Banking Union and then to have sought to ensure that the elements of Banking Union were designed in such a way as to minimize the risks of moral hazard. The German banking system had the lowest rate of internationalization on a range of measures and the lowest foreign penetration, despite some exposure to euro periphery debt. Germany had a structurally undercapitalized banking system—due to the very large presence of alternative banks. However, Germany also had the highest 'manageability' of real and potential bank losses—given the comparative rude health of its banks and public finances.

Despite very limited overall internationalization levels, we would expect the Netherlands—with its two very large cross-border banks and a strong reach of internationalization into the alternative bank sector—to support Banking Union, but with preference to proceed with caution on support mechanisms.

We would expect French interest in Banking Union given the presence of large cross-border banks, a comparatively high exposure to euro periphery debt, potentially under-capitalized banks (due to double counting)—despite the overall good health of the banking system—and the questionable 'manageability' of potential bank losses due to the large size of the banking sector (relative to GDP) and the increasingly worrying state of public finances.

With its highly internationalized banking system and the presence of four 'too big to fail' banks, the interest of British policy-makers in Banking Union might have been expected—regardless of sovereignty concerns. However, the high level of internationalization beyond the EU and the strong presence of non-EU-headquartered banks decreased the relevance of Banking Union for the UK. While the health of the British banking system was mixed and the 'manageability' of potential bank losses was an important political concern, the ability of the Bank of England to manipulate monetary policy to the benefit of banks and the sovereign remained. The support of British policy-makers for the Banking Union project—albeit without British participation—reflects the relatively high exposure of the British banking system to the euro area.

Clearly, in terms of banking system structure, there are good reasons to have expected lukewarm Italian and Spanish interest in Banking Union. Overall internationalization levels (especially if we exclude the very largest banks) and the reach of internationalization were low. Yet, the health of the banking system in the two countries—according to a range of measures—and the 'manageability' of real and potential bank losses, in the context of the sovereign debt crisis, encouraged energetic support for Banking Union. The loss of power over bank supervision was the price to be paid for the creation of euro area-level support, resolution, and deposit guarantee mechanisms.

5

Supervision

Introduction

The first key component of Banking Union to be agreed was the SSM. As explained in Chapter 3, the acute financial trilemma in the euro area manifested itself with the sovereign debt crisis. The need to break the sovereign debt–bank doom loop provided the functional rationale for Banking Union, which complemented the financial support mechanisms made available in the euro area with the supranationalization of banking supervision that was transferred from the national level to the Banking Union level.

The internationalization of national banking systems (one element of the trilemma) explains interest in supranational supervision. However, policy-makers in different countries had different preferences concerning important aspects of the SSM. In order to explain national preferences on the SSM, two main factors are considered. First, moral hazard concerns pushed otherwise disinterested policy-makers—notably in the German government—to accept the need for supranational supervision especially for member states in need—or potentially in need—of financial support for banks. While northern euro area and other member states agreed on the problem of moral hazard and the need to harmonize supervisory standards, they disagreed significantly on the scope of ECB direct supervision—a divergence due principally to different national banking systems. However, with regard to the threshold for ECB direct supervision, the 'domestic reach of internationalization' is the key feature to consider. Countries in which the reach of internationalization in banking systems—mainly through consolidated and semi-consolidated groups of alternative banks—was high favoured a low threshold for direct ECB supervision (and vice versa).

This chapter begins by examining the concerns of a number of euro area policy-makers, notably the Germans, who took an interest in supranational supervision in order to avoid national supervisory forbearance and potential moral hazard created by support mechanisms for banks without reinforced supervision. After a brief overview of the intergovernmental negotiations on the SSM, this chapter elucidates the preferences of national policy-makers on the scope of ECB direct supervision that was of primary importance during the SSM negotiations. It then discusses the preferences of British policy-makers and other euro area outsiders with regard to their accession to the SSM (and Banking Union). Finally, it briefly reviews the Comprehensive Assessment carried out in the summer and autumn of 2014, which highlighted the problem of national supervisory forbearance and the legacy problems plaguing national banking systems.

Challenging Supervisory Forbearance: Concerns with Moral Hazard and Divergent Supervisory Practice

As explained in Chapter 3, the Banking Union proposal was triggered by the sovereign debt crisis in the euro area and the need to break the sovereign debt–bank doom loop. However, the German and other northern euro area member states had moral hazard concerns with regard to the establishment of euro area support mechanisms for banks in periphery member states. The Netherlands government pointed out that 'Europe-wide burden sharing could increase incentives for banks and national governments to engage in risky, undesirable behaviour. To mitigate such risk of moral hazard it is essential to introduce effective and independent banking supervision that functions properly in practice. It is also important to make sure that national governments still have incentives to keep their national banks healthy' (Netherlands Government 2012).

As a precondition for establishing support mechanisms, the Germans, the Dutch, and the Finnish demanded the establishment of the SSM. Euro area member states with the strongest banking systems (highest relative return on equity/assets, best relative capital positions—as explained in Chapter 4) and in the best fiscal position to manage their own domestic bank failures were the most preoccupied with the moral hazard created by inadequate national supervision combined with euro area funds. The Netherlands government also argued that supranational supervision 'should start not with all banks receiving public support but with those banks receiving European support', given the problem of 'moral hazard' (Netherlands Government 2012).

In late September, the German, Dutch, and Finnish governments made it clear that they opposed any agreement to allow the ESM to recapitalize banks without prior agreement on an adequate regulatory and supervisory framework and reinforced fiscal policy rules (Finnish Ministry of Finance 2012; *Financial Times*, 18 October 2012). These three governments also insisted that the banks in difficulty in those member states with fragile banking systems—notably Spain and Ireland—remained primarily the responsibility of the governments of those member states. The ESM was only to be used to help banks facing difficulties in the future, arising under the supervision of the ECB in the new banking union.

However, the euro area member states had significantly different supervisory practices, with supervision in some member states potentially considered forbearance in others. Indeed, some leading NCA and ECB officials warned about different definitions on a range of matters (see Mersch 2013b). For this reason, several member states—led by Germany—and several of the large euro area cross-border banks insisted upon harmonized supervisory standards. All the largest German and Dutch commercial banks supported the SSM, which they regarded as 'key to diminish discrepancies between national supervisory practices' (ING 2013).

The main Dutch bank, ING, was adamant that 'Important tasks like the authorization of credit institutions, assessment of acquisitions and disposals, the authority to ensure compliance for capital, liquidity regime and leverage ratios, and the imposition of additional capital buffers for prudential and countercyclical reasons should be the *exclusive responsibility* of the ECB for *all banks* in the participating member states' (ING 2013: 13; emphasis added). The logic of extending ECB direct supervision in order to boost international investor confidence in the quality of bank supervision in the euro periphery was also not lost on periphery policy-makers. The Spanish government argued that the fact that such a large percentage of national bank assets would be subject to direct ECB supervision represented a 'solid guarantee' for Spanish banks, which 'would be supervised according to very high standards' (Rajoy 2013).

The Intergovernmental Negotiations on the Single Supervisory Mechanism

In September 2012, the Commission adopted a set of legislative proposals concerning the establishment of the SSM, as the first step towards Banking Union: a regulation giving strong powers for the supervision of all banks in the euro area to the ECB (European Commission 2012a); a regulation with limited specific changes to the regulation setting up the EBA to ensure a balance in its decision-making structures between the euro area and non-euro area member states (European Commission 2012b); and a communication on a roadmap for completing Banking Union over the coming years, covering the Single Rulebook, common deposit protection, and a single bank resolution mechanism (European Commission 2012c).

The Commission and French policy-makers called for an end-of-year deadline to finalize the first element of Banking Union, the SSM. However, it became clear in the autumn that implementation would be delayed until the spring of 2014. There were two main controversial issues concerning the SSM. The first one was the scope of direct ECB supervision, in particular whether the ECB should directly supervise all banks in the euro area or only the main (cross-border) banks. The second one was whether non-euro area member states should be allowed to join the SSM and the relationship of the new mechanism with non-euro area countries.

The Commission and the French, Dutch, and Italian governments were in favour of the SSM covering all 6,000 euro area banks, which the Commission also suggested in its September draft of the SSM regulation (European Commission 2012a, d; *Financial Times*, 5 December 2012). Other member states and a range of observers questioned the ability of the ECB to handle the supervision of so many banks without a massive transfer of resources (*Financial Times*, 5 December 2012). The Germans sought real investigation and auditing powers to be assigned to the ECB—but only over the biggest banks. The French preferred a 'licensing' system that would enable national supervisors to act on behalf of the ECB (*Financial Times*, 5 December 2012). Italian policy-makers also separately called for 'delegation' provisions to be inserted into the draft regulation (Signorini 2012).

Negotiations on the scope of direct ECB supervision focused on the threshold that would trigger it. This is important because it concerns the degree of supranational bank supervision and thus the actual power of the ECB in relation to both national supervisors and national governments. A very high bank-size threshold (by bank assets and/or by assets as a percentage of national GDP) would result in only the very largest banks being subject to direct ECB supervision. A cross-border threshold (notably, foreign held assets as a percentage of total bank assets) would lead to only banks with a certain level of cross-border activity being subject to ECB supervision. A combination of size and cross-border criteria would further limit the number of banks—depending on the precise levels set. Thus, threshold was about the reach of supranational supervision and the design of the SSM, namely the relative supervisory powers assigned to the ECB and to NCAs.

National preferences on the reach of the ECB's direct control over bank supervision varied markedly. France, the Netherlands, Italy, and Spain (joined by Luxembourg) supported direct ECB supervision over all euro area banks. The French government expressed concern over unequal treatment of member states given that its banking system was dominated by five very large institutions which would all end up being directly supervised by the ECB (*Financial Times*, 14 November 2012). Germany (joined by a number of other euro area member states, including Austria, Belgium, and Finland) preferred ECB supervision of only the largest systemically important banks.

For policy-makers from the latter countries, preferences on threshold were driven—at least officially—by efficiency concerns: they argued that it was impractical to extend direct ECB supervision over thousands of smaller banks given staffing, travel, and language concerns. However, such concerns were downplayed by French and Dutch negotiators, who called for a gradual transfer. Italian and Spanish negotiators were willing to compromise on this point—the threshold was not a deal-breaker for these two countries—and both accepted the possibility of ECB supervision for most if not all euro area banks, although Italy's preference was for a delegation mechanism to ensure de facto ongoing national control under supranational 'guidance'.[1] Several governments publicly criticized the German negotiators over their determined position on threshold and on sheltering small alternative (cooperative and savings) banks from direct ECB supervision, and called for compromise (*Euronews*, 4 December 2012). This German position aligns with long-standing government efforts to protect the country's cooperative and savings bank sector from EU Commission efforts to liberalize it (see Deeg 1999; Smith 2001).

The compromise reached on the SSM foresaw that the ECB would be 'responsible for the overall effective functioning of the SSM' and would have 'direct oversight of the euro area banks' (European Council 2012a: 2). This supervision, however, would be 'differentiated' and the ECB would carry it out in 'close cooperation with national supervisory authorities'. Direct ECB supervision (through Joint Supervisory Teams) was to cover those banks which met the following four criteria: one of the country's three largest banks by assets; assets exceeding €30 billion; assets representing at least 20 per cent of their home country's annual GDP, except if the bank's assets amount to less than €5 billion; any other bank with a high level of cross-border exposure (although no precise figure was established).

This direct supervision would, it was later decided by the ECB, concern 128 euro area banks, holding slightly more than 80 per cent of euro area bank assets. However, the agreement also permitted the ECB to step in, if necessary, and supervise any of the 6,000 banks in the euro area to bring about the eventual restructuring or closure of banks that found themselves in difficulties. The licensing/delegation systems proposed by the French and Italians were dropped. Rather, NCAs would have to ensure that a single set of supervisory

[1] This claim has been confirmed in interviews with a large number of national ministry of finance and permanent representation officials from nine different member states. While less specific, several public statements by ministers and ministry officials of these three countries at the time of the negotiations also appear to confirm this point.

rules—outlined in the supervisory manual—was applied to all banks under their purview. The European Council agreed that the SSM would allow the ESM to recapitalize banks in difficulties—but deemed to be solvent by the ECB—directly, subject to 'double majority' voting in both the ECB (Single Supervisory Board [SSB]) and the EBA. The SSM was to begin operation on 1 March 2014 or twelve months following the entry into force of the legislation, whichever was later, subject to operational arrangements (European Council, 2012a). The SSM officially began operating on 4 November 2014.

The European Central Bank's Positioning on the Single Supervisory Mechanism

Prior to the debate on Banking Union, some senior ECB officials (e.g., Tommaso Padoa-Schioppa) expressed support for the ECB to take over supervisory functions (Howarth and Loedel 2005). This was not official ECB policy. Nonetheless, the ECB endorsed the initial Commission's proposal of allocating all supervisory competences to the ECB, regardless of the size of banks (Epstein and Rhodes 2016). President Mario Draghi made clear that being a decisive supervisor included oversight of all 6,000 banks to ensure a level playing field (*Financial Times*, 8 November 2012). But in several speeches he also reiterated that day-to-day tasks would remain with national supervisors (see, e.g., ECB 2012c).

He argued that the ECB should be in a position to carry out its new functions 'in a decisive, firm, complete and strong manner without any reputational risks' and 'new tasks should not be mixed with [the central bank's] monetary policy tasks—delivering price stability in the medium term—which for [the central bank] remains the primary task' (ECB 2012c). The ECB welcomed the 13 December agreement on the SSM. However, there were ongoing concerns about the operation of the ESRB—the body established in 2011 to monitor trends in European financial markets—which was chaired by the ECB President and supported by the analytical, statistical, administrative, and logistical assistance of the ECB. Critics claimed that the close ECB–ESRB ties already gave the central bank a role in macroeconomic supervision that could compromise its monetary policy functions (*EUObserver*, 1 February 2012).

The December agreement involved the creation of a planned mediation committee between the banking supervisory board and the ECB's Governing Council. This was a last-minute compromise introduced to satisfy the German government, which was opposed to assigning automatic responsibility to the ECB for mishaps it could not directly supervise (*Financial Times*, 17 December 2012). It was agreed that the mediation committee would intervene when the banking supervisory board (which could potentially include both euro area members and non-members) disagreed with the ECB's Governing Council on the supervision of a specific bank. The consultancy hired by the ECB proposed that the administrative head of the supervisory arm should be a member of the central bank's executive board who would also serve as a vice-chair of the supervisory board. This powerful figure would likely come from one of the larger member states—Danièle Nouy, a senior official from the Bank of France, was eventually appointed (*Financial Times*, 4 February 2012).

The Bundesbank maintained its reputation for rigorous critique of proposed solutions to the euro crisis by issuing an opinion that the December deal on the ECB's role in supervision lacked 'a long-term solid legal basis' and that the mediation committee operating between the bank supervisor and the Governing Council could be attacked in the courts (*Financial Times*, 17 December 2012). The Bundesbank President, Jens Weidmann, also challenged the logic of transforming the ECB into a prudential supervisor and expressed concern that the ECB's new supervisory role would not be sufficiently separate from its monetary policy role (and the goal of price stability) to ensure independence (*Financial Times*, 27 September 2012; *WirtschaftsWoche*, 22 December 2012).

Many other observers and policy-makers, including the EP's Economic and Monetary Affairs Committee, expressed similar concerns (*Financial Times*, 29–30 November 2012). Weidmann, however, argued that at best the ECB should operate as a transitional supervisor until another entirely independent body was set up. Weidmann was also opposed to the creation of a 'resolution' authority able to use taxpayer money to shut down banks, until a fund based on bank contributions was established, on the grounds that this would spread risks to taxpayers yet without adequate democratic controls.

National Banking Systems and Preferences on Direct European Central Bank Supervision

This section teases out and explains national preferences on the scope of ECB's direct supervision, and, more precisely, the threshold for it. While some national governments sought to extend ECB's direct supervision of many (if not all) banks, including small parochial entities, others maintained a policy in favour of covering only the biggest banks regardless of the actual level of their cross-border activities. Given the important presence of smaller alternative banks in all five of the euro area member state banking systems examined here, a more uniform preference in favour of a high threshold for direct ECB supervision might have been expected. In particular, the juxtaposition of the German and French positions on threshold merits further exploration: alternative banks held respectively the same percentage of total assets (43 per cent) in the two countries (central bank data). The bulk of these banks were very small institutions.

The crucial explanatory variable for the preferences of national policy-makers on ECB's direct supervision concerns what we label as 'the reach of internationalization'. We develop Schoenmaker's understanding of cross-border banking in order to better understand national preference formation on supranational bank supervision. Schoenmaker seeks to explain the contribution to international financial instability that large cross-border banks can make. Supranational supervision has also been explained and justified in interviews and public statements by national governments in all five of the euro area member states selected as case studies on the grounds that large cross-border banks escaped effective supervision.[2]

All six countries had large institutions with significant exposure to other EU member states (see Table 1 and Figure 3). However, Schoenmaker's econometric analysis and his focus upon very large, globally important cross-border banks only provides a limited picture of the variable of internationalization that created interest in supranational supervision and fails to provide an effective guide to national preferences on the threshold for direct ECB supervision which concerns the potential supervision of smaller banks. There is some correlation between the presence of large cross-border banks and their relative presence in the national banking system and national preferences on the threshold for direct ECB supervision.

The most concentrated of the five banking systems were the Dutch and the French—the Dutch with three very large banks with a strong cross-border presence, and the French banking system with five systemically important banks with significant cross-border operations. Dutch and French policy-makers advocated direct ECB supervision of all euro area banks, in part on the grounds of unequal ECB supervision. With less concentrated banking systems, containing more middle-sized and small banks, Spanish, Italian, and German policy-makers sought a higher threshold and/or a mechanism of 'delegation' from the ECB to national supervisors, proposed by the Italians. As policy-takers, Spanish and, to a lesser extent, Italian policy-makers were willing to compromise. German policy-makers were more stubborn on the question of threshold.

We should also consider the internationalization (exposure to other EU member states) of the entire banking system as an indicator of national preferences. It can be hypothesized that if overall internationalization levels are high, then support for ECB supervision of more banks—beyond the largest—should be greater and, if internationalization levels are lower, the

[2] All five national finance ministers/ministries confirmed this logic publicly. On Wolfgang Schäuble's support for ECB supervision of the biggest cross-border banks, see 'ECB should only supervise big banks: Schaeuble', at Reuters.com, 3 September 2012, available at <http://www.reuters.com/article/2012/09/03/us-eurozone-banks-schaeuble-idUSBRE88204U20120903>.

opposite should apply. However, on a general internationalization index (see Table 1, Chapter 4) there is no correlation with stated national preference on threshold. Thus, among the countries with lower levels of overall internationalization, France and the Netherlands supported the transfer of supervision of all banks to the ECB, while Germany, joined by Italy and Spain, sought a high threshold. Among the other countries with a very high level of internationalization (not examined further in this research), three sought a high threshold—Austria, Belgium, and Finland—but were willing to compromise, while Luxembourg sought full transfer to the ECB (see Howarth and Quaglia 2016).

Rather than discard internationalization as an explanatory variable, we next consider the 'reach' of internationalization into the banking system to explain varying national preferences on the threshold for supranational supervision. If internationalization is limited to a small number of large institutions, while a large number of smaller banks are more domestically focused, we would expect support for a higher threshold for supranational supervision. This then leads to the main hypothesis tested in this section: that the greater the reach of internationalization into the national banking system, the greater the support for direct ECB supervision of a larger number of smaller euro area banks.

These smaller banks were both commercial and 'alternative' banks. In all five of our euro area cases, there were a large number of alternative (mostly cooperative and savings) banks. These banks historically had an important social function, and most continued to have a strong connection to a locality, which often had a clear political, if not politicized, dimension—most obviously in Germany (Ayadi et al. 2009; Bülbül, Schmidt, and Schüwer 2013; Simpson 2013). Most alternative banks, especially savings banks, continued to be the main lenders to SMEs in these countries. We consider the extent to which small and parochial alternative banks were affected by internationalization in order to explain the willingness of some member state governments to allow them to be subject to direct ECB supervision. The relevant difference here is due to the structure of the alternative bank sector. In several countries, alternative banks operated joint liability schemes, which meant that if one institution collapsed, other banks would come to its rescue. The precise details of these schemes varied.

Moreover, in certain countries, small alternative banks (cooperatives or savings banks, or both) established central financial institutions in the context of partial or far-reaching consolidation in the 1980s and 1990s. These central financial institutions engaged in a larger range of commercial and investment banking activities than their much smaller associated banks. They engaged in significant international activities and, in a number of cases, were among the most internationalized of large EU banks. The structure of these part-consolidated banking groups and the internationalization of their central financial institutions is outlined in Table 3.

Part consolidation meant that smaller banks would be subject to direct ECB supervision by virtue of their legal and financial relationship with the larger central financial institution, if the latter met the agreed threshold. Joint liability schemes created a financial commitment of a large number of very small and parochial banks to internationalized and systemically important institutions, the collapse of which would impose massive costs upon the smaller entities. A spectrum can be drawn between, at the one extreme, the Netherlands, with one remaining large semi-consolidated alternative bank, and, at the other extreme, Germany, with 1,500 non-consolidated small alternative banks with a looser relationship with and financial commitment to central financial institutions. France, with three large semi-consolidated banks, was closer to the Netherlands, while Italy and Spain, with a number of middle-sized regional savings banks, were in between.

Germany

Unlike France, the German position on the threshold for direct ECB supervision corresponded closely to aggregate figures on both internationalization and concentration (Table 2 and Figures 3 and Figure 6). German policy-makers consistently supported ECB direct supervision of the country's two largest commercial banks, both with a very high international presence—Deutsche Bank and Commerzbank (*Financial Times*, 5 December 2012; interviews German Federal Financial Supervisory Authority (BaFin) official, Berlin, 30 October 2014). These two banks were also themselves strongly in favour of their direct supervision by the ECB, which would also simplify the supervision of their numerous subsidiaries in the euro area (Deutsche Bank 2012, 2013).

The opposition of the German authorities to lowering the supervision threshold also aligned with the position of associations representing the publicly owned Landesbanks and savings banks (the VOB) and Cooperatives (the BVR), which were clear in their opposition to the extension of direct ECB supervision to smaller German banks (BVR/VÖB/DSGV 2012; *Financial Times*, 9 September 2012; *Financial Times* 2 December 2012). In the meantime, Deutsche Bank and Commerzbank actively supported direct ECB supervision of all euro area banks in order to avoid the differential treatment of bank supervision (Bloomberg 2012; Deutsche Bank 2012, 2013).

Determined German opposition to extending ECB direct supervision beyond the largest banks reflects the limited reach of internationalization into the German banking system. Despite waves of consolidation, there were still 1,104 very small/small cooperative banks and 423 saving banks in Germany in 2012 (Bülbül, Schmidt, and Schüwer 2013). Collectively, the smaller cooperative and savings banks (excluding central institutions) held 22 per cent of total assets. However, their role in the German economy was far greater than their balance-sheet size would suggest (see also Chapter 4). Small cooperative and savings banks provided, respectively, 13 and 21 per cent of loans to NFCs in Germany and held, respectively, 16 and 24 per cent of the country's bank deposits (Bundesbank, various years). With associated institutions, German alternative banks held 40 per cent of total assets and provided 51 per cent of lending to NFCs.

The cooperative banks included two central financial institutions—DZ Bank and WGZ Bank—and a number of specialized service providers operating nationwide. DZ Bank, the fourth-largest bank in Germany at the end of 2012, also operated as a commercial bank and had a significant international presence (21 per cent in the EU and a total of 27 per cent internationally). It was very likely to be covered by direct ECB supervision. However, the cooperatives' joint liability scheme did not cover these larger institutions and, with the exception of DZ Bank, their focus was overwhelmingly domestic. The absence of a joint liability scheme that included these much larger entities stands in marked distinction to the Austrian cooperative banks and their highly internationalized mother institution (Fonteyne 2007).

Savings banks maintained joint liability schemes but only with other small, locally focused entities. Importantly, they had a reputation for being financially stable banks—none had needed to be bailed out by governments since the 1950s. The savings banks in certain regions had ties to regional Landesbanks, some of which had a strong international presence, notably LB Baden-Württemberg. However, as with the cooperatives, there were no joint liability schemes that bound the savings banks to Landesbanks. Rather, many savings banks contributed to Landesbank funding and benefited from some of their services (Ayadi et al. 2009; Bülbül, Schmidt, and Schüwer 2013).

The close connections between the savings bank and local and other German politicians encouraged federal government support for the protection of existing practices and the policy of extending direct ECB supervision only to systemically important banks. The German government's willingness to compromise on the inclusion of the DZ Bank (the central financial institution to the cooperative banks) and the Landesbanks in the remit of direct ECB supervision confirms the internationalization argument in that DZ Bank and the Landesbanks all held a significant percentage of their assets in other EU member states.

The damage caused to some Landesbanks during the financial crisis, large government bail-outs, Commission-imposed restructuring, and stagnant lending placed them in a politically weakened position (Deeg and Donnelly 2016). The German federal government and the Bundesbank have long called for the consolidation of banks in this sector (Hardie and Howarth

2009, 2013; *Financial Times*, 14 September 2010). Clearly, the German preference to extend ECB direct supervision to the unstable Spanish *cajas* (see 'Spain', below) also encouraged compromise on a threshold, even if that meant direct ECB supervision also for the above-mentioned German banks.

France

French policy-makers, the main peak banking association, and a number of individual French banks expressed concern over the unequal treatment of member states given the size of the five largest French institutions, which would all likely end up being directly supervised by the ECB (Crédit Agricole 2014; *Financial Times*, 14 November 2012; French Banking Federation 2012). In addition to 'fairness' concerns, the French government and banks also argued that the division into larger and smaller banks made little economic sense, given that banking crises often originated with smaller, fast-expanding banks (French Banking Federation 2012).

Despite the strong French preference in favour of the transfer of full supervisory oversight to the ECB, it is clear that the French would have preferred a mandate system whereby national supervisors would have maintained a large degree of autonomy over supervision. The French Finance Minister also argued that ECB supervision must consider the specificity of French banks (*Bloomberg*, 26 October 2015). Michel Sapin argued in favour of an SSM approach that takes 'into account the real risks of each bank and [does] not judge them by the mere size of the banks', reflecting the dominance of the French banking system by large universal banks. For the French, the size of a bank did not, per se, create specific risks.

In accordance with the financial trilemma, French interest in supranational supervision was sparked by the internationalization of the five largest French banks, which all held a significant percentage of the assets in other EU member states and in the euro periphery specifically (Howarth 2013). However, the low aggregate internationalization and moderate concentration figures for the French banking system appear to contradict French Ministry of Finance preference on the transfer of all bank supervision to the ECB (Figures 3 and 6). French preferences can be explained in terms of the semi-consolidated nature of French cooperative banks which meant that even with a relatively high threshold, a very large percentage of French bank assets would likely be subject to direct ECB supervision. All French cooperatives were in one of three large centralized semi-consolidated groups, in which small banks advertised as distinct entities at the local and regional level but had very limited autonomy from the mother bank. The central institutions and, in the case of the part-listed Crédit Agricole and BPCE specially created investment banks (CACIB and Natixis) were highly internationalized (see Chapter 4).

French opposition to differential treatment also reflects French government insistence on a lack of a 'too big to fail' problem facing the large French banks given their 'mixed business' model and a long-standing strategy of constructing national champions engaged in a range of banking activities (Howarth 2013). The three largest alternative banking groups in France—Crédit Mutuel and BPCE (a federation of cooperative and former savings banks), and Crédit Agricole—also expressed concerns about direct ECB supervision, given their funding structure, but not outright opposition (Crédit Agricole 2014). Overall, though, French policy-makers preference in favour of direct ECB supervision of all euro area banks was flexible. France was one of the main member state drivers behind Banking Union and the SSM, and President François Holland placed great emphasis on the rapid construction of the SSM (see Donnelly 2014; Howarth and Quaglia 2013a; Moscovici 2012; interviews with German policy-makers 30 October 2014; interviews with Commission officials 13–14 November 2014; *Reuters*, 12 December 2012).

The Netherlands

Dutch policy-makers were well disposed towards Banking Union, arguing that

> it could promote a level playing field and help mitigate (cross-border) systemic risks more effectively, as well as help reduce the risk of contagion by breaking the link between national governments and their banking sectors. Given these benefits, the openness of the Dutch economy, and the size of the Dutch banking sector, a banking union could potentially offer the Netherlands significant advantages (Netherlands Government 2012).

This speaks to the logic of the financial trilemma, and it chimes well with the highly consolidated nature of the Dutch banking system and the high internationalization of the three largest banks, which created a very strong interest in the supranationalization of supervision. The Netherlands was home to two of the world's thirty largest banks (by asset size) (ING and Rabobank) and a third very large bank that had previously been one of the world's largest (ABN). All the small and locally focused Dutch cooperative banks (Raffeisen) formed part of a semi-consolidated group and participated in a joint liability scheme with a mother bank (Rabobank) with a very strong international presence.

Dutch policy-makers thus supported direct ECB supervision of all euro area banks, which was presented, as in France, as the best way to even out ECB supervisory control among the different member states (Netherlands

Government 2012; Dutch Ministry of Finance interview, 22 June 2015). However, they believed that supervision should be 'phased in' on the grounds that 'extending the scope of supervisory authority on a step-by-step basis would give the ECB the chance to build up the required capacity and experience'.

Italy

Italian policy-makers were very much in favour of Banking Union, not least because Italy was the first euro area member state threatened by contagion from other euro periphery member states and, notably, Spain. Despite, the comparative stability of the national banking system and fiscal position, Italy was hit by rising bond yields in the summer of 2011. Thus, like the Spaniards, the Italians were 'demanders' of Banking Union. On the specific issue of the SSM, they supported the transfer of supervisory powers to the ECB for all the banks in the euro area and potentially to other countries that wanted to join the SSM (Grilli 2012). They opposed a 'two-level system', whereby a 'small number of internationally active banks' would be subject to SSM supervision and a 'large number of small domestic banks' would not—a dual system would cause 'supervisory dishomogeinity' (Signorini 2012). However, they also called for a 'strong involvement' of national supervisory authorities in the operational activities of the SSM, whereby national supervisors should be involved in decision-making processes concerning non-systemic banks. The Bank of Italy in particular proposed a formal 'delegation' to national supervisors to be inserted in the SSM regulation, so as to allow a more 'flexible' management of supervisory processes concerning small banks (Signorini 2012).

Similarly, Italian banks, like the Italian authorities, called for SSM supervision to encompass the entire banking system, opposing a 'dual system' in which only large cross-border banks would fall under the ECB supervision, as this would generate 'competitive disparities'. For the Italian Banking Association, the 'optimal solution' was to centralize supervision at the ECB for the entire banking system, but with a 'compulsory delegation' to national supervisors of 'discretionary powers' for non-systemic banks, in line with the principles of 'subsidiarity' and 'proportionality' (Mussari 2012).

The preferences of Italian policy-makers and banks were shaped by the configuration of the national banking system. Italy had a handful of large cross-border banks, of which only the two largest ones, Unicredit and Banca Intesa San Paolo, were highly internationalized and were also adamantly in favour of the SSM and ECB's direct supervision. Italy had a large number of very small savings banks, which, however, were not publicly owned and were not subject to specific regulation and supervision. In 2011, Italian savings banks held only 5 per cent of total Italian bank assets (European Saving

Banks Group 2013). They were subject to the same regulation as commercial banks and were supervised by the Bank of Italy.

Italy also had a large number of cooperative banks, which held 16 per cent of total national bank assets (down from over 20 per cent in the early 2000s) and about 30 per cent of Italian loans and deposits (European Association of Cooperative Banks 2013). There were two types of cooperative bank in Italy: mutual banks (formerly rural and artisans' banks) and people's banks (*banche popolari*). Italian cooperatives were far less integrated than those in other countries (e.g., in Germany and Austria)—none of the alternative bank groups was subject to joint liability/support schemes (Gutiérrez 2008). Ayadi and Lastra (2010: 21) describe Italian cooperatives as 'less centralized than the Austrian, German, Dutch, Finnish and, to some extent, French cases'. The credit cooperatives maintained their separate DGS, but this was funded ex post. Italian alternative banks also did not have central financial institutions, which might link these institutions to more internationally focused trading and investment banking activities.

The small banks mutual focused largely on lending to SMEs (about 70 per cent of assets). Tax rules encouraged them to retain their profits and to build up reserves. People's banks were larger operations—the Banco Popolare was Italy's fifth largest bank by assets in 2012, following the merger of smaller banks—able to expand their business beyond previous geographic restrictions and less reliant on SME lending (about a third to a half by 2012) (Bülbül, Schmidt, and Schüwer 2013). However, the focus of all these banks remained domestic. Hence, alternative banks were clearly an important part of the Italian banking sector, which explains Italian policy-makers' concerns for 'flexibility' and 'proportionality' in dealing with them within the SSM.[3] Interestingly, though, Italian policy-makers did not follow the German position of shielding these banks entirely from supranational interference—a difference owing to the Italian desire to move ahead quickly with Banking Union.

Spain

Among the country studies examined, Spain needed Banking Union the most. Hence, in the SSM negotiations, Spanish policy-makers were the least outspoken on the SSM and the most flexible about the scope of direct ECB supervision. For them, the priority was to link the establishment of the SSM to the possibility of using the ESM to directly recapitalize ailing banks in crisis-stricken countries, first and foremost Spain (Rajoy 2014). For this reason,

[3] This concern was reiterated by an Italian policy-maker, who pointed out that without sufficient proportionality, most of the small Italian banks would not be able to withstand/cover the costs of reporting obligations and the likes in the SSM (Brussels, June 2015).

Spain supported France on the speedy creation of the SSM. Spain also joined France in advocating ECB supervision of all euro area banks. For Spain, the creation of the SSM was not only about boosting confidence to tackle the sovereign debt–bank doom loop which threatened to engulf the country; it was also closely linked to preserving what was left of the savings bank sector that had played such an important role in the economic fortunes over the previous three decades.

Prior to 2010, Spanish savings banks were widely considered to be successful according to a range of measures. Bülbül, Schmidt, and Schüwer (2013) and Manghetti (2011) called them a model of successful savings banks, with profit levels similar to two giant Spanish commercial banks. In 2011, the *cajas* held 35 per cent of total banks assets, down from a high of 39 per cent in 2006 (European Savings Banks Group 2013), and they held around 50 per cent of Spanish deposits. From the 1970s, the *cajas* had been privatized and merged, while the regional principal was ended allowing their expansion throughout Spain and they transformed themselves into universal banks. With one of the largest branches-to-population ratios in the EU, the *cajas* turned to high-risk commercial real-estate investments in order to maintain their high profit margins (IMF 2012a, b). At the same time, they were still subject to considerable local political interference and, in effect, supervisory forbearance (Bülbül, Schmidt, and Schüwer 2013; Royo 2013c).

The abrupt end of the real-estate boom hit the *cajas* particularly hard, and non-performing loans rose dramatically. They were rescued with public funds and/or were forced to merge with other *cajas*—the total number of savings banks had dropped from 45 to 11 by 2012. Most infamously, Bankia was a new bank formed by the government through the forced merger of several failing savings banks from the Madrid metropolitan area. There were also numerous small cooperatives in Spain with strong local roots. However, these held only 4 per cent of total Spanish bank assets in 2012 (European Association of Cooperative Banks 2013), and, although they were negatively affected by the Spanish bank crisis, their more conservative lending practices maintained comparatively high repayment rates (Bülbül, Schmidt, and Schüwer 2013). As in Italy—unlike Germany—neither the savings banks nor the cooperatives in Spain were subject to joint liability schemes.

Very strong Spanish support for the SSM and direct ECB supervision of all euro area banks are a direct result of the desperate situation of the national banking system, the devastation of the *cajas*, and Spanish government reliance on ESM funds to help break the sovereign debt–bank doom loop. Spanish policy-makers sought early access to ESM funds in 2012 with an emergency recapitalization of the *cajas*. This exposed the affected banks to strong conditionality imposed by the ESM, eliminating much national margin of manoeuvre. German policy-makers were also keen to ensure that all ailing *cajas* that received ESM funds fell under direct ECB supervision (German Ministry of Finance, interview, 8 October 2015).

In the Spanish case, restricting direct ECB supervision to only the largest cross-border banks made little sense. The two large internationalized Spanish banks, Santander and BBVA, were comparatively stable entities. They were also very supportive of the SSM. However, they demanded the transfer of full supervisory powers to the ECB, as a means to achieve a level playing field among euro area countries and among all banks (*El Pais*, 8 April 2014). Clearly, the devastation of the crisis effectively reduced the political influence of the *cajas*, which did not even take a position on ECB direct supervision.

Euro Outsiders and the Single Supervisory Mechanism

The second main issue in the SSM negotiations was the treatment of and relations with euro outsiders, which in turn were divided into two groups: those that considered joining the SSM (maybe at a later date), and would-be permanent outsiders. Euro area outsiders interested in participating in the SSM were opposed to the Commission's proposed regulation of September, which placed the ECB at the centre of the mechanism. The wording of the draft suggested that non-euro member states would be excluded from decision-making as they lacked a vote on the ECB's Governing Council.

The Commission's draft also appeared explicitly to limit membership by defining 'participating Member State' as a 'Member State whose currency is the euro' (European Commission 2012a). The euro outsiders were supported by the EP's Economic and Monetary Affairs Committee, which formed its own position on the status of the ten EU member states not in the euro area, deciding that 'opt-in' countries should be able to sit on a new ECB supervisory board with equal voting powers but not on the decision-making Governing Council (*EUObserver*, 29 November 2012). The December Council agreement on the SSM satisfied some euro-outsider concerns.

The revised regulation changed the definition of 'participating Member State' to 'a Member State whose currency is the euro or whose currency is not the euro which has established a close cooperation', defined as adopting the necessary legal framework and cooperating with the ECB along the lines codified in the draft regulation. Opening the SSM to non-euro member states made good sense in that more member states sharing common supervisory frameworks, rules, and mechanisms would further strengthen stability (*EU Observer*, 29 November 2012). Not including them would potentially create a more difficult situation in case of (financial) problems and the necessity of extra financial assistance. Furthermore, if different rules were to apply in these member states, the Banking Union might find itself confronted with regulatory and supervisory arbitrage on its doorstep.

The main priority of the British government—which had no intention of joining the SSM—was to avoid a potential euro area block within the single financial market. The British, supported by seven other non-euro member state governments, threatened to block Banking Union if there were insufficient safeguards put in place for the 'euro-outsiders' (*Financial Times*, 8 November 2012). Crucially, the British feared the adoption of subsequent financial legislation that would be detrimental to the British financial sector. However, the broader issue of concern was the satisfactory co-existence of a more integrated euro area core and the non-core member states. Banking Union became a kind of test case for the UK's role in a two-speed Europe (*Financial Times*, 13 December 2012). In the EBA—the supervisory body responsible for EU-wide bank stress tests—the British feared a euro area majority able to impose its rules on non-euro area members. Hence, as early as the summer of 2012, the British demanded an EBA voting reform: that any decision by the EBA should be approved by a minimum number of member states outside the Banking Union and thus effectively by a 'double majority' of member states inside and outside the Banking Union.

Germany, the Netherlands, and Austria all broadly accepted British-led requests for so-called double majority voting. However, most euro area member states expressed concern that in the event that the number of non-Banking Union member states dwindled, the UK would enjoy effective veto powers (*Financial Times*, 8 November 2012). The Commission opposed EBA reform because it would result in the creation of two forums for decision-making: those inside and outside the euro area (*Financial Times*, 13 December 2012). The outcome was a compromise involving the creation of a double majority system until the number of non-Banking Union member states dwindled to fewer than four. The EP retained amendment and veto powers on the EBA regulation, which was to be adopted in 2013.

National Banking Systems and Non-Euro Area Country Preference on Single Supervisory Mechanism Participation

Non-euro area countries had a choice about joining the SSM (or not). They faced incentives and disincentives concerning SSM membership, which are discussed in turn. SSM membership could provide a way to improve relations between home and host supervisors, which was particularly important for countries that had a high degree of (euro area) foreign bank penetration, which is traditionally a 'tricky' issue. SSM membership could also improve the effectiveness of supervision because the ECB would possess information about the banks' headquarters and subsidiaries. Furthermore, non-participation in the SSM could have detrimental effects on domestic banks if depositors shifted their accounts to banks headquartered in Banking Union member states.

However, there were also reasons not to participate in the SSM. Non-euro member states were worried about their second-class status, with limited decision-making power compared with that of euro area members and no access to the ECB's funding. There was the concern that the ECB could be less prone to focus on the risks building in non-euro and smaller member states, not least because branches and subsidiaries of foreign banks could be systemic for the host but not for the home country. Finally, banking nationalism in some CEECs played a role. Overall, the balance between costs and benefits mostly ensued from the configuration of national banking systems and the effectiveness of the national supervisory framework.

The UK's banking system was dominated by one large, nationally focused bank (Lloyds-TSB) and three large, highly internationalized and well-capitalized institutions with limited reliance on the domestic real economy. British-headquartered bank assets were the most international (extra-European) of any EU member state. Had the UK opted to participate in the SSM, over 90 per cent of its retail bank assets would have been held by banks subject to direct ECB supervision. Yet, at the same time, domestic lending formed only a small part of most of these banks' assets—the principal exceptions being Lloyds-TSB and the much smaller British subsidiary of Santander (Santander 2014). The three largest British-headquartered banks were major international players and were among the world's ten largest banks in terms of asset size throughout most of the 2000s. All three held a majority of their assets internationally and a large majority of these international assets beyond Europe (Table 1). British banks had some exposure to the euro periphery, but this was comparatively limited (Tables 4 and 6).

Overall, the UK government was by and large supportive of Banking Union—and specifically the SSM—for euro area member states, notably as a way to tackle the sovereign debt crisis afflicting the euro area periphery and to ensure financial stability therein (see, e.g., *The Telegraph*, 13 December 2012; 19 December 2012). However, it was clear that the UK did not want to be part of the new institutional arrangements (see, e.g., *Financial Times*, 11 October 2013; House of Lords 2012a). Its banking system was not only the most 'Europeanized' of the six largest EU member state banking systems in terms of the holdings of other EU-headquartered banks in the UK (as both a percentage and in total terms) and British bank holdings elsewhere in the EU (in total terms), but it was also very internationalized in terms of non-EU-headquartered banks active in the UK and the activities of British banks abroad. The UK was most exposed to the potential instability of globally systemic banks, which affected the British banking system more than others in Europe, in relative terms. Hence, British policy-makers did not campaign for supranational solutions in the EU. Similarly, all the large British banks by and large supported the creation of the SSM, but none sought British participation (BBA 2012).

The Swedish government's decision not to participate in Banking Union was largely due to the fact that no major banks in the country were owned by banking groups headquartered in another EU member state (Darvas and Wolff 2013). The Swedish government also expressed concern about the second-class position of non-euro member states in the SSM (*Financial Times*, 11 December 2012). The possibility of Swedish banks switching subsidiaries in other member states to branches also diminished the potential impact of Banking Union for Swedish banks.[4] Finland and Estonia—with banking systems dominated by Swedish-owned banks, notably Nordea in Finland and Swedbank in Estonia—had a strong vested interest in reaching a compromise to ensure Swedish participation. Latvia and Lithuania, also dominated by subsidiaries of Swedish banks, had less interest in joining Banking Union given Swedish non-membership, although Latvia's intention to enter the euro area in 2014 pushed its government to support the form of membership on offer. Similarly, Lithuania joined the SSM when it adopted the euro in 2015 (*Financial Times*, 11 December 2012; Spendzharova and Bayram 2016).

Denmark, which had a formal opt-out on EMU, stated that it would consider its stance after the ECB's Comprehensive Assessment. Only approximately 16 per cent of total Danish bank assets were held by EU-owned subsidiaries (2012 figures), and a significant percentage of these by Swedish banks. Only 29 per cent of Danish assets abroad were in the euro area (less than Danish assets in Sweden and Norway alone), and only 5 per cent of total Danish bank assets. By late 2013, only 1.5 per cent of Danish bank assets were in the euro periphery, and these principally in Ireland. Despite its EMU opt-out, Danish policy on the SSM and other elements of Banking Union can be described as positive 'wait and see'. This stance stemmed from limited monetary policy autonomy (Denmark maintained its currency in the ERM II), the large size of the country's banking sector (four times GDP at the end of 2012), and the even bigger relative size of the country's financial sector (the third highest in the EU compared with GDP) (interview with Danish central bank official, March 2014).

In the CEECs, there was some concern that non-participation in the SSM (Banking Union) might have a devastating effect on domestic banks as

[4] In July 2015, Nordea announced that it would transform its large Finnish subsidiary into a branch, thus extending the supervisory control of the Swedish supervisory body over its Finnish operations and escaping ECB supervision (*Reuters*, 21 October 2015).

depositors shifted their accounts to banks headquartered in Banking Union member states (Darvas and Wolff, 2013). Nonetheless, three CEECs made clear their opposition to SSM/Banking Union membership: Hungary, Poland, and the Czech Republic (Epstein and Rhodes 2014; Spendzharova 2014). Compared with most CEECs, where foreign bank penetration from EU banks typically exceeded 70 per cent, in Hungary and Poland it was 'only' 54 and 56 per cent, respectively, in 2012. Participation in the euro area was not a priority for the policy-makers of either of these member states. The significant presence of foreign financial institutions also provided an incentive to national policy-makers in these countries to promote domestic banks and other forms of 'banking nationalism' (Johnson and Barnes 2014; Mero and Piroska 2016).

Both the Hungarian and the Polish governments had been public about their objective to increase domestic ownership of banks to at least 50 per cent (MTIE 2013, *Bloomberg*, 22 July 2015). Indeed, in large part due to a range of discriminatory measures and notably punitive taxes, the foreign bank presence in Hungary had declined significantly from 85 per cent of total bank assets in 2005 to 56 per cent by 2012. The Hungarian and Polish governments were worried that joining the SSM would have resulted in the ECB interfering with the authorization of bank mergers which had been manipulated by national authorities to promote domestic banks as 'national champions' (Mero and Piroska 2016).

These governments and authorities sought to develop domestic banks, whereas the explicit objective of Banking Union was to loosen the ties between national banks and governments (Epstein and Rhodes 2016; Mero and Piroska 2016). Regarding the Czech Republic, where foreign ownership by EU banks was very high, the country expressed no intention of joining the SSM. Determined Czech reluctance to joining the single currency shaped Czech policy on the SSM. The Czech authorities might also have sought to encourage euro area banks to convert their Czech branches into subsidiaries so as to gain from favourable Czech fiscal and regulatory conditions.

The Bulgarian government maintained a positive 'wait and see' approach to Banking Union. In July 2014, following a massive run on deposits, President Rosen Plevneliev announced the intention to start accession procedures to join the SSM. The announcement largely coincided with plans to resolve the Corporate Commercial Bank AD, the nation's fourth-largest bank, after it had suffered substantial losses. Once the domestic financial turmoil was over, the Bulgarian government commitment to join the SSM declined (Mero and Piroska 2016). Except for the Corporate Commercial Bank and First Investment, Bulgaria's major banks were foreign owned: Italy's UniCredit SpA, Hungary's OTP Bank Nyrt, Greece's Eurobank Ergasias SA, National Bank of Greece SA, and Austria's Raiffeisen Bank International AG were among the largest by assets in the country (*Bloomberg*, 15 July 2014).

In the summer of 2014, Romania announced its intention to start the procedures to join the SSM, planning to undertake an exercise similar to the ECB's Comprehensive Assessment in 2016 and join the SSM afterwards (Mero and Piroska 2016). The Romanian banking sector, like that of Bulgaria, was dominated by the subsidiaries of euro area banks; these subsidiaries were of systemic importance for the host country (Romania) but not for their home countries; namely Austria, France, and Italy.[5] Some commentators argued that the home–host coordination problem between national regulators would be better addressed within the SSM.

In 2014, a policy forum organized by the IMF brought together representatives of six CEE countries that were EU members but were not yet in the euro area—Bulgaria, Croatia, the Czech Republic, Hungary, Poland, and Romania—as well as the ECB and the Commission. On 'Opting into the Banking Union before euro adoption', the report concluded that

> the lack of equal (or fully equivalent) treatment of the Banking Union members and non-euro area opt-ins—regarding their role in the Single Supervisory Mechanism (SSM), as well as access to common liquidity and fiscal backstops—makes opting into the Banking Union before euro adoption less attractive. Countries that would benefit most from early opt-in are those that see the Banking Union as a way to enhance the quality and credibility of bank supervision or to gain access to larger industry-funded common backstop (IMF 2015: 1).

As the vice-deputy governor of the Czech central bank put it 'Entering the SSM means transferring powers... not necessarily responsibilities and costs in bad times' (Hempl 2015). He argued that for euro area countries, this transfer was somewhat compensated for by ultimate power/burden-sharing within the ECB and in the ESM. This was not the case for non-euro area countries.

The Comprehensive Assessment 2014

The Comprehensive Assessment, which subsequently took place in the summer and autumn of 2014, assumed considerable practical and symbolic importance with regard to the harmonization of euro area supervisory standards (Gren, Howarth, and Quaglia 2015). In October 2013, the EBA laid down two new stricter definitions for non-performing loans and for loans subject to forbearance—that is, when a bank gives a borrower leeway in repaying loans (*Financial Times*, 21 October 2013). The EBA's draft standards defined non-performing loans as those that were more than ninety days past due. These

[5] Austria's Erste Group Bank AG owned the biggest lender, which in the summer of 2014 wrote down its subsidiary with a loss of €1.6 billion.

standards were subsequently incorporated into the ECB's Asset Quality Review (AQR) of 2014 which formed part of the Comprehensive Assessment. The EBA's official aim was to generate a more coherent picture of the health of EU national banking sectors, and it was very likely that the new standards could lead to higher figures for non-performing loans for a number of EU banks, hitting specific member states hard—notably Italy.

Forbearance had been widely used by some lenders as a way of avoiding the recognition of losses. Previously, EBA stress tests had also been widely criticized for being too lenient and for giving national authorities too much discretion in setting standards for non-performing loans. However, some observers noted that the new definitions still left room—grey areas—for interpretation (*Financial Times*, 21 October 2013). The definitions were to apply to all loans and debt securities on bank balance sheets and some off balance sheet, but were to exclude those held for trading. Further, the new EBA rules could not supersede existing national accounting and regulatory definitions.

The ECB's AQR further improved the transparency and comparability of bank data across the then eighteen euro area member states plus Lithuania (which joined at the start of 2015). The AQR manual (ECB 2014b), published on 11 March, included the first set of mandatory bank supervision rules ever produced specifically for euro area NCAs—which were considerably more detailed and directing than existing EBA guidelines. The manual contains methodology for the AQR's 'phase 2' (the on-site inspection of banks), with detailed guidance on a range of matters, including procedures for validating data and checking model inputs; the valuation of material exposures and collateral, and the determination of provisioning needs; the processes for quality assurance and progress tracking to ensure timely completion; when to use independent, external valuations for assets; and the use of industry benchmarks to assess market values.

The AQR harmonized even more than the EBA's guidelines the definition of non-performing loans and uncovered hidden losses. In doing so, the ECB found massive shortfalls—€136 billion—in the loans that banks and national regulators classified as non-performing (i.e., bad). This figure amounted to 15 per cent more than the total previously announced by NCAs. The ECB found that banks had over-valued their assets by a total of €48 billion, pointing especially to an over-valuation of commercial loans (*Financial Times*, 26 October 2014). The EBA also reinforced its 2014 stress tests, imposing harmonized definitions. Both the ECB President, Mario Draghi, and the Head of the SSM, Danièle Nouy, argued publicly that some banks would have to fail the stress tests in order to ensure the credibility of the new system.

The twenty-five named banks that failed the Comprehensive Assessment (fourteen after earlier capital-raising in 2014) were widely predicted, and suspicions about the stability of some of these institutions had been present for years (*Financial Times*, 27 October 2014). Therefore, while criticized by some for being insufficiently rigorous (de Groen, 2014; Finance Watch 2014), the Comprehensive Assessment was clearly an improvement on what had come before in a number of member states—notably in the periphery. Italian and Greek banks were the most exposed, with, respectively, nine and four failing, followed by three Austrian banks and two from each of Cyprus, Slovenia, and Spain. Italian banks were responsible for a quarter of the total over-valued assets, just less than 1 per cent of their risk-weighted assets. Greek banks were responsible for €7.6 billion of the total over-valued assets, or almost 4 per cent of their risk-weighted assets. Once capital injections in early 2014 were taken into account, four Italian banks still faced shortfalls, including the country's third-largest and fourth-largest institutions: the MPS and Banco Popolare. MPS, which needed to cover a shortfall of €2.1 billion, was the largest failure of the Comprehensive Assessment (*The Economist*, 26 October 2014; *Financial Times*, 26 October 2014).

Only one German bank failed—Münchener Hypothekenbank—but it had raised sufficient capital in 2014 to avoid additional capital action. German banks would have to reduce the value of their assets by €6.7 billion, while French banks would only have to do so by €5.6 billion. Italian banks were hit particularly hard by the harmonized definition of non-performing loans. In 2014, bad loans reached a total of €160 billion—more than double their level in 2010—and they were expected to rise to nearly €200 billion in 2015 (*Bloomberg*, 16 April 2015).

About 17 per cent of Italian bank loans—€333 billion—were non-performing according to the IMF (Jassaud and Kang, 2015; *New York Times*, 13 February 2015). Obviously, the conditions of the Comprehensive Assessment (the ECB's AQR and the EBA's stress tests under stricter rules combined) were set a year or more after the negotiations on the SSM in the autumn of 2012 (see Tables 14 and 15). However, they should be seen as a reflection of German and other northern euro area member state preferences with regard to ensuring an SSM design that challenged head on supervisory forbearance that was long-standing in a number of euro area member states and thus the conditions that facilitated moral hazard.

Conclusion

This chapter has discussed the establishment of the SSM, which transferred banking supervision to the supranational level and was the first significant step in the making of Banking Union. This change could only ever have been achieved in exceptional circumstances—which the sovereign debt crisis created, as explained in Chapter 3. However, the EU's response to the crisis, especially the possibility of financial assistance to ailing banks, raised issues related to moral hazard, which explains why policy-makers in Germany, Finland, and the Netherlands supported the establishment of the SSM.

The second rationale for the establishment of the SSM derived from the financial trilemma, which was particularly acute and ultimately untenable in the euro area. Thus, the logic behind a move to supranational supervision was that national control of large ('systemically important') cross-border banks was bound to be sub-optimal. There were, however, significant differences in the internationalization patterns of the national banking systems of the six countries covered in this book. France, Germany, the Netherlands, Spain, and Italy were dominated (more than 80 per cent) by national banks, but these banks also had a very large presence through subsidiaries in other EU member states. The UK was both home to large, highly internationalized banks, and host to a larger number of major banks headquartered in both the EU and beyond. The British banking system was by far the most internationalized of the six country cases considered in this study.

All the countries examined—except for the UK—had a significant alternative banking sector, where the large majority of small and medium-sized banks were cooperatives and/or savings banks. However, these alternative banks differed in several important respects. In France and the Netherlands, most alternative banks were in consolidated or semi-consolidated groups with joint liability schemes that exposed them directly to much larger internationalized institutions. Although German alternative banks were in a similar structure, with large central financial institutions, attached entities, and tied Landesbanks engaged in a range of international banking activities, Germany was the only country where joint liability schemes covered only smaller institutions. These institutions were thus sheltered from the international operations of their central financial institution. Italian and Spanish alternative banks did not have joint liability schemes, but the Spanish *cajas* had been severely disrupted by a domestic banking crisis, whereas many small alternative banks in Italy suffered major losses from non-performing loans, as later revealed by the EBA's stress test and the ECB's AQR in 2014.

In terms of the position of the banks themselves, larger institutions in all five euro area case study countries supported the transfer to the ECB of supervisory powers over all banks in participating countries. The largest banks uniformly opposed uneven supervision. They feared that they would be subject to stricter ECB control, while smaller institutions continued to benefit from a national supervision that was potentially more favourable and informed by specific local concerns and, thus, benefit potentially from supervisory forbearance.

The reluctance of smaller alternative banks in France and the Netherlands to accept the potential extension of direct ECB supervision to even the smaller entities of semi-consolidated banks was sidelined by the support from mother banks (central financial institutions) with a stronger international presence. In Germany, the representative associations for the cooperatives and savings banks succeeded in presenting a strong opposition to the extension of ECB supervision to all banks. Alternative banks in Spain and Italy were in a weak economic and (ultimately) political position to make their case to be excluded from the ECB's direct supervision. In 2014, fourteen Italian banks subject to SSM supervision failed the first Comprehensive Assessment.

In the summer of 2012, the IMF came out as a vocal champion of Banking Union as an essential step to resolve the sovereign debt crisis (Goyal et al. 2013; IMF 2012c, 2013a). Like the Bundesbank, the IMF expressed its concern over a 'half-finished' project, arguing that the 'SSM, the single resolution mechanism with common fiscal backstops (mutualization), a single authority with the power to shut down banks and common safety nets were *all* required to ensure a successful Banking Union' (Goyal et al. 2013, 22). The preferences of national policy-makers on the establishment of the other components of Banking Union will be examined in the following chapters.

6

Resolution

Introduction

Even prior to the finalization of the SSM in December 2012, negotiations had begun in earnest on the SRM and the use of the ESM as a common fiscal backstop. Resolution is the process by which the authorities intervene to manage the failure of a bank. The main objective of resolution rules for financial institutions is to ensure that they can fail in an orderly fashion—that is, without excessive disruption to the financial system, without avoidable interruption to the critical economic functions that banks provide, and without exposing taxpayers to losses deriving from public bail-outs. The organization of a system-wide resolution regime is also important in order to avoid competitive distortions among banks.

A resolution regime is ultimately a political solution to underlying distributive conflicts surrounding bank failure. Who should pay for a collapsed bank: the private sector—banks, their shareholders, bondholders, owners of large bank deposits—or the taxpayer? Whereas during the international financial crisis it was mainly taxpayers who propped up banks through state-led bail-outs, after the crisis, resolution regimes were reformed with the explicit aim of making shareholders, bondholders, and large depositors pay for the bulk of the resolution of banks through 'bail-in' and resolution funds, rather than forcing governments (and thus, ultimately, taxpayers) to do so. Banks may also be required to contribute funds in advance to a resolution fund that can be drawn upon by banks that are being resolved.[1]

This chapter begins by discussing the negotiations on the BRRD agreed in May 2013 that applied to all EU member states. It then examines the negotiations on the SRM agreed in July 2014. This examination is followed by an explanation of national preferences on the main issues in the SRM negotiations

[1] The contribution of depositors and bondholders to resolution is referred to as a 'bail-in'.

by considering the 'manageability' of real and possible bank losses, and the configuration of national banking systems.

In the negotiations on the BRRD, initially the controversial issue was the creation of national resolution funds—to be precise, their level, financing (ex post or ex ante), and the possibility of borrowing between national funds. Later on, the discussions focused on one specific tool for bank recovery and resolution, namely the bail-in of creditors, whereby the controversial issues were the flexibility left to national authorities and the hierarchy in the bail-in of creditors, in particular the treatment of non-insured personal deposits and deposits by SMEs. Whereas the German-led coalition (including the Netherlands, Austria, and Finland) advocated fixed rules and no special treatment for certain kinds of creditors, France, the UK, and Mediterranean countries called—for varying reasons—for more flexibility to be left to national authorities and a special treatment for personal deposits of any amount.

In the negotiations on the SRM, the main issues concerned the centralization of decision-making power, the sources of funding, and the legal basis of the new mechanism. The initial legislative proposal assigned the Commission the power to decide whether to enter a bank falling under the scope of the SRM into resolution. Some member states (first and foremost Germany) argued that decision-making power should rest with national resolution authorities. As for the funding of the new mechanism, the Commission proposed the creation of a Common Resolution Fund, funded by industry, but some member states (first and foremost Germany) opposed this. The third issue concerned the legal bases of the SRM, in particular whether it required treaty revision, as requested by German policy-makers, or not—as argued the Commission, the ECB, France, Italy, and Spain, which were keen to accelerate the establishment of the SRM. Once an agreement on the SRM regulation was reached, negotiations focused on implementing legislation to calculate financial industry contributions to the SRF.

Moral hazard concerns, linked to the 'manageability' of current and possible bank losses (see Figures 8 and 10, and Table 12), and the structure of national banking systems—especially the domestic reach of internationalization and distinctive national joint liability schemes for alternative banks (see Table 3)—explain member state preferences on the BRRD (specifically, the flexibility left to national authorities and the hierarchy of creditors in the bail-in), the SRM (specifically the centralization of decision-making authority, the sources of funding, and the legal bases), and the use of the ESM as a common fiscal backstop (specifically, the conditionality attached to it), which is discussed in Chapter 8. Member states that were least likely to need recourse to the SRF and the ESM insisted upon necessary treaty change, decision-making power to be assigned to national resolution authorities, and strict conditionality to be imposed upon banks and member state governments in exchange for ESM funding. Countries that were more likely to benefit from the creation of the SRM and the use of the ESM as a common fiscal backstop—both through their role as confidence-building mechanisms and through eventual recourse—ruled out the need for treaty change, supported the transfer of resolution powers to supranational bodies, and opposed conditionality for the use of the ESM as a common fiscal backstop to recapitalize ailing banks (see Chapter 8). In the subsequent negotiations concerning the calculation of financial industry contributions to the funds, the configuration of national banking systems was a major factor in shaping member state government preferences.

The Negotiation of the Bank Recovery and Resolution Directive

After prolonged consultations, the Commission presented a formal legislative proposal for the BRRD in June 2012 (European Commission 2012g). The proposed directive had been in the making since the international financial crisis that reached its peak in the autumn of 2008. However, the legislative proposal by the Commission had been delayed for two main reasons. First, international regulatory fora were discussing this issue and the Commission wanted to put forward EU legislation in line with what had been agreed internationally. Indeed, EU legislative activity on bank recovery and resolution regimes aligned closely with international regulatory initiatives in this field undertaken by the Financial Stability Board (FSB)[2] and the Basel Committee on Banking Supervision (BCBS).[3]

In November 2011, the FSB issued the 'Key Attributes of Effective Resolution Regimes for Financial Institutions' (FSB 2011), which mainly focused on global systemically important cross-border financial institutions. The attributes outlined twelve essential features that should be part of the resolution regimes of all jurisdictions, concerning the scope of application; the resolution authority and resolution powers; recovery and resolution planning;

[2] The FSB comprises treasuries, central banks, and supervisors of the main Group of Twenty (G20) countries as well some international financial organizations, such as the IMF. It is based at the BIS. The FSB's predecessor was set up in 1999, and in 2009, after the international financial crisis, it was transformed into the FSB, with an enlarged membership and enhanced resources.

[3] The BCBS was established by the central bank governors of the Group of Ten countries in 1974. After the international financial crisis, the membership of the BCBS was extended to all countries of the G20. Countries are represented by their central bank and by the authority with formal responsibility for the prudential supervision of banking activities, whenever this is not the central bank.

legal framework conditions for cross-border cooperation; crisis management groups; and institution-specific cross-border cooperation agreements. The FSB drew upon the work carried out by the BCBS. In March 2010, the Cross-Border Bank Resolution Group of the BCBS published its own report, which included a set of ten recommendations (BCBS 2010c). At the June 2010 Toronto Summit, the G20 leaders endorsed the BCBS recommendations and expressed their commitment to implementing them. Several of the FSB and BCBS standards or recommendations informed specific features of the EU legislation, such as recovery and resolution planning, resolution powers, the inclusion of bail-ins, and crisis management groups.

The second main reason for the delay of the Commission's proposal until June 2012 is that the issue of banking resolution was controversial in the EU and thus subject to extensive consultation. The first consultation document was issued by the Commission in October 2009 ('Public Consultation Regarding an EU framework for Cross-Border Crisis Management in the Banking Sector'). This was followed by a Commission communication on bank resolution funds in May 2010 and a communication on a new EU framework for crisis management in the financial sector in October 2010. In January 2011, the Commission organized a further consultation on the technical details of a possible European crisis management framework.

The BRRD had the same scope of application as the CRD IV (hence, it applied to credit institutions and certain investment firms). It distinguished between powers of 'prevention', 'early intervention', and 'resolution'. In the case of prevention, banks were required to draw up recovery plans, and national resolution authorities were required to prepare resolution plans for all national banks, both at group level and for the main individual institutions within the group. Authorities could require a bank to change its legal or operational structures to ensure that it could be resolved with the available tools. Financial groups could enter into intra-group support agreements in the form of loans or the provision of guarantees. The framework envisaged early supervisory intervention whereby the authorities could require banks to implement measures set out in the recovery plan and would have the power to appoint a special manager at a bank for a limited period (European Commission 2012g). The harmonized resolution tools and powers outlined in the directive were designed to ensure that national authorities in all member states had a common toolkit and roadmap to manage the failure of banks.

There were two main controversial issues in the negotiations on this directive. The first to emerge was the proposal to establish national resolution funds, which would raise contributions from banks proportionate to their liabilities and risk profiles, and would not be used to bail out banks. There was a link between this piece of legislation and the DGS Directive, which was designed to provide funding for the protection of retail depositors. Member states were allowed to merge these two funds, provided that the scheme remained in a position to repay depositors in case of failure (European Commission 2012g). When the directive was proposed in July 2012, the Commission noted that, ideally, a single pan-European fund should be established with a pan-European resolution authority to manage its disbursal. However, at the time of the proposal, the Commission recognized that the absence of a single European banking supervisor and insolvency regime would make this unworkable (European Commission 2012g). As in the case of the DGS Directive, the obstacles to these far-reaching changes were ultimately political, with the main line of division running between those member states that were more likely to need to access a pan-European fund and those that were less likely because of the relative 'manageability' of real and possible bank losses.

The Commission proposed that all countries should set up national resolution funds worth up to 1 per cent of national bank deposits, paid for by the banks, to cover the costs of ailing banks. During the EU legislative process the EP supported this provision, whereas the Council of Ministers—and the majority of member states—favoured a lower coverage (interview, Brussels, 2013). Moreover, the UK insisted on an exemption, arguing that it already collected £2.5 billion annually from a temporary government bank levy introduced in 2010. The UK, with a domestically headquartered banking sector dominated by a handful of very large institutions, also claimed that a resolution fund would not be big enough to prop up any of its major banks (*EUObserver*, 21 June 2013).

In the end, the directive required member states, as a general rule, to set up ex ante resolution funds (i.e., the funds had to be set up in advance of entering a bank into resolution) to ensure that the resolution tools could be applied effectively. These national funds would have to reach, within 10 years, a target level of at least 0.8 per cent of covered deposits of all the credit institutions authorized in their country (the initial Commission's draft stated 1 per cent). To reach the target level, banks would have to make annual contributions based on their liabilities, excluding their own funds, and adjusted for risk. An exemption to this rule allowed member states to establish their national financing arrangements through mandatory contributions without setting up a separate fund—this was the case for the UK. However, the member states opting for their own arrangements had to raise at least the same amount of financing and make it available to their resolution authority immediately upon request (Council 2013).

Member states were free to choose whether to merge their funds (or not) for resolution and DGSs. In both cases, the combined target level had to be the same. Lending between national resolution funds was possible on a voluntary basis (Council 2013). Resolution funds were available to provide temporary support to banks via loans, guarantees, asset purchases, or capital for bridge banks. Resolution funds could also be drawn on to compensate shareholders or creditors if and to the extent that their losses under bail-in exceeded the losses they would have undergone under normal insolvency proceedings, in line with a 'no creditor worse off' principle (Council 2013). Resolution colleges were to be established under the leadership of the group resolution authority and with the participation of the EBA, which was to act as binding mediator if necessary (European Commission 2012f, g).

The second controversial issue that emerged later on in the BRRD negotiations concerned the bail-in tool, whereby banks would be recapitalized by wiping out shareholders' stakes, and creditors would have their claims reduced or converted into shares. At stake in the negotiations was how much flexibility governments should be granted in making decisions on winding down banks as well as on the hierarchy in the bailing in of creditors. The Commission's proposal envisaged that only 'deposits that are guaranteed in accordance with Directive 94/19/EC' and certain kinds of liabilities (e.g., 'secured liabilities') would be excluded from the bail-in (European Commission 2012g). Indeed, the Commission and the ECB initially argued that almost all creditors, including depositors, should share the bank's losses equally, with guarantee schemes reimbursing deposits under €100,000. This form of burden-sharing would not alarm senior bondholders and hence would not increase the bank's funding costs.

During the financial crisis in Cyprus in early 2013, uninsured depositors were hit, starting a bank run, and capital controls had to be imposed in the euro area. This event suggested that relying solely on the guarantee for deposits under €100,000 was insufficient to preserve stability and prevent bank runs, unless bigger deposit-holders were reassured (*Financial Times*, 13 May 2013). The most noticeable change of mind over what protection was necessary for depositors in order to prevent bank runs concerned the ECB and the European Commission. After the bank run in Cyprus, the ECB and the Commission argued for a US-style 'depositor preference', whereby uninsured deposits (above €100,000) would be the last ones to suffer losses (*Financial Times*, 13 May 2013). Support built up among several finance ministers in favour of some form of depositor preference.

A coalition led by France and the UK wanted—for different reasons—national authorities to have flexibility when using a bail-in. They wanted national authorities to have the freedom to decide when, and on whom, losses were to be forced. Germany, Denmark, the Netherlands, and Finland favoured harmonized rules with no special treatment for uninsured deposits in order to reduce legal uncertainty for investors. They insisted that the bail-in rules be of limited flexibility, giving national authorities little choice as to when to force losses on equity and bondholders after a bank collapse, as well as limited room to choose which kinds of liability could be exempted from such bail-ins.

Spain, in the midst of a severe banking crisis, wanted deposits of all sizes to be excluded (*Financial Times*, 24 June 2013).

Commissioner Michel Barnier argued that too much flexibility would create a system wherein wealthy countries could use public money for bail-outs while poorer countries would have to force losses on bank owners, creditors, and, potentially—as in the case of Cyprus—deposit-holders (*Financial Times*, 24 June 2013). Depositors in poorer member states would have an incentive to transfer to the branches of banks headquartered in wealthier member states. In the end, it was agreed that small depositors with less than €100,000 would be guaranteed in the event of a bank bail-out. Individuals with more than €100,000 in deposits, and SMEs with more than €100,000 in deposits, were given greater protection. Large companies and institutional investors with more than €100,000 in deposits were given the least protection. National resolution authorities were given some flexibility, notably the power to exclude liabilities on a discretionary basis for one of four reasons: if they could not be bailed in within a reasonable time; to ensure continuity of critical functions; to avoid contagion; and to avoid value destruction that would raise losses borne by other creditors (Council 2013).

This was a partial victory for France, the UK, and all the countries that advocated flexibility. However, such flexibility would only be available after a minimum level of losses (equal to 8 per cent of total liabilities, including their own funds) had been imposed on a bank's shareholders and creditors, or under special circumstances—20 per cent of a bank's risk-weighted assets where the resolution financing arrangement had at its disposal ex ante contributions which amounted to at least 3 per cent of covered deposits. The contribution of the resolution fund was capped at 5 per cent of a bank's total liabilities. In extraordinary circumstances—such as when this limit had been reached, and after all unsecured, non-preferred liabilities other than eligible deposits had been bailed in—the resolution authority was allowed to seek funding from alternative sources (Council 2013).

In the negotiations on the final text of the BRRD, the EP and some member state governments were keen to maintain a degree of national discretion to protect some creditors from haircuts (*Financial Times*, 13 October 2013). The EP pressed for governments to be given an option to temporarily renationalize or recapitalize banks during a systemic crisis. However, the European Commission warned that there were unavoidable limits to bail-out powers because EU treaty articles restricting state support to the private sector (state-aid rules) prevailed over any exemptions passed in legislation. The Commission made clear that it would monitor such interventions and require them to be fully subject to EU state-aid rules and, therefore, the burden-sharing requirements. This would involve, at a minimum, converting junior debt into equity and, if necessary, wiping out bondholders and shareholders before state funds could be used (*Financial Times*, 13 October 2013).

The Negotiations on the Single Resolution Mechanism

In July 2013, the Commission proposed the establishment of the SRM (European Commission 2013), designed to complement the SSM. The Commission's draft regulation envisaged the establishment of a Single Resolution Board (SRB), consisting of representatives from the ECB, the Commission, and the national resolution authorities of the countries where the bank had its headquarters as well as branches and/or subsidiaries. The ECB, in its role in the SSM, would signal when a bank headquartered in a Banking Union member state was in 'severe financial difficulties' and needed 'to be resolved'. The SRB would prepare the resolution of a bank and would be 'responsible for the key decisions on how a bank would be resolved' (European Commission 2013), with national resolution authorities 'closely involved in this work'. The Commission assigned to itself the power to decide whether to enter a bank into resolution. The Commission, which drafted the proposal, argued that this decision could not rest with the SRB 'for legal reasons' (European Commission 2013). According to the treaty, only an EU institution could make such a decision at the European level, precluding an agency (e.g., the EBA) from fulfilling this role.

National resolution authorities would retain responsibility for executing the resolution actions, with the SRB having an oversight role, monitoring the implementation by national authorities. If the national authorities did not comply with SRB decisions, the board would have the power to 'directly address executive orders to the troubled banks' (European Commission 2013). A SRF would be established under the control of the SRB to provide financial support during the restructuring process. It was envisaged that this fund would be created from contributions from the banking sector, through the pooling of resources of national resolution funds of member states participating in Banking Union. While these funds were being built up, the Commission proposed that it should be able to borrow from the markets (European Commission 2013). The Commission's fund proposal was supported by the ECB, the French government, and euro area periphery member states.

However, several elements of the Commission's draft legislation for the SRM were widely criticized. For some, it did not go far enough because it did not propose the establishment of a true Single Resolution Authority, which would have required a treaty revision (Speyer 2013; see also Zavvos and Kaltsouni 2015). As noted above, the Commission assigned responsibilities to several bodies. Furthermore, the actions of the SRB were contingent on the decision of the ECB to signal that a bank within the SSM was in difficulty, implying that the SSM's internal decision-making structure and its interaction with national authorities would form a further layer within the SRM (Deloitte 2013). Clarity and speed in decision-making are crucial for crisis management, but this multi-layered structure for the SRM created several veto points.

Critics challenged the initial SRM's proposal on legal grounds: the Commission based its proposal on Article 114 TFEU, designed to protect the Single Market, whereas German policy-makers, for example, argued that a treaty change was required. Moreover, critics argued that draft legislation gave too much power to the Commission, which would decide whether and when to place a bank into resolution. They were thus concerned that the Commission would gain the power to make decisions that could have fiscal implications for the member states. Should national and the SRFs not have enough financial resources to resolve a bank, national governments (and, ultimately, taxpayers) would have to provide support, notably through the ESM. The Germans argued that the SRM should begin as a network of national authorities (*Financial Times*, 8 November 2013).

Underlying these legal concerns, German policy-makers feared that their national banks would be the largest contributors to the resolution fund and gain little in return. German Finance Minister Wolfgang Schäuble opposed a model for a single European bank rescue fund financed by levies on banks. German policy-makers favoured a network of national funds in the medium term and argued that the setting up of a common fund required treaty change (*Financial Times*, 6 December 2013). Germany also insisted on bringing forward rules to impose losses on senior creditors in banks to 2015, especially the bail-in measures, which were included in the BRRD and would reduce the need for public funding to prop up banks (this point was restated in the German non-paper in the autumn of 2015, when the discussion of the CDGS regained momentum in the EU: see Chapters 7 and 10).

In October 2013, an opinion from the European Commission's legal service shed serious doubt on the legality of giving a new agency wide discretion to close troubled banks under EU treaties: 'The legal service considers that the powers which would be conferred by the proposal of the board . . . need to be further detailed in order to exclude that a wide margin of discretion is entrusted to the board' (*EurActive*, 8 October 2013). Almost all member states also opposed the allocation of new resolution power to the Commission. However, Germany was left almost alone in demanding that any resolution decisions were taken by ECOFIN, which lacked the structures to make rapid decisions (*Financial Times*, 6 December 2013).

In April 2013, all six of the ECB Executive Board members had come out publicly in favour of a rapid move to an SRM even though this was clearly at odds with the German government's more gradualist version (see, e.g., Mersch 2013a; *Financial Times*, 29 April 2013). In November 2013, the ECB issued a 32-page opinion signed by Mario Draghi, which stated that the SRB should be, from the start, a single 'strong and independent' body, thus directly challenging the German position in favour of a network of national authorities (*Financial Times*, 8 November 2013). The ECB argued that 'co-ordination between national resolution systems has not proved sufficient to achieve the most timely and cost-effective resolution decisions, particularly in a cross-border context' (*Financial Times*, 8 November 2013). The ECB also insisted that treaty change was unnecessary to create the new body (*Bloomberg*, 17 December 2013).

In the run-up to the decisive ECOFIN meeting in December 2013, Dutch policy-makers floated the idea of splitting the SRM proposal into two parts, to be discussed in parallel negotiations. One part concerned the scope and decision-making mechanism of the SRM; the other part concerned the SRF (*Bloomberg*, 10 December 2013). With reference to the SRF, a compromise solution proposed by Dutch policy-makers was a system whereby the resolution fund of the bank's home state would be used before other member states' funds were utilized. The *Financial Times* also reported a possible compromise on the banks covered by the system, leaving national authorities in the lead in resolving smaller banks, as favoured by German policy-makers (*Financial Times*, 6 December 2013). In December 2013, German Finance Minister Schäuble invited Michel Barnier and the finance ministers of France, the Netherlands, Spain, and Italy to an informal negotiating session in Berlin (*Financial Times*, 6 December 2013).

Another contentious issue in the negotiations on the SRM was how to proceed if national resolution funds were insufficient to deal with a big bank's failure. German government officials argued on the grounds of moral hazard that if the resolution funds were insufficient to resolve an ailing bank, the national authorities (and, in the end, the taxpayers) of the home country should cover the costs. France and some Southern European countries called for the use of the ESM as a common backstop. For example, French Finance Minister Pierre Moscovici reiterated his support for a SRF with a 'unique backstop' to cover shortfalls while the fund was set up by collecting levies from the banking industry (*Bloomberg*, 10 December 2013).

In December 2013, an agreement was reached in the Council of Ministers on the SRM regulation (Council 2013). In addition, a decision was adopted by euro area member states that committed them to negotiate an intergovernmental agreement on the functioning of the SRF by March 2014. The draft regulation agreed by the Council established that 'upon notification by the

ECB that a bank was failing or likely to fail, or on its own initiative, the SRB would adopt a resolution scheme placing a bank into resolution' (Council 2013). The Board would decide on the application of resolution tools and the use of the SRF. 'Decisions by the Board would enter into force within 24 hours of their adoption, unless the Council, acting by simple majority on a proposal by the Commission, objected or called for changes' (Council 2013). Assigning the Board such powers—albeit with potential Council interference—was an important change, advocated first and foremost by Germany, compared with the original Commission draft, which gave the Commission the power to decide to enter a bank into resolution.

It was agreed that the SRB would consist of an executive director, four full-time appointed members, and the representatives of the national resolution authorities of all the participating countries (Zavvos and Kaltsouni 2015). The Commission and the ECB would only have observer status. Any decisions with significant financial implications for the SRF would be taken by a two-thirds majority of the Board members, representing at least 50 per cent of contributions. According to the version of the regulation agreed in December 2013, a decision to close down a bank would need the approval of a large number of actors, including the European Commission, the Council of Ministers, and the SSB (in effect the ECB), as well as the SRB and its plenary council.

The SRM was to cover all banks in the member states participating in Banking Union. However, the Germans succeeded in getting adopted their position that the Board would be responsible for the resolution only of those banks directly supervised by the ECB. National resolution authorities would be responsible for the resolution of all other banks, except if a bank required access to the SRF. National authorities would also be responsible for executing bank resolution plans under the control of the SRB (Council 2013). In order to guarantee member state budgetary sovereignty, the SRB was not empowered to require governments to provide extraordinary public support to any bank under resolution (European Commission 2013c; Zavvos and Kaltsouni 2015).

The version of the regulation agreed by the member states in December 2013 created an SRF that would be financed by bank levies raised at the national level. It would initially consist of national compartments that would be gradually merged over ten years. During this period, mutualization between national compartments would progressively increase (Council 2013). Thus, while during the first year the cost of resolving banks (after bail-in) would mainly come from the compartments of the member states where the banks are located, this share would gradually decrease and the contribution from other participating countries' compartments would increase.

The December 2013 regulation also endorsed the bail-in rules set by the BRRD as applicable to the use of the SRF. The SRM would gradually merge national resolution funds into a single European one over a decade, with the target funding level of €55 billion by 2026 or about 1 per cent of all insured deposits (*The Guardian*, 19 December 2013). In the end, it was decided that during the building up of resolution funds, member state governments would collectively have to provide the extra funding to resolve national ailing banks, if necessary by requesting a loan from the ESM. A fully shared backstop would be available only once national resolution funds reached their target level and were fully merged (*Wall Street Journal*, 18 December 2013; *The Guardian*, 19 December 2013). From 2026 onwards the SRM could no longer borrow from the ESM.

The German government refused to include in the December 2013 regulation the most legally sensitive elements of the SRM package, notably specific provisions on the transfer and pooling of member state funded compartments into a single mutualized fund. These were placed in an intergovernmental side agreement. The Germans sought an intergovernmental agreement in order to eliminate EP involvement on these matters and minimize the Commission's role (*European Voice*, 12 December 2013). Moreover, the December 2013 compromise ensured that the SRM regulation was not to apply before the intergovernmental agreement entered into force—which was to take place following ratification by participating member states representing 80 per cent of contributions to the SRF. The Germans insisted upon subsequent intergovernmental agreements among participating member states to permit the transfer of national funds towards the SRF and the activation of the mutualization of the national compartments.

The ECB, the Commission, and the EP joined forces in challenging elements of the regulation/intergovernmental agreement compromise of the December European Council. Vitor Constâncio, a member of the ECB's Executive Board, expressed the ECB's fear that the markets would find the proposed resolution process insufficiently credible because it was too complex and involved too many policy-makers to work with the necessary speed in crisis situations (ECB 2013). Constâncio also warned that to be credible, the national bank-resolution funds needed to have access to outside financing, especially in the period when national resolution funds were being built up (*Wall Street Journal*, 18 December 2013; *The Guardian*, 19 December 2013). He criticized the December agreement because it did not allow the resolution funds to borrow on the financial markets to raise extra funding: 'We are talking here not about a final backstop, we are talking here about a credit line, which is a system that exists for instance in the US . . . You should flesh out the possibility of the fund borrowing in the markets to have bridge financing to complete the resolution process' (*The Telegraph*, 18 December 2013).

Michel Barnier, the EU Commissioner responsible for financial services, remained concerned about the ability of the SRM to make difficult decisions to close a bank quickly or secretly enough. He argued that 'decision-making within the SRM [was] still too complex with a consultation system which [slowed] down the process unnecessarily' (*The Telegraph*, 18 December 2013). Concerns similar to those expressed by the ECB and the Commission were also aired by policy-makers outside the EU. Jack Lew, the US Treasury Secretary, stated: 'We don't think it's big enough. We don't think it's fast enough' (*Financial Times*, 16 January 2014).

The EP questioned the need for an intergovernmental agreement to formulate the details on the functioning of the SRF to be used in bank resolution (EP 2014a). In a letter sent to the EU's rotating presidency of the Council, the EP argued that the 'intergovernmental agreement on Single Resolution Fund is illegal because it bypasses the established legislative processes of the Union' (*Financial Times*, 16 January 2014). The EP did not even formally recognize the Council text of the side agreement—regarding which it had no formal role. However, the EP retained some leverage on the side agreement because of its co-decision power on the SRM regulation.

To further complicate negotiations, the version of the regulation adopted by the EP in January 2014 was significantly different from that agreed by the Council. MEPs restated the requests that 'all banks must be treated equally, irrespective of which country they are established in, and that the system must be credible and efficient' (EP 2014a). They called for a simplification of the resolution decision-making process by creating a stronger, more centralized authority, with the SSB (and thus the ECB's Governing Council) possessing the final say over bank resolution without political interference. They also wanted to remove Germany's safeguards so that the SRF would be available sooner, with access to a centralized/common credit line. A further EP demand was to accelerate the mutualization of the SRF so as to complete it by 2018 rather than 2026. Informal 'trialogue' negotiations between the EP and the Council, assisted by the Commission, began in early 2014 with a view to reaching a first reading agreement on the proposal before the parliamentary dissolution in May 2014 (Febelfin 2013).

The EP unsuccessfully attempted to bring the elements of the December intergovernmental side agreement into the regulation, winning only limited concessions in the 20 March 2014 compromise with the Council: a decreased period of eight years during which the national compartments would merge; an increased proportion of the SRF shared at an earlier stage; and a marginally increased role performed by the Commission in the SRB—allowing the Council to reject resolution proposals only under certain conditions (*Financial Times*, 20 March 2014). Although the Commission was to have a limited role in the SRM, member state governments retained their vetoes on mutualization and an important say on the use of resolution funds. A messy compromise was reached on triggering the resolution process. It was agreed that the SSB (and, ultimately, the ECB's Governing Council) would hold the trigger, being responsible for deciding whether or not a bank should be resolved. The SRB would ask the SSB to make such a decision; if it declined to do so, then the SRB itself would take the decision. The SSB (and thus the ECB) was therefore to be the main 'triggering' authority, but the SRB might also play a role if the SSB (ECB) was reluctant or hesitated to act (EP 2014b).

After the agreement was reached on the BRRD and the SRM regulation, implementing delegated legislation had to be adopted for both acts. In October 2014, the Commission adopted a BRRD delegated act establishing the yearly contributions of individual banks to their respective national resolution funds. It established a fixed part of the contribution on the basis of the institution's liabilities, excluding own funds and guaranteed deposits (thus, the larger the bank, the higher the fixed part of the contribution), and a variety of risk indicators to be used to adjust the basic contribution to the risk posed by each bank. Finally, it established a special lump-sum regime for small banks that were seen as having a lower risk profile and hence less likely to use resolution funds. Banks representing 1 per cent of the total assets would pay 0.3 per cent of the total contributions (in the euro area). The October 2014 delegated act laid down the basic rules on how to calculate the contributions of individual banks to twenty-eight national resolution funds. Under the BRRD, the target level of the national resolution funds was set at the national level and calculated on the basis of covered deposits.

In October 2014, the Commission also adopted a draft proposal for a Council implementing act specifying the methodology for the calculation of contributions of banks to the SRF in member states participating in Banking Union, whereby a unified system of contributions would be pooled in the SRF on the basis of a European target level (European Commission 2014a). Under the SRM, the target level of the SRF was the sum of the covered deposits of all institutions of member states participating in Banking Union. This resulted in changes to the contributions banks would have to make under the BRRD alone. In December 2014, the Council reached a political agreement (compromise) on the implementing regulation determining the contributions to be paid by banks to the SRF, to be built up over a period of eight years to reach a target level of at least 1 per cent of the amount of covered deposits of all credit institutions in all the participating member states (Council 2014).

In the political agreement reached by the Council, member states agreed to mitigate any abrupt increase in fees for Banking Union headquartered banks when switching from a national to the European target level (Council 2014). In this regard, the implementing regulation provides for an adjustment mechanism during the initial eight-year period when the SRF is to be built up. This phase-in period mirrors the eight-year mutualization phase during which national compartments in the SRF are to be gradually merged. Between 2016 and 2023, annual contributions by banks are to be calculated in a manner that is increasingly based on the SRM target level. Therefore, while in the first year 60 per cent of bank contributions are to be calculated in accordance with national target levels, this share is to decrease annually. By the eighth year, all bank contributions will be calculated on the basis of the SRM target level. Bank contributions raised in 2015 under the BRRD are to be deducted from the amount due from each institution (Council 2014).

According to the Bundesbank, banks in France and Germany would have to contribute the bulk of the SRF's financial resources (€55 billion), with each country's banking sector set to pay just under €15.5 billion by the end of 2023 (Bundesbank 2014). The two biggest euro area economies would thus together finance more than 55 per cent of the SRF. Under that option, Italy, the third biggest euro area economy, would contribute €5.8 billion, Spain €5.4 billion, and the Netherlands €4.2 billion. Ireland would pay €1.8 billion, Greece only €629 million, and Cyprus €113 million. The smallest contribution would come from Estonia—€23 million (Reuters, 18 December 2014). Smaller banks—broadly defined as those with total assets of up to €1 billion—are to pay a lower flat contribution rate. Participating member states can lift this size threshold to €3 billion in total assets by 2023 during the transitional phase (Bundesbank 2014). Banks will not be required to make all their contributions ex ante, but can provide irrevocable payment commitments, though these must be adequately backed by collaterals and convertible into funding at all times.

Explaining National Preferences on the Single Resolution Mechanism

This section spells out and explains national preferences on the main issues in the negotiations on the SRM. The UK is not considered in this section as it was not involved in the negotiations on the SRM. The UK also maintained its own resolution mechanism which, nonetheless, met EU requirements (Bank of England 2014). Countries with massive cross-border banks, such as France and the Netherlands (see Tables 1 and 2), supported the SRM because they needed it more than countries with fewer large cross-border banks—such as Germany, which had its own liability schemes already (see Table 3)—and a smaller percentage of banking assets were held by the biggest players. The euro periphery, such as Italy and Spain, which might have been less interested under normal circumstances but whose banks were in bad shape (see Figure 8 and Table 12), needed the confidence boost that their banks could be resolved without excessive disruption to national finances.

Germany

The German government challenged the Commission's draft SRM regulation on legal grounds, arguing that the Commission had overstepped its authority and that a treaty change was required (*Financial Times*, 6 December 2013). The head of a Bavarian banking association went so far as to liken the Commission's proposals to 'enabling acts', the laws that the Nazis used to seize power (*Financial Times*, 11 July 2013). As noted earlier, the German government was also concerned with the legal implications of mutualizing resolution funds in the SRF, given that this had potential fiscal policy implications and thus required parliamentary approval. As far as the decision-making of the SRM/SRB was concerned, German policy-makers demanded that resolution decisions should be taken by the Council (*Financial Times*, 6 December 2013), which was to operate by unanimity, allowing each member state to retain its veto. Finally, Germans policy-makers successfully argued that the Board would be responsible for the resolution only of those banks directly supervised by the ECB.

German preferences on the BRRD and SRM were driven by moral hazard concerns, but they also reflected a desire to protect German cooperative and savings banks. There were several moral hazards that preoccupied the German government: for bank shareholders, bondholders, and depositors; for the banks themselves; and for governments. A core element of the German political discourse on Banking Union was that (German) taxpayers should be protected against future public bail-outs of banks, the keyword being 'Haftungskaskade' (liability cascade) (Schild 2015). Strong German government support for the BRRD was notably due to the requirement that banks facing resolution would first have to undertake 'bail-in'—a requirement later integrated into the SRM regulation—then recourse to national resolution funds, financed through bank levies. In the SRM, the SRF should only be used for systemically important banks with important transnational activities, and only after the requirement that member state governments provide funds. Germany (joined by the UK and 'core' euro area member states) supported an early entry into force of the BRRD in 2016 instead of 2018—specifically to protect German taxpayers.

With the aim of preventing a moral hazard for euro area member states, the German authorities argued that if national resolution funds created because of the BRRD were insufficient to resolve an ailing bank, the national authorities (and, in the end, the taxpayers) of the home country should cover the costs, otherwise a moral hazard would arise for NCAs in the supervision of less significant banks and for governments with regard to resolution decisions (*Financial Times*, 6 December 2013). A further moral hazard concern can be seen in German government demands for the SRM to cover the resolution of only the largest euro area banks directly under ECB supervision and not of the banks still subject to national supervision (and thus potential forbearance and political interference). Furthermore, the German government accepted the creation of a common fiscal backstop during the transition period to the creation of the SRF. However, the Germans insisted that the banking sector would ultimately be liable for repayment by means of levies in all participating countries with the aim of fiscal neutrality 'over the medium term so that taxpayers will be protected' (Eurogroup 2013).

With savings and cooperative banks in mind, German policy-makers also sought to exclude smaller banks from SRM coverage and thus contributions to the SRF (*Financial Times*, 6 December 2013; *European Voice*, 19 September 2013). In this respect, Germany favoured a compromise that would mirror the deal reached with reference to the direct supervision of banks by the ECB in the SSM which deprived the ECB of involvement in the direct supervision of all but 130 banks—although the ECB retained the power to intervene in any bank if necessary, subject to a majority vote in the SSM's supervisory board. The Germans wanted national resolution authorities to be responsible for the resolution of all smaller euro area banks, except if national authorities required access to the SRF, which in the case of Germany was highly improbable given the existence of well-funded joint liability schemes for the savings banks and cooperatives.

According to the Commission's June 2013 proposed legislation, contributions to the SRF would be smaller for banks funded mainly through deposits and undertaking lower risk activities. However, despite the large number of small banks engaged in 'traditional' banking activities in Germany, this did not result in German government support. Most likely, this was because the two largest German commercial banks, Deutsche Bank and Commerzbank, opposed this proposed funding scheme which would hit them on two fronts—that is, size and risk activities (*Wall Street Journal*, 10 July 2013).

France

The French authorities pointed out that Banking Union, which was designed to break the 'vicious circle between sovereigns and banks', was based on three pillars: the SSM, the SRM, and the CDGS, all regarded as essential to 'sever the link between the bank and sovereigns and hence lead to the normalization of interest rates in the euro area' (Agence France Trésor 2013: 2). The French were joined by the large majority of euro area member states in this assessment, including the Dutch, Italian, and Spanish governments. Finance Minister Pierre Moscovici in an article in *Le Monde* (20 December 2013, authors' translation) argued that, in addition to the SRM and the SRF, 'a common public safety net' was needed to ensure that the SRF would be able to finance its operations even in the event of a systemic crisis. Moscovici argued that 'in the transitional phase, the ESM should be the lender of last resort'. French policy-makers sought a simplified SRM that allowed for quick and effective decision-making and that could be implemented as soon as possible by revising the Treaty Establishing the European Stability Mechanism (ESM treaty) and pooling national funds over a period of five years (French Senate 2013).

French policy-makers and banks were also concerned that the SRF contribution rules should not create distortions between national banking systems both within the Banking Union and in relation to the banking systems of countries not participating in the Banking Union (French Senate 2013). BNP Paribas Chief Executive Jean-Laurent Bonnafe regarded as 'exorbitant' the €16 billion figure reported by the media as the likely contribution of French banks to the SRF and argued that such contribution should be lower because of the relatively low-risk profile of French banks (*Reuters*, 4 November 2014). French policy-makers wanted to make sure that the criteria for the contributions of individual banks to the fund, to be subsequently defined by a delegated legal act of the Commission, should not weigh heavier on the French banking sector than the national fund to be built up in accordance to the BRRD, which in France was to reach €13 billion (Marc 2013: 31).

The French advocated an approach that took the risk structure of the bank's assets into account more than the bank's size—which would penalize the four large French banks. The French were also concerned that less concentrated banking systems (notably the German, Austrian, and Italian systems; see Figure 6) would contribute far less if the scope of the SRM did not include all banks regardless of size. The French thus sought to force all euro area banks to contribute to the SRF, as they all might get money from it in the event of resolution (Marc 2013: 23). Notably, French policy-makers expressed concern that French banks would end up contributing more than German banks despite the larger size of the German banking system (French Senate 2013). The use of a risk-weighted model to determine bank contributions would hit hardest those euro area headquartered banks—notably Deutsche Bank—which relied most heavily on investment banking activities.

The Netherlands

The Netherlands government was officially in favour of creating an SRM, arguing that in

> a European resolution mechanism, the taxpayer is better protected against the cost of failing banks than if member states take individual actions... therefore transferring resolution at the European level is a logical step following the decision to

> move banking supervision at the European level... only by transferring resolution to the European level, a Banking Union can function properly and the link between national governments' vulnerable and fragile banking sectors can be reduced (Netherlands Government 2013b, authors' translation).

Dutch policy-makers were in favour of a European resolution authority 'as independent as possible' and 'ideally... placed in a new European institution' (Netherlands Government 2013b). However, they also noted that this would require a treaty change and this was, in the short term, unfeasible.

The Dutch authorities pointed out that a 'good balance' needed 'to be struck between national and European interests' in order to avoid problems of moral hazard for banks and sovereigns (Netherlands Government 2013b). They sought an SRM design that would prevent banks from claiming from the European resolution fund 'too fast and too much', leaving the 'burden of resolution to be quickly passed on to other banks' (Netherlands Government 2013b). The Dutch authorities and all three big Dutch banks also insisted upon the complete independence of the SRB in order to minimize political influence over resolution decisions (Netherlands Government 2013b; Rabobank 2013). Reiterating a constant position shared with the German government, the Dutch authorities insisted that banks covered by the SRM 'should start with a comparably healthy position', which thus required an ECB-led comprehensive assessment which would bring to light 'any as yet unidentified losses on bank balance sheets' and written off or covered by a 'bail-in of private creditors and not by national [public] resources' (Netherlands Government 2013b). 'Derogation from bail-in' should be allowed only in exceptional situations.

The very high concentration of the Dutch banking system (see Figure 6), the high level of internationalization of the largest Dutch banks (see Table 1), and the impact of the financial crisis on the Netherlands (see Tables 10 and 11) explain the national position in favour of the BRRD and SRM which aligned closely with the position of the country's three largest banks (see, e.g., ING 2014: 12; Rabobank 2013; see also Dutch Banking Association 2013). The three largest Dutch banks were 'too big to fail' and could easily overwhelm national resources. Thus, the Dutch authorities sought EU-wide bail-in rules (that would not create the competitive disadvantage of specifically national rules), the possibility of resolution support funds at the supranational level, and the ESM backstop. Clearly, the Netherlands did not face the immediate threat of sovereign default which encouraged euro periphery support for the SRM. However, the comparatively large size of the banking sector and largest banks relative to GDP (see Figure 11 and Table 16), and huge real and relative losses during financial crisis, meant that the Netherlands government was particularly sensitive with regard to the construction of a credible resolution regime (Netherlands Central Bank officials interviews, 10 October 2014;

Netherlands Government 2013b). The Netherlands government accepted the need for bank contributions to reflect risk weights—and thus the extent to which bail-in could be effective given bank balance sheets and likelihood of recourse to the SRM to resolve a bank—to avoid competitive distortions among banks and banking systems (Netherlands Government 2013b).

Italy

Italian policy-makers supported the SRM as a way to 'avoid the pursuit of domestic interests and negative externalities among banking systems' (Szago 2013: 10, authors' translation). They also argued that 'the supranationalization of resolution was a more adequate way (compared with domestic action) to deal with large cross-border banking groups, avoiding overlapping among national authorities' (Szago 2013: 10, authors' translation; see also Italian Senate 2013). Both the Bank of Italy and the Italian Banking Association (ABI) pointed out the need to establish the SRM to complement the SSM, arguing that 'the transfer of supervisory functions to the ECB, in the absence of mechanisms for crisis management, would not break the vicious circle between banks and sovereign and would curtail the ECB's action... There could be a potential conflict of national interests, which would make it impossible to start the resolution process of an ailing bank' (Sabatini 2013: 4, authors' translation; similar points were also made by Szago 2013).

As for decision-making, the Italian authorities called for a system able to 'make quick decisions' and to 'swiftly manage any resolution procedure', arguing that 'governance arrangements should be streamlined, rather than made more complicated' (Saccomanni 2013). The SRF and the common fiscal backstop of the ESM were a priority for the Italian government. In the final stage of the negotiations in December 2013, the Italian Finance Minister, Saccomanni (2013), sent a letter to the other EU finance ministers, stressing that in order 'to break the nexus' and 'reduce the risk of contagion' the system had to rely on 'common financial resources, so that the risks are mutualised'—thus effectively reversing the German logic of moral hazard regarding banks and sovereigns. Saccomanni (2013) called for a 'common backstop' to 'provide contribution to the cost of resolution without conditionality'.

For the Italian government, the overriding importance of EU-level support mechanisms was to bolster international financial confidence in the Italian banking system. Like the French, they argued in favour of the participation of all banks in the SRM—whether supervised directly by the ECB or not. Like Germany, Italy had many smaller and medium-sized banks which escaped ECB direct supervision (see Figure 6). However, unlike Germany, the Italian government wanted to ensure the access of all Italian banks to the SRF. Banking system structure shaped the details of the Italian position, notably on bank contributions to the SRF. The Italian authorities and ABI raised the issue of the 'contributions to be paid by banks participating in private systems of insurance recognized by law' (Sabatini 2013, authors' translation). The reference was to the institutional protection schemes established on the basis of a contractual arrangement whereby member banks protected each other against the risks of illiquidity and insolvency (see Table 3). The ABI sought to avoid what could become a 'double contribution' by securing a 'reduction' of the ordinary ex ante contribution. The Italian authorities and the ABI also raised the issue of rules for ordinary ex ante contributions to the SRF. The ABI proposed to finance the SRF through 'commitments to pay' guaranteed by government bonds. This would have come close to a de facto ex-post contribution—which most struggling Italian banks (see Figure 8 and Table 12) would have preferred to true ex ante contribution.

Spain

The Spanish Prime Minister, Mariano Rajoy, stated that the 'creation of the SRM was a Spanish "request"' in order to build an effective Banking Union (Rajoy 2012, authors' translation). The Spanish saw the creation of the SRM as an 'essential element to break the tie between sovereign risk and risk in the banking sector' and to end 'financial sector fragmentation' in the euro area (Rajoy 2014, authors' translation). The Spanish position was thus very close to those of the French and Italian governments. Overall, the Spanish authorities were not very vocal during the SRM negotiations, for two reasons. First, the Spaniards, like the Italians, did not have much bargaining power. Like the Italians, the Spanish were demanders of the SRM, but, unlike Italian banks, Spanish banks had already received euro area financial assistance. Second, given that the Spanish banks had already been directly recapitalized by the ESM, they were in less immediate need of potential access to a large SRF (Spanish Ministry of Finance official, interview, February 2015).

Conclusion

This chapter has discussed the second core component of Banking Union, namely the design and funding of bank resolution—both the SRM and the BRRD, which applies to the entire EU and is part of the Single Rulebook. The resolution of ailing banks is a thorny issue (not only in the EU or in Banking Union) because it often involves the use of taxpayers' money if a bank is bailed out, as happened during the international financial crisis. Moreover, resolution is strictly interconnected with deposit protection (discussed in Chapter 7), and the fiscal backstop and LLR (discussed in Chapter 8). Resolution is particularly tricky during a crisis—notably because it can worsen financial panic—and particularly in the case of large cross-border banks, especially those that are too big to fail. For all these reasons, the Commission took several years to propose the BRRD even though it began consulting on this issue shortly after the crisis. The BRRD might not have been agreed without the Banking Union and SRM negotiations.

The main issues in the negotiations on the SRM concerned the centralization of decision-making power, the scope of the SRM, the sources of funding, and the legal basis of the new mechanism. German opposition to the Commission's draft directive on the SRM stemmed from legal difficulties; concerns over moral hazard created for banks, sovereigns and creditors; and the structure of the German banking system. Clearly, the German government disliked both having to pay for the closure of foreign banks and empowering foreigners to close German banks. However, legal, moral hazard, and banking-system-specific concerns shaped the contours of German government preferences.

The Commission proposal of June 2013 envisaged assigning to the Commission itself decision-making power to enter a bank into resolution. Some member states, first and foremost Germany, argued that decision-making power should rest with national resolution authorities individually and then collectively in the EU Council of Ministers, with member state veto. The Commission pushed for SRM coverage of all EU banks, whereas the Germans insisted upon the coverage of only the largest systemically important cross-border banks, keeping in mind the aim to shelter smaller German alternative banks both from contributions and supranational interference, and to maintain existing joint liability schemes that created considerable confidence in the stability of these. As for funding the SRM, the Commission initially proposed the creation of a Common Resolution Fund, funded by industry, but some member states (particularly Germany) opposed this idea. The fourth issue concerned the legal basis of the SRM, in particular whether it required treaty revision, as requested by German policy-makers, or not—as argued by the Commission, the ECB, France, Italy, and Spain, which were keen to speed up the establishment of the SRM.

By March 2014, euro area member states had agreed the SRM, less than two years after the June 2012 agreement by heads of government and state to 'complete' EMU by creating Banking Union. Yet most observers were highly sceptical of the institutional design of the agreed SRM—and its potential contribution to banking and financial system stability (see, e.g., Münchau 2014). Many observers, including the IMF (2014), the ECB (2013), and the Commission (*The Telegraph*, 18 December 2013) feared that the decision-making system of the SRM was too 'convoluted' and too characterized by multiple veto points to permit the effective and timely resolution of ailing banks—in resolution, timing is of the essence. Moreover, observers queried the limited size of the SRF and the eight-year process for the full merger of national compartments of the SRF, which further threatened its credibility. The failure to agree a common DGS (discussed in Chapter 7) created further concern. Finally, the lack of clarity regarding a common fiscal backstop remained a major obstacle to breaking the sovereign debt–bank doom loop.

7

Deposit Guarantee

In June 2012, the Van Rompuy report (also known as the Four Presidents report) included a common DGS as a key component of Banking Union. The report stated that 'A European deposit insurance scheme . . . would strengthen the credibility of the existing arrangements and serve as an important assurance that eligible deposits of all credit institutions are sufficiently insured' (2012: 4). It also noted that the scheme

> and the resolution fund could be set up under the control of a common resolution authority. Such a framework would greatly reduce the need to make actual use of the guarantee scheme. Nevertheless, the credibility of any deposit guarantee scheme requires access to a solid financial backstop. Therefore, as regards the euro area, the European Stability Mechanism could act as the fiscal backstop to the resolution and deposit guarantee authority (p. 4).

A DGS provides protection to bank depositors, reimbursing the deposits of clients of a failed bank up to a certain amount. It is designed to prevent a 'bank run'—that is, panic withdrawals by customers of their bank deposits because of fear of collapse. In so doing, it also supports the overall stability of the financial system (FSB 2012: 8). The issue of DGSs is related to the creation of a resolution framework for banks. A range of expert observers (including IMF economists) and the EU four presidents argued for a CDGS to be a key component of Banking Union. In July 2012, the IMF executive board argued in favour of Banking Union 'comprising a pan-European DGS and a pan-European resolution scheme—both backed with common resources'. ECB Vice President Vitor Constâncio (2014) stated:

> Such a scheme would have several benefits. It would be commensurate to the centralized supervisory regime, and ensure that decisions that are taken on a centralized level affect depositors in all countries in the same way, thus ensuring a level playing-field. Depositors would be treated in a uniform way across countries, independently of their location and the location of the bank to whom they have entrusted their savings.

Moreover, a CDGS could be more credible and better able to mobilize financial resources than national schemes. The CDGS could also undermine the potential distortions to the Single European Market created by different national schemes, as highlighted by the international financial crisis.

In its September 2012 communication 'A Roadmap towards Banking Union', the Commission argued that '[s]hifting the supervision of banks to the European level is a key part of this process, which must subsequently be combined with other steps such as a *common system for deposit protection*, and integrated bank crisis management' (emphasis added, p. 2). The Commission also noted that '[t]his future system will help build the necessary trust between Member States, which is a pre-condition for the introduction of any common financial arrangements to protect depositors and support orderly resolution of failing banks' (p. 3). However, the communication only made specific reference to the revision of the DGS Directive under negotiation in the EU since 2010.

By December 2012, the establishment of a CDGS had disappeared from the policy agenda. The so-called Van Rompuy report issued in December 2012 only made reference to the '[a]greement on the harmonisation of national resolution and deposit guarantee frameworks, ensuring appropriate funding from the financial industry' (p. 4). Only in the autumn of 2015 did the European Commission renew its campaign to encourage member state governments to adopt a European Deposit Insurance Scheme (EDIS). This chapter explains why the creation of a common DGS has been so particularly challenging for euro area member states.

It is argued that obstacles to harmonization of national DGSs and the failure of member states to agree to create a CDGS were due to two main reasons. Principally, the different configuration of existing national DGSs blocked progress. Different national DGSs were in turn linked to the different configuration of national banking systems. Second, there was the perennial problem of moral hazard concerning the 'manageability' of real and possible bank losses and the fact that countries with healthier banking systems—first and foremost Germany—would inevitably become net contributors to any mutual/common fund. This commitment to potential financial transfer—even via the banking system as opposed to the public purse—was politically unpalatable for policy-makers in these countries.

This chapter first outlines the purpose and main types of DGS. It then traces the evolution of EU legislation on DGSs from the first directive issued in 1994 to its revision in 2014. This overview is followed by a discussion of the negotiations on a CDGS in the context of Banking Union. Finally, this chapter outlines the main features of existing DGSs in the six member states in order to better understand national preferences in the negotiations on the revised DGS Directive and on the proposal for a CDGS.

The Main Functions and Features of Deposit Guarantee Schemes

Most of the world's wealthier countries long had statutory DGSs, while some also had voluntary schemes (Demirgüç-Kunt et al. 2006, 2008, 2014). In the EU, all schemes had to meet minimal standards set in the DGS Directive adopted in 1994 (European Commission 1994) and then in the revised version, which was finalized in June 2014. The original DGS Directive required all member states to operate a scheme for at least 90 per cent of the deposited amount, up to at least €20,000 per person. Most EU member state DGSs far exceeded this minimal amount. Despite changes to the 1994 directive in the aftermath of the international financial crisis and the 2014 revision, national DGS specificities continued.

Some countries had multiple statutory public or private deposit insurance schemes for different types of financial institution. The DGS could be organized as a separate legal entity, or could be under the jurisdiction of the banking supervisor, the national central bank, or the Ministry of Finance. Countries could choose to fund DGSs ex ante by collecting premiums on a scheduled basis; others did that ex post from surviving institutions once a bank had failed. Some countries had contingency plans that included government support in the case of a shortfall of funds to cover deposits (Demirgüç-Kunt et al. 2006, 2008, 2014). Some DGSs used different measures to calculate the premiums for different banks so as to take into account the level of risk. Domestic banks were covered by the DGS, but not necessarily subsidiaries or branches of foreign banks. In the EU, deposits in foreign branches were covered by the home-country DGS, and deposits in foreign subsidiaries were covered by the host-country DGS (IMF 2013b). Deposits in branches of non-EU-headquartered banks were required to join the host-country DGS, unless the home (non-EU) countries were recognized as having national DGSs similar to the EU's (IMF 2013b; Demirgüç-Kunt, Kane, and Laeven 2008).

DGSs usually insured deposits up to a statutory coverage limit. The level of coverage was the level of protection granted in the event of deposits being unavailable under national law, not applying co-insurance. The most common form of DGS coverage was at the 'per depositor per institution' level. However, some countries covered deposits per depositor or per depositor account. Different types of deposit were affected differently by DGSs. Eligible deposits (or protected or insured deposits) were deposits repayable by the guarantee scheme under national law, before the level of coverage was applied. Covered deposits (or guaranteed, reimbursable, or repayable deposits) were deposits obtained from eligible deposits when applying the level of coverage provided for in national legislation (Bernet and Walter 2009; Cannas et al. 2014). Coverage of interbank deposits was less common than that of retail deposits, the assumption being that financial institutions should be capable of monitoring the level of risk of their deposits. However, in times of financial market stress, interbank deposits could be guaranteed to encourage the free flow of liquidity across banks.

The adequacy of national DGSs was severely tested during the international financial crisis of 2007–8. In April 2008, the FSB (2008) pointed out that the international financial crisis had stressed the importance of effective DGSs. In 2009, the BCBS and the International Association of Deposit Insurers jointly issued *Core Principles for Effective Deposit Insurance Systems*. Together with the IMF, the World Bank, the European Commission, and the European Forum of Deposit Insurers, they also issued in December 2010 a methodology to enable assessments of compliance with these core principles. In February 2011, the FSB agreed to include the *Core Principles* in the list of key standards for sound financial systems that deserve priority implementation depending on country circumstances. The IMF and the World Bank included the assessment of the compliance with these standards in their Reports on Observance of Standards and Codes programme (FSB 2012: 2–3).

The Negotiations on the Revision of the Existing Deposit Guarantee Scheme Directive

The DGS Directive of 1994 set the minimum level of deposit protection schemes in the EU at €20,000 per depositor. However, as the 1994 directive was based on minimum harmonization, national DGSs continued to differ in several important respects, such as the definition of eligible deposits, the level of cover, the types of funding mechanism, and the calculation of bank contributions. The international financial crisis that accelerated in late 2008 with the collapse of the US investment bank Lehman Brothers brought into the spotlight the inadequacy of the 1994 directive (Ayadi and Lastra 2010).

To begin with, the minimum level (€20,000) was too low to placate fears of a bank run. Moreover, the deposit protection coverage varied markedly across the EU, ranging from the legal minimum in most of the new member states and the UK to more than €100,000 in Italy and France. Furthermore, uncoordinated decisions on deposit guarantees taken by some member states at the height of the crisis in late 2008 (notably in Ireland and Germany) worsened the crisis (Quaglia, Eastwood, and Holmes 2009). It became evident that different national schemes across the EU potentially distorted level-playing-field competition and created the potential for bank runs because, in the event of financial crises, customers in some member states were prone to shifting deposits to banks headquartered in those member states with more generous guarantee schemes.

At the peak of the international financial crisis in late 2008, the Commission proposed legislative changes to the DGS Directive. These changes—agreed hurriedly in 2009—represented an emergency measure designed to restore depositors' confidence by raising the minimum level of coverage for deposits from €20,000 to €50,000, and subsequently to €100,000. The need for swift action meant that several controversial issues were not tackled, and hence the directive contained a clause providing for a broad review of all aspects of DGSs. By 2010, the schemes continued to vary markedly across the member states, and only sixteen out of twenty-seven applied the coverage level of €100,000, or had legislation in place to do so (European Commission 2010a).

When the sovereign debt crisis broke out in the euro area in late 2009, the issue of a CDGS came back onto the agenda. In July 2010, the Commission put forward a legislative proposal to amend the DGS Directive with a view to promoting the 'harmonization and simplification of protected deposits, a faster pay-out, and an improved financing of schemes' (European Commission 2010a: 5). The proposal aimed to establish a network of guarantee schemes as a first step towards a 'pan-European deposit guarantee scheme' to cover all EU-based banks (European Commission 2010a: 5). Such a pan-European scheme, however, presupposed full harmonization of national schemes and could only enter into force after a minimum fund of 1.5 per cent of eligible bank deposits had been reached in all the member states.

One of the most contentious provisions in the Commission's proposed 2010 directive was the establishment of a mandatory mutual borrowing facility, whereby if a national DGS was depleted it could borrow from another national fund. Several member states tried to remove this provision during negotiations in ECOFIN. It was feared that the mutual borrowing facility would be the first step towards a pan-EU DGS, as explicitly stated by the European Commission (2010b) in its memo accompanying the proposal—which was even more controversial.

Indeed, during the preparation of the proposal for the revised directive in 2010, the Commission considered the establishment of a single pan-EU scheme. However, it soon realized that there were complicated legal issues that needed to be examined (European Commission 2010b) and thus shelved a pan-EU scheme for the time being. Ultimately, though, the problem was political. The creation of a pan-EU DGS would have implied pooling national sovereignty to an extent unacceptable to most member states in 2010. The main line of division was between those countries that feared that their banks would become net contributors to the scheme (e.g., Germany), and those countries experiencing major problems in their banking system (e.g., Spain and Ireland), the banks of which were more likely to resort to the scheme (Howarth and Quaglia 2014).

Effectively, the German government baulked at the prospect of German taxpayers underwriting depositors in other member states with unstable banking systems. The British government similarly opposed the proposal of a mutual borrowing facility on the grounds that it posed 'an unpredictable and unacceptable fiscal risk to the British Treasury' (House of Commons, European Scrutiny Committee 2010–11: 39). Given strong member state opposition, the right-to-borrow proposal was dropped in 2013. Moreover, the Germans were concerned about protecting the country's self-regulated voluntary DGS (Moloney 2011). German commercial, savings, and cooperative banks, which each had their own sector-specific institutional protection schemes which also provided funds for deposit guarantees, opposed the Commission's proposal because they feared that they would be forced to establish a second fund based on ensuring deposits (Donnelly 2014). These voluntary sectoral schemes provided indirect protection to depositors, whereas the Commission's proposal called for the creation of funds that specifically covered depositors.

The Commission's push in favour of ex ante funding for DGSs stemmed from widespread economic opinion (IMF 2013b). The IMF (2013b) discouraged schemes based on ex-post funding on the grounds that failing banks would not contribute to the guarantee of their own depositors. Moreover, the IMF (2013b) feared that ex-post schemes could be damaging to a banking system by potentially hitting up banks for contributions to support depositors of a failed bank in difficult economic times when banks could least afford it. Opponents of the introduction of ex ante schemes argued that ex ante payments would hit banks hard during a difficult period and would further destabilize euro periphery banking systems (IMF 2013b). Moreover, the UK, Italy, and the Netherlands, which had national DGSs based on ex-post funding, were unhappy about the Commission proposal on the compulsory adoption of ex ante funding for DGSs, as this would have meant having to raise funds from the national banking industry, hence imposing extra costs for the banks (interview, Brussels, May 2013).

Finally, all member states, but particularly those with low existing coverage and ex-post-funded DGSs, opposed the target level and transition period proposed by the Commission. The initial proposal had been 1.5 per cent of eligible deposits in ten years, whereas the EP sought a target level of 1.5 per cent of covered deposits in fifteen years, and the compromise text agreed by the Council indicated a target level 0.5 per cent of covered deposits in fifteen years. On pay-out, the Commission proposed seven days, the EP five working days (with some national discretion until 2016 and an immediate emergency payment of €5,000), while the Council agreed a pay-out in fifteen to twenty working days.

The initial Commission proposal contained 'risk-adjusted premiums' with a strict EU-wide model. Most member states (and the Council) argued in favour of full flexibility in the choice of model, with different degrees of EBA involvement in the establishment of DGS guidelines. The Commission proposed a limited use of funds, whereas most member states (and the Council) sought unlimited use. The most contentious issue concerned the organization of credit transfers between national DGSs in the case of insufficient funds. The Commission proposed mandatory credit transfers between DGSs from 2020. The EP proposed ongoing voluntary credits, while ECOFIN called for no provision on credit transfer, either mandatory or voluntary. The clause agreed (Article 9a) allowed DGSs to transfer credits to other national DGSs on a voluntary basis.

The final stage of the negotiations on the revision of the DGS took place in 2013 in a trialogue between ECOFIN, the EP, and the Commission, with several controversial issues outstanding. The revised directive was eventually agreed in April 2014 by including several compromises in order to iron out the most controversial issues between the EP and the Council, as well as among member states. The target level for ex ante funds of DGSs was set at 0.8 per cent (in between what was proposed by the EP and ECOFIN) of covered deposits (i.e., about €55 billion) to be collected from banks over a ten-year period. Repayment deadlines were to be gradually reduced from twenty working days to seven by 2024 (here again, the gradualness was a compromise) (European Commission 2014c).

The target funding level of 0.8 per cent of covered deposits was the minimum level required by EU law. Member states were left free to set higher target levels for their national DGSs. In 2014, schemes in about half of the member states had already reached the target level (or were above or relatively close to it). According to the European Commission (2014c), in a third of member states, DGS funds were above 1 per cent of covered deposits, and in a few of them they were even above 2 per cent. Upon the approval of the Commission, member states could set a target level lower than 0.8 per cent (but not lower than 0.5 per cent of covered deposits) if the characteristics of the banking sector (e.g., concentration of most assets in a few banks) made it unlikely that banks would be liquidated using the DGS—rather, they would be resolved (European Commission 2014c). This was a concession to the Netherlands, with its highly concentrated banking system, but also to France, with its five very large banks (*Bloomberg*, 18 December 2013).

In order to appease those member states with ex-post payment systems—notably the UK, Italy, and the Netherlands—the revised directive envisaged the possibility of 'payment commitments' of a bank towards a DGS fully collateralized by low-risk assets. The total share of payment commitments was not to exceed 30 per cent of total DGS funds. In order to appease countries such as the UK that had adopted bank levies in the aftermath of the international financial crisis, member states were allowed to consider bank levies as equivalent to ex ante funds.[1]

In order to cater for the needs of sectoral protection schemes in place in Germany and Austria, the revised directive gave them the choice of being officially recognized as a DGS (and thus being subject to all provisions of the DGS Directive), or continuing their activity as purely institutional protection schemes. In the latter case, they would not be subject to the directive, but its member banks would have to also contribute to an official DGS in that member state. In order to appease banks that were members of voluntary sectoral schemes, their lower risk linked to mutual protection could be taken into account when risk-based contributions to DGSs were calculated. Article 12 stipulated that national DGSs could borrow from each other on a voluntary basis if a number of conditions (seven in total) were met. Moreover, the borrowing DGS would be under legal obligation to repay the loan within five years, paying interest on the amount borrowed.

The contributions to DGSs were to be based on the amount of covered deposits and the degree of risk incurred by the respective bank member. Member states could set lower contributions for low-risk sectors governed by national law. In order to ensure consistent application of the DGS Directive in member states, the EBA was to issue guidelines to specify methods for calculating the contributions to DGSs. These guidelines were published in May 2015 (EBA 2015b). In its 'feedback on the public consultation' (pp. 66ff), the EBA noted that respondents supported the mandatory ex ante collection of contributions on the grounds that this would work to strengthen confidence in DGSs across EU member states.

However, the EBA also noted the importance that respondents placed upon flexibility, 'due to the variety of national banking structures throughout the Union' (p. 66). The EBA 'acknowledge[d] the difficulty of developing a methodology which [would] cater for the specific features of banking structures of all Member States' (p. 66). There was also concern that the EBA guidelines would not allow sufficient flexibility for voluntary sectoral protection schemes (as for German savings banks) since the formulae for the guidelines were based predominately on covered deposits. The EBA responded by promising further modification to the guidelines so that they would be amended to take into account important features of institutional protection schemes (e.g., their business model and risk profile).

In 2015, there were ongoing debates about the composition of EU-wide core risk indicators to determine bank contributions to DGSs. Differing bank and

[1] The term 'bank levies' refers to, for example, the mandatory contributions paid by banks to the state budget for the purpose of covering the costs related to systemic risk, failure, and resolution of institutions.

government positions stemmed from bank business models and structural differences in national banking systems and/or different regulatory and supervisory practices. The absence of a universal definition of the non-performing loan ratio was seen as a major problem that could undermine harmonized implementation. The EBA had initially proposed a non-risk-weighted leverage ratio (in addition to risk-weighted measures). However, several member state authorities and numerous banks criticized this proposal, especially given that the introduction of a non-risk-weighted leverage ratio would disadvantage undercapitalized banks, and in particular alternative banks that did not issue equity, thus hitting different EU banking systems unevenly—notably, Germany more and the UK less. There were similar debates on the respective merits of Return on Assets measures (adopted by the EBA)—which might disfavour alternative banks—versus Return on Equity. It was also argued that using risk-weight assets would favour banks that used the Internal Ratings-Based approach and disfavour banks that used the standardized approach when calculating risk-weight assets (EBA 2015b: 67). In each case, the precise standard adopted would have a significant effect upon the contributions of individual banks, and member state banking systems more generally.

Negotiating the Common Deposit Guarantee Scheme

In theory, three main options could have been pursued: a pan-EU DGS for all banks in Banking Union; a pan-EU DGS for all systemically important banks in Banking Union; and a system of 'solidarity' between national DGSs, similar to that initially proposed by the Commission for the revision of the DGS Directive in 2010. In fact, none of these options was pursued: determined German hostility forced the Commission to drop the CDGS from its agenda in 2012 (*Financial Times*, 12 September 2012; House of Lords 2012b: 37, 2014a: 45). German banking associations and individual banks feared that any CDGS would impinge upon their sectoral institutional protection schemes (*Handelsblatt*, 7 November 2012; Kaiser 2012). Moreover, German banks feared that they would likely become net contributors to a CDGS—bailing out depositors in other euro area member states.

As for resolution funds and the fiscal backstop, discussion on the creation of a CDGS pitted countries expected to make net contributions to common rescue funds—either from taxpayers or from banks—against those that expected to be the principal recipients (Donnelly 2014). The German government criticized the CDGS as an unacceptable step towards debt mutualization (*Financial Times*, 13 September 2012). Hence, all the main political parties in Germany opposed it. The coalition agreement between the Christian Democratic Union, the Christian Social Union, and the Social Democratic

Party explicitly rejected the idea (*Koalitionsvertrag* 2013: 94). Similarly, the Netherlands government pointed out the risk of 'moral hazard', arguing that 'a final condition for full burden sharing is that banks which are to participate in a European DGS and resolution fund must have equal starting positions. Before banks can qualify for a European resolution fund and DGS, their financial positions must be comparable' (Netherlands Government 2012, authors' translation). By contrast, France and euro area periphery countries regarded a CDGS as the final pillar of Banking Union, necessary to sever the doom loop between banks and sovereigns, preventing deposit flights in countries hit by the sovereign debt crisis (*Reuters*, 11 September 2015). For example, the Italian authorities repeatedly pointed out that the SSM should be complemented by an SRM and a CDGS because 'coherence was needed between the centralization of supervision and the management of financial difficulties' in order to achieve the objectives of Banking Union (Szago, 2013: 7, authors' translation). Similarly, the Spanish government emphasized the need to agree the basis and the date for the CDGS to complete Banking Union (Rajoy 2013). However, these countries focused their efforts on the creation of the SRM (and SRF) (Saccomanni 2013), on which there was a proposal under negotiation—rather than lobby for a CDGS, which was seen as a lost battle.

According to the *Financial Times* (13 September 2012), the Commission had prepared a draft proposing a new agency—the European Deposit Insurance and Resolution Authority (EDIRA)—which would control a new European Deposit Guarantee and Resolution Fund. EDIRA would be financed through a regular levy on euro area banks and would become the 'single resolution authority' for Banking Union, replacing national DGSs. Due to German opposition, the proposal for EDIRA was removed, and the final Commission document, 'A Roadmap Towards Banking Union', only discusses DGSs briefly (*Financial Times*, 13 September 2012).

The ECB regarded the CDGS as an important component of Banking Union, but one that could be implemented at a later date. The ECB Vice President, Vitor Constâncio (2014), argued that what

> was achieved in December 2013, when the co-legislators agreed on the Deposit Guarantee Scheme Directive (DGSD) was only a little part of what in the end will be necessary.... [A] full-fledged scheme to foster financial integration would imply the setting up of a euro area wide deposit protection scheme. From a central bank perspective, the establishment of a common deposit insurance scheme is of less urgency than the other components of a Banking Union. Still, it is an important element that that should be pursued later, as it will be important to fend off bank runs on cross-border banks, thereby enhancing trust in the European banking sector.

In June 2015, EU leaders—including ECB President Mario Draghi and Commission President Jean-Claude Juncker—endorsed the creation of a CDGS in the so-called Five Presidents' report on the future of the euro. In the autumn of 2015, the European Commission, with the keen support of the ECB, reintroduced the creation of a CDGS to the EU-agenda (*Reuters*, 11 September 2015; *Financial Times*, 21 October 2015). Commission Vice President Valdis Dombrovskis pledged the launch of draft legislation on the common DGS by the end of 2015 as part of a broader policy package he unveiled designed to reinforce the euro. The Commission proposal would, as a first step, involve the establishment of a mandatory 'reinsurance' scheme that would 'contribute under certain conditions when national deposit guarantee schemes are called upon', and thus in effect act as a backstop to national DGSs (*Financial Times*, 10 September 2015).

These initiatives took place despite explicit German opposition. The German Finance Minister, Wolfgang Schäuble, presented classic moral hazard concerns to oppose the creation of a CDGS, arguing that it was unacceptable that the 'backstopping of depositors [could] become an excuse for banks to behave irresponsibly, potentially leaving German taxpayers to foot the bill' (*Financial Times*, 10 September 2015). Schäuble placed priority on measures to ensure that banks had big enough buffers of capital and debt to absorb financial shocks, and that authorities could force losses on creditors without facing litigation (cited in *Financial Times*, 10 September 2015). Schäuble argued that '[the German] objective [was] to further reduce banking risks as well as separate the risks of banks and state.... The creation of a single deposit guarantee scheme [was] not adequate for this objective' (*Financial Times*, 11 November 2015). For Schäuble, '[t]here [was] a moral hazard problem. As soon as you share risk, the decisiveness to reduce risk is lessened. That is what happened over the past few years' (*Financial Times*, 8 December 2015). The German government also had good reason to fear that a number of member states would have difficulty meeting the target level for ex ante contributions from banks to national DGSs agreed in the 2014 revised directive. The likelihood existed that a CDGS would be created even though some member states had very little in the way of ex ante funds. The potential for moral hazard for both depositors and governments in euro periphery countries was clear. In September 2015, the German government produced a non-paper which pointed out several forward steps deemed necessary to make Banking Union a success, without mentioning a CDGS (German Federal Government 2015).

In order to make progress on the DGS and overcome German opposition, the European Commission proposed that savings and cooperative banks be made exempt from having to contribute to the CDGS (*Reuters*, 2 November 2015). Commission President Juncker argued that it was 'people who did not follow the virtues of a social market economy' who caused the financial crisis, and that cooperative banks and savings banks were not to blame (*Frankfurter Allgemeine Zeitung*, 2 November 2015).

National Preferences and Divergent Deposit Guarantee Schemes across the European Union

In Europe, most national DGSs were set up as a consequence of a series of banking failures in the late 1970s and early 1980s, although some countries (e.g. Germany) had set up their system earlier.[2] In 1994, the EU issued the DGS Directive, which was based on minimum harmonization. The directive also established harmonized rules concerning the compulsory participation of branches of non-EU banks in national DGSs in the host country and the non-participation of branches of EU banks in national DGSs in the host country, unless they sought to opt in with the aim of obtaining extra coverage. However, member state implementation of the directive was largely undertaken in ways that were suitable to national banking systems and the existing national DGS. Hence, the revised national DGS remained distinctive (see Garcia and Prast 2004).

Germany

The most obvious examples of national banking systems shaping national DGSs were in EU member states with distinct banking pillars—notably Germany and Austria—where separate DGSs and institutional protection schemes were set up by commercial, savings, cooperative, and other public banks. The German and Austrian authorities were particularly concerned about the impact of a CDGS upon their sectoral schemes. Furthermore, the German schemes were largely funded through ex ante bank contributions—that is, in advance. This funding model reflected the small size of the savings and cooperative banks where ex ante contributions helped to build confidence in the deposit guarantee and ex-post contributions might be financially unmanageable (IMF 2011d).

Germany had two mandatory DGSs (private/public banks), two voluntary DGSs (private/public banks), two institutional protection schemes (one for saving banks, Landesbanks, and Landesbausparkassen, with several regional and national sub-schemes, and one for cooperative banks), and one voluntary

[2] Between 1977 and 1983, France, the Netherlands, Spain, and the UK set up national DGSs, and Germany revised its existing system. Following the European Commission's (non-binding) recommendation concerning the establishment of national DGSs, Italy set up a voluntary scheme for commercial banks in 1987, while Italian cooperatives had set up their own voluntary scheme in 1978 (Garcia and Prast 2004).

DGS for building and loan associations (Bausparkassen). Commercial banks were part of a statutory, legally enforceable but privately run scheme supervised by the BaFin. The coverage provided for deposits was €100,000 and estimated at more than 90 per cent of retail deposits with commercial banks. The German Banking Association offered its private commercial bank members additional coverage through a private voluntary scheme amounting to 30 per cent of the bank's capital per depositor, constituting a de facto full compensation scheme. This voluntary system did not have administrative powers or legal claim to compensation and was not supervised by BaFin.

Savings banks and Landesbanks had largely ex ante funded (risk-based) institutional protection schemes which were set up under regional arrangements and were coupled with additional ex-post burden-sharing provisions. Further, support could be provided through an inter-regional arrangement among the regional schemes and an additional arrangement (that included the Landesbank schemes and the state building society schemes), although there was no legal obligation to provide assistance (IMF 2011d). Cooperative banks (Volks- and Raiffeisenbanks) were members of their own institutional protection scheme run by the Association of German Cooperative Banks, which took the lead in resolving failed member banks. Ex ante funding (risk based) could be complemented by ex-post funding from member banks, although there was no legal obligation to provide assistance. Savings and cooperative banks did not participate in the statutory national DGS except if the national supervisor (BaFin) decided that their own schemes failed to fulfil the required conditions.

The ratio of retail deposits protected under the institutional protection schemes of savings and cooperative banks was even higher than in the private sector (IMF 2011d). The total coverage under these schemes was also very high in comparison with other countries and very broad—it included all the liabilities of participating institutions. The institutional protection schemes attracted criticism for weakening market discipline and lacking close oversight by BaFin due to their private legal nature (see, e.g., IMF 2011d). The IMF (2011d) and FSB (2012) both recommended the move towards a more uniform statutory deposit insurance regime—strongly resisted by both the savings and cooperative banks, and German regional and federal governments.

France

The DGS in France was managed by the Fund for the Guarantee of Deposits and Resolution (FGDR), which, prior to 2013, was the *Fichiers des Guichets Domiciliatires*. The French DGS operated through three mechanisms created to protect both depositors and investors: a 'pay-box' scheme for pay-outs to depositors in failing insured banks up to a maximum of €100,000 per depositor within twenty days, which was in line with the existing EU legislation on DGSs; a resolution mechanism for ailing banks, designed to reduce the risk of loss to depositors; and an investment guarantee scheme providing compensation to clients affected by fraud or other losses. French law provided for no 'depositor preference' prior to the adoption of the revised DGS Directive in 2014 (IMF 2012c), which meant that shareholders could be compensated over depositors.

The FGDR was a privately owned institution funded by approximately 582 participating banks (end-2014 figures). Banks paid in a one-time contribution to the FGDR, a yearly fee based on the amount of deposits covered in each institution by the fund, and exceptional contributions if it was depleted due to pay-outs. The FGDR could also raise funds in the financial markets. There were no contingency credit lines from the government. At the end of 2010, the FGDR held slightly above €2 billion or 0.21 per cent of total covered deposits, rising to just above €3 billion at the end of 2014 (IMF 2012d; FGDR 2015). The implementation of the revised DGS Directive was to raise the recommended ex ante funding target level significantly.

Prior to the implementation of the revised DGS Directive agreed in late 2014, the FGDR was limited in relation to the total amount of covered deposits. The FGDR took the view that resolution of a systemically important French bank would not lead to a pay-out to indemnify depositor claims, but rather to resolution measures—for instance, facilitating a sale of some assets and liabilities (FGDR 2015). This requirement of selling off assets (rather than raising the deposit cover provided) was a reflection of the large size of the biggest French banks, which were better positioned to sell off assets than, for example, small German banks. Financial support from the FGDR could be used either for compensation to depositors or for recovery actions in order to prevent the disorderly failure of a bank. This financial support was not subject to an explicit 'least cost' criterion—whether the cost of providing financial support was likely to be lower or higher than that of a pay-out to depositors in liquidation. However, in practice, a 'least cost' consideration was seen as inevitably shaping FGDR decisions (IMF 2012d).

The Netherlands

The Dutch DGS, the Collective Guarantee Scheme, was established in 1978 and existed until reforms in mid-2013 designed to implement the revised DGS Directive (Garcia and Prast 2003). The scheme was funded ex post (through a 'pay-box' system) and, in the event that available funds were insufficient for the full coverage of insured deposits, public authorities were not explicitly authorized to provide additional funding. As in France, insured depositors were not given priority over shareholders. Ex-post assessments were made case by case based on several items of data reported to the central bank. The contribution amounts were determined after consultation with the Bankers' Committee. Only deposits of small enterprises, small foundations, and households were protected. The coverage limits were €20,000 from 1998 to 2008, conforming to the minimum established in EU legislation, and then expanded to follow required EU minimum amounts. The Netherlands, with a highly concentrated banking system and a few big banks, only just met the EU legal minimum and only ex post. The Rabobank ran its own institutional protection scheme with its component banks (small cooperatives), thus rendering less necessary additional deposit guarantee requirements, and making the Dutch authorities less well disposed towards a CDGS.

Italy

As in Germany and Austria, the Italian DGS for banks consisted of two schemes covering different banking types. One DGS, the Interbank Fund for Deposit Guarantee (Fondo Interbancario di Tutela Dei Deposit), was set up by banks incorporated as joint-stock companies and cooperative banks; a second, the Fund for Deposit Guarantee of Cooperatives (Fondo di Garanzia dei Depositanti del credito cooperative), was set up by mutual banks. The two DGSs were initially established as private-law consortia and voluntary systems supervised by the Bank of Italy, but membership became compulsory with the passage of the first DGS Directive in 1994. As of 31 December 2012, there were 241 banks participating in the Interbank Fund for Deposit Guarantee and 398 in the Fund for Deposit Guarantee of Cooperatives (IMF 2013c).

The two sectoral schemes were primarily entrusted with depositor pay-out in the context of bank liquidation, but had a broad mandate to provide guarantees and credits, acquire equity and fund purchase and assumption transactions (which concern resolution), provided that they were less costly than a pay-out. Such interventions were subject to Bank of Italy approval. The DGSs were both ex-post funded, with contributions provided by participating banks as and when required. For the Interbank Fund for Deposit Guarantee, this amount varied between 0.4 per cent and 0.8 per cent of the total covered deposits (end-2012 figures). The total value of covered deposits as a percentage of eligible deposits covered by the Interbank Fund for Deposit Guarantee was 68.7 per cent, while that of the Fund for Deposit Guarantee of Cooperatives is 65 per cent (end-2012 figures; IMF 2013c). The revised DGS of 2014 changed the level of covered deposits, and bank contributions became ex ante in Italy.

The Italian national DGS was one of the few nationwide schemes providing deposit guarantees over the €100,000 set by EU legislation, although with no ex ante bank contributions, which meant that the de facto coverage was likely to be lower than the nominal amount guaranteed. The comparative generosity of the Italian national system was ascribed to the 'Italian saving culture', and the fact that the DGS could transfer assets and liabilities, and provide financial support to banks placed under special administration, as an alternative to the reimbursement to depositors, on the basis of the 'least cost' principle (European Commission 2007: 64). Moreover, in Italy, the DGS for cooperatives could intervene even when a procedure had not been formally initiated (De Polis 2015). The Italian government sought to amend the Commission's proposal revising the 1994 directive in order to preserve these distinctive features of the national DGS, and specifically their 'social functions' and 'their ability to engage in early intervention in case of crisis' (Sabatini 2013, authors' translation; De Polis 2015).

Spain

The DGS in Spain was administered by the Deposit Guarantee Fund (Fondos de Garantía de Depósitos), which was a private-law entity wholly prefunded by the member credit institutions. Until 2011, there were three Deposit Guarantee Funds: one for each sector of the banking industry (commercial banks, savings banks, and credit cooperatives). In the context of the Spanish banking crisis, the three sectoral funds were merged into a single fund and the premiums were made uniform across the board. From 2011, the Deposit Guarantee Fund Management Board consisted of twelve members: six from the Bank of Spain and two from each of the three banking sectors, with the Bank of Spain's Deputy Governor serving as chair (IMF 2012b).

The Deposit Guarantee Fund could be funded in four ways: by ordinary annual contributions, by extraordinary contributions, by issuing bonds, or by borrowing from third parties, including the government or Spain's Fund for Orderly Bank Restructuring created in 2009 to transfer public funds to Spanish banks. When the Deposit Guarantee Fund assets reached a level equal to or greater than 1 per cent of total deposits (approximately €10 billion), bank contributions were to be discontinued. The accumulated assets of the Deposit Guarantee Fund remained low because of the poor state of the Spanish banking system. In 2012, the IMF recommended an explicit backstopping from the Spanish state (IMF 2012b).

The Deposit Guarantee Fund had the objective of guaranteeing bank depositors either through pay-outs or through financial support—subject to approval by the Bank of Spain based upon a 'least cost' analysis—aimed at restoring the viability of banks. The range of financing mechanisms that the Deposit Guarantee Fund could deploy was broad and included both liquidity and solvency support (IMF 2012b). Such financing varied from credit lines, guarantees, subordinated loans, or subsidies to a bank, to the acquisition of bad assets, to the injection of capital for mergers take-overs, or support for asset and liability transfers. In the case of bankruptcy, the Deposit Guarantee Fund was to appoint the liquidator, thus controlling the pay-out process. In the case of bank liquidation, neither the Deposit Guarantee Fund nor depositors enjoyed any preferential rights over the estate of a failed bank (IMF 2012b)—at least prior to the implementation of the revised DGS Directive.

The UK

The Financial Services Compensation Scheme (FSCS) was independent of both government and the financial industry but accountable to the Prudential Regulatory Authority of the Bank of England (and previously, to 2012, the independent Financial Supervisory Authority). The FSCS managed five protection schemes for different categories of customer, one of those being insured depositors in deposit-taking institutions (IMF 2011b). As in France, there were no distinct schemes for specific categories of bank. The scheme for insured depositors was an ex-post-funded scheme in that when it incurred costs, the member banks would be required to cover the costs on a pro-rata basis (a share of protected deposits up to the compensation limit per individual depositor per authorized bank). In a pay-out situation the FSCS also had unlimited access to borrow from the National Loans Fund administered by the Treasury, with the accounts maintained at the Bank of England. Thus, unlike the euro area member state DGS, the FSCS had a fiscal backstop, like the Federal Deposit Insurance Corporation in the US. This is an important point that will be discussed further in the concluding section of this chapter.

FSCS funds could be used to pay out to depositors if a bank failed; finance the transfer of insured deposits to another institution under the bank insolvency procedure; and, using the FSCS's stabilization powers, contribute to a non-payout resolution of a failed bank. In this last case, the FSCS could only act upon the order of the British Treasury, and intervention had to be based on the 'least cost' option (IMF 2011b). In the context of bank resolution, the FSCS ranked pari passu with unsecured creditors. As in France and the Netherlands (and a number of other EU member states), the UK did not have official depositor preference prior to the finalization of the DGS Directive in June 2014—that is, the FSCS did not give depositors a preferential ranking in insolvency (PRA 2014). However, the Bank of England's Special Resolution Regime's tools and powers were expected to be used so as to achieve a similar outcome to depositor preference. All banks were required to have account systems allowing a 'single depositor view'—that is, that all deposits pertaining to a depositor could be easily summed up and presented in a list (IMF 2011b).

Conclusion

This chapter has examined the—to date—missing component of Banking Union. The CDGS was initially listed as one of the four pillars of Banking Union but was subsequently shelved because of disagreement among the member states, and notably because of German opposition. In 2014, the 1994 directive harmonizing national DGSs was substantially revised. In the negotiations concerning both the revision of the directive and the failed attempt to set up a CDGS, national preferences were determined largely by the structure of existing national DGSs, which in turn were closely linked to the configuration of national banking systems. All this made EU negotiations particularly 'complex'.

The second important element shaping national preferences was the concern for moral hazard, which was in turn linked to the health of national banking systems (see Figure 8 and Table 12), the sustainability of national public finances (see Figure 10), and, ultimately, the 'manageability' of real and potential bank losses. In countries with ailing banking systems, the risk of having to resolve banks by resorting to, among other things, resolution funds and DGSs was much greater than in countries with healthier banks. The poor state of public finances in the euro area periphery increased the likelihood that the costs of resolving ailing banks would have to be mutualized and born by all the euro area member states, not just by the home country. All this made EU negotiations politically contentious.

Finally, the credibility of the CDGS was linked to the possibility of accessing a common fiscal backstop and/or LLR. In many countries, national DGSs could have access to additional financial support from the Treasury if needed, or they could raise funds on the market, bolstered by a backstop and/or LLR in the event of market difficulties. Euro area membership and the sovereign debt crisis undermined this national backstop, especially in the euro area periphery countries, but did not replace it with clear supranational support mechanisms. The next chapter examines the development of the fiscal backstop and LLR in Banking Union.

8

Lender of Last Resort and the 'Fiscal Backstop' in Banking Union

This chapter examines the fourth component of Banking Union: the fiscal backstop which relates implicitly to the issue of the LLR in the euro area. This chapter first outlines the concept and the functions of LLR. It then analyses the central role performed by the ECB in boosting stability during the international financial and sovereign debt crises—culminating in ECB's promise in July 2012 to 'do whatever it takes' to save the euro. The second part examines the construction of the 'fiscal backstop' of Banking Union by looking at the temporary EFSF and its permanent successor, the ESM, which were set up to help tackle the sovereign debt crisis in the euro area. Finally, the chapter outlines the reform of fiscal policy coordination in the EU and especially in the euro area, which is linked to the discussion concerning the fiscal backstop. Indeed, the reforms introduced in the fiscal domain were intended to limit the moral hazard potentially created by ECB extraordinary monetary policy to help banks and sovereigns, and by the euro area funding mechanisms established as part of Banking Union.

In the operations of the ECB and the establishment of support mechanisms, two competing rationales were at stake. On the one hand, there was the need to deal with the sovereign debt crisis and 'save the euro', preventing the breaking up of EMU. This was an immediate priority for the countries in the euro area periphery that had been badly hit by the crisis (see Chapter 3). Yet, these concerns were shared by other euro area member states—notably France and Germany, whose banks and financial institutions were significantly exposed to the countries directly hit by the sovereign debt crisis (see Chapter 4). On the other hand, policy-makers in Germany and other 'core' euro area member states sought to limit the moral hazard created through intervention to help banks and sovereigns. Although the function of LLR at the national level had traditionally been shaped by moral hazard concerns (which accounts for the Bundesbank's reluctance to endorse the LLR concept), these concerns were compounded in the multi-level governance of the EU/euro area.

Lender of Last Resort: Definitions and Functions

There is no commonly agreed definition of LLR and its functions. Indeed, Charles Goodhart (1999) writes of the 'myth' of LLR, given the ambiguity of the concept and the difficulty in operationalizing it (see also Domanski and Sushko 2014). Michael Bordo (1990) puts forward four alternative views on LLR. First, according to the 'Classical view', LLR should provide whatever funds are needed to stave off financial panic. Bagehot argued that in times of financial distress, LLR should freely provide liquidity to illiquid but solvent financial institutions at a penalty rate against good collateral. A second view—which has been ascribed, for example, to Goodfriend and King (Bordo 1990) and the Federal Reserve of Richmond (Tucker 2014)—argues that LLR should provide liquidity to the financial system (e.g., through open market operations), not to individual institutions, in order to stave off a liquidity crisis. This definition mostly coincides with the ELA elaborated below. A third view, attributed, for example, to Goodhart (Bordo 1990) and the Federal Reserve of New York (Tucker 2014), postulates that LLR should assist illiquid and insolvent banks. Finally, according to 'Free Banking' supporters, no authority is needed to serve as LLR (Bordo 1990). According to Tucker (2014), LLR, which is often but not always the central bank, is a 'liquidity reinsurer' whose function is to provide liquidity insurance to the banking system, which in turn provides liquidity insurance to the rest of the economy (households and firms). Moreover, during the sovereign debt crisis, the debate on LLR also extended to the function of providing funding to illiquid but solvent governments in the euro area, and arguably also to insolvent ones (see Gros 2012b; De Grauwe 2013), as elaborated in the following section.

The ECB prefers the concept of ELA, which consists of lending to the financial system through open market operations, rather than lending to individual institutions, which according to the ECB is the function of LLR strictu sensu (Papadia 2014). This distinction is important for the ECB because it is in charge of providing ELA to the system, whereas ELA to specific institutions (the traditional LLR) is performed by national central banks, which bear potential losses resulting from the operations undertaken. When the provision of funding to specific institutions involves large amounts, the ECB is involved in the decision taken by national central banks (see Chapter 3).[1] Indeed, during the international financial crisis,

[1] Following the establishment of the ECB, there was an intense debate about the function of LLR in the euro area, whereby the bank preferred to maintain some constructive ambiguity (Buiter 1999: 21).

the ECB provided system-wide ELA, whereas national central banks provided liquidity to specific banks in their jurisdiction. According to the ECB's definition of LLR, the ECB's Single Market Programme (SMP) and Outright Monetary Transactions (OMTs) (described below) are not functions of LLR; they are instead instances in which the central bank (ECB) provides intermediation to substitute for impaired market functioning (Papadia 2014: 95) (what Tucker [2014] called the 'market-maker of last resort'). Moreover, the ECB is reluctant to accept the concept of LLR for sovereigns because this implies 'fiscal dominance' (Papadia 2014: 95) and consequently the infringement of the no monetary financing rule in the TEU.

It should be noted that there are important links between LLR and fiscal policy. On the one hand, even if the monetary authority (the central bank) can in principle print as much liquidity as needed to act as LLR, ultimately there has to be a fiscal authority behind the central bank to compensate for potential losses incurred by the central bank. Losses related to LLR functions are a 'fiscal issue' because they have to be borne by taxpayers (Tucker 2014). On the other hand, the provision of liquidity during a crisis in many cases requires the central bank to design and implement operations jointly with the fiscal authority, involving some risk-sharing.[2] In this respect, Tucker speaks of the 'fiscal carve out', which delineates the space in which an independent central bank can operate vis-à-vis the fiscal authorities (Tucker 2014). Moreover, LLR needs to address the problem of moral hazard because banks might engage in risky behaviour if they know that LLR would step in in case of problems. Indeed, this has traditionally been a concern of the Bundesbank, which prior to the establishment of EMU never openly admitted its willingness to act as LLR (Goodhart 1995, 326; Goodhart and Eric 2000).[3] However, de facto the Bundesbank acted as LLR to several German banks during the international financial crisis (see, e.g., Hardie and Howarth 2013).

The Measures Taken by the European Central Bank During the Crises

Following the bankruptcy of Lehman Brothers in the US in September 2008, unsecured interbank money markets froze in the euro area and banks became

[2] Furthermore, the operations of LLR can have distributive consequences stemming from the decisions to provide liquidity to some financial institutions but not others.

[3] During the negotiations on the provisions concerning EMU in the TEU, the German central bank governor opposed the assignment of the function of LLR to the ECB because of moral hazard concerns and the risk of potential inflation (Goodhart 1995: Goodhart and Schoenmaker 1995: 326).

increasingly dependent on ECB liquidity operations and overnight borrowing (ECB 2008b; Gros, Alcidi, and Giovanni 2012). In October, the ECB expanded its list of assets eligible for use as collateral in its credit operations and increased the provision of longer-term liquidity by fully meeting banks' demands for liquidity at maturities of three and six months (ECB 2008a). Indeed, the ECB revisited its collateral policy repeatedly during the crisis, allowing banks to use a wider range of assets as collateral when borrowing from the ECB at below market rates.[4] Overall, the ECB's liquidity management during the international financial crisis was evaluated as 'timely' and 'proactive', and its framework as 'flexible' and 'robust' (IMF 2008, 22).

After the sovereign debt crisis began in Greece, in May 2010 the ECB's Governing Council adopted the SMP to purchase bonds—especially sovereign bonds—on the secondary markets. No purchases were made on the primary market because of the ban on monetary financing in the TEU. According to the ECB, the SMP was designed to counteract disruptions in the monetary policy transmission mechanism. The programme envisaged that central bank money created from the purchase of securities would be 'sterilized' through specific operations to re-absorb the liquidity injected and thereby ensure that the monetary policy stance was not affected. The SMP was replaced by OMT in September 2012, as explained below.

Throughout the unfolding of the sovereign debt crisis, the ECB's extraordinary monetary policy decisions were the subject of intense disagreement among Governing Council members and euro area member state governments (Howarth 2012). Debates focused on the ECB's liquidity boosting measures (notably, the purchase of covered bank bonds), and later the ECB's purchase of sovereign and other debt from the euro area member states most at risk of default and facing high bond yields. The ability of the ECB to neutralize fully the inflationary impact of its sovereign debt purchases was the subject of increased scrutiny. Despite the ad personam rule assigned to the ECB's Governing Council members, several 'Northern' European members expressed concerns that were widely shared in their home member states. Although the full details cannot be known because of ECB secrecy, a growing number of unilateral public announcements by executive board members and national central bank governors that criticized ECB policy could be seen as the clearest indication of discord.

The German Governing Council members and the Bundesbank, like the German government, typically argued for further fiscal consolidation in the besieged Southern European member states and criticized ECB action to reduce their bond yields. From the outside, Otmar Issing, the former German

[4] There were allegations that some banks, especially Spanish banks, were gaming the system: see *Reuters*, 28 January 2008, and *The Daily Telegraph*, 29 January 2008.

executive board member, repeatedly challenged the bank's purchase of Greek and other sovereign debt on the grounds that it took pressure off governments to engage in reform (*Bloomberg*, 3 September 2011). The resignations of Axel Weber from the Bundesbank and Jürgen Stark from the ECB's executive board demonstrated the intensity of internal discord.

In February 2011, Weber announced his intended departure at the end of April. He publicly explained his departure in terms of the impossibility of leading an organization in which his policy preferences placed him in a small minority (*Financial Times*, 13, 16, and 21 February 2011). Weber publicly opposed ECB emergency bond buying from its start in May 2010, and was joined by up to four other Governing Council members who remained anonymous (*Financial Times*, 12 May 2010). Weber's opposition reflected widespread German concern over what the conservative newspaper *Frankfurter Allgemeine Zeitung* referred to as the 'Americanisation of monetary policy' (10 May 2010). In early April 2011, the Dutch central bank Governor, Nout Wellink, also went public with his concerns over bond purchasing (*Central Banking*, 4 April 2011) and called for a reduction. There were additional hints at deeper tensions within the Eurosystem. Sources from within the Bundesbank complained that French banks—the most heavily exposed to Greek debt—were using the ECB purchase programme to clean their balance sheets of Greek debt, while German banks had reached an agreement with the German Ministry of Finance to hold on to Greek debt until 2013 (*Der Spiegel*, 31 May 2010).

The decision to temporarily halt the emergency purchase of bonds in late January 2011 was the ECB's response to the rise in inflation, especially in Germany. It also potentially reflected a battle within the Governing Council over the prioritization of inflation (Howarth 2012). By early 2011, the bank's measure of inflation (Harmonised Index of Consumer Prices) reached 2.4 per cent, the highest level for over two years. The ECB had consistently insisted that it could 'sterilize' the purchase of Greek debt and that its monetary policy remained focused upon its core goal (*Financial Times*, 31 January 2011). However, there was concern over the repeated failure to neutralize fully the inflationary impact of the ECB's bond buying and the fact that financial markets would not take seriously a threat to raise interest rates if the ECB was still intervening heavily in debt markets.

A second temporary halt in late March 2011 reflected ongoing concerns. By May 2011, the ECB had failed five times to neutralize fully the inflationary impact of its debt purchases (*Financial Times*, 3 May 2011), thus reflecting directly the tensions between the two ECB roles of financial and euro area stability and combating inflation and, most certainly, between Governing Council members—as demonstrated most clearly in the resignations of Weber and Stark. While some economists have insisted that the amounts involved in the debt purchases were very small in relation to the ECB's overall operations, 'sterilization' was an important political message to the Germans that the bank's actions would not create inflation (*Financial Times*, 3 May 2011). The extension of sovereign debt purchases to additional euro area member states from August 2011 undermined further the thrust of this message. At the same time, the ECB pursued its traditional anti-inflationary interest rate policy. In early April 2011, and again in July, the ECB twice raised interest rates by 25 basis points. While the move reflected standard ECB reaction to inflationary pressures, it was widely criticized for having increased pressure on struggling euro area member states at risk of sovereign default.

As the sovereign debt crisis intensified in the summer of 2011, the Bundesbank held firm in its opposition to the ECB's SMP. Jens Weidmann publicly queried the legality of the ECB's 'monetary financing' of debt as contrary to EU treaty provisions (*Financial Times*, 7 December 2011), and a German economist brought a case against the ECB to the European Court of Justice. There was speculation that the Bundesbank could even move to undermine any possible ECB action on reducing bond yield differentials by casting doubt on its willingness to defend this action (*Financial Times*, 29 November 2011). Weidmann publicly argued that Italy could 'handle even an interest rate that remains over 7 per cent for a while' (*Financial Times*, 29 November 2011): its bond yield would lower in time following what Weidmann saw as long-overdue structural reform. Yet criticism has not all been in one direction. In the aftermath of Stark's resignation, the former Italian executive board member Lorenzo Bini Smaghi publicly challenged criticisms of the ECB's bond buying as the result of 'inadequate economic analysis' (*Financial Times*, 15 September 2011; Bini Smaghi 2013)—a direct jab at German Governing Council members.

Despite disagreements on the ECB's bond-buying programme, Governing Council members embraced a uniform position on the fiscal policies to be pursued by the member states most at risk of default. The ECB criticized member states for engaging in insufficient austerity; it took a strong position on the operation of the EFSF (that it not be allowed to purchase debt directly from the markets); and it strongly opposed the move by member states to push for a 'selective' default on Greek sovereign debt. However, even on some of these highly sensitive policies, apparent disagreements appeared.[5] In August 2011, in two confidential letters, the ECB's Governing Council

[5] For example, in July 2011, Ewald Nowotny, the Austrian Central Bank Governor, announced in an interview with a US television news channel that a short-term 'selective default' by Greece might *not* have 'major negative consequences' (*Financial Times*, 19 July 2011). Nowotny subsequently retracted his statement.

asked the governments of Spain and Italy for specific commitments on structural reforms and the consolidation of public finances. The ECB would intervene on the markets to stabilize the yields on government bonds only if these commitments were publicly accepted, which they were. Conventional monetary policy was accompanied by a number of unconventional measures.

In December 2011, in order to counteract the spread increase on Italian and Spanish government bonds in addition to the increased capital outflows, the ECB launched a programme of LTRO, issuing loans to European banks at a 1 per cent interest rate for a three-year period, requiring government bonds, mortgage securities, and other commercial papers in bank portfolios as collateral. Concurrently, the ECB changed its collateral rules, accepting lower-quality collateral in return for loans. Gros (2012b) points out that the banks depositing their funding at the ECB (receiving only 0.25 per cent interest) were not the same ones that were taking out three-year loans from the ECB at 1 per cent. The deposits came largely from Northern European banks (mainly German and Dutch), and LTRO loans went largely to banks in Southern Europe (mainly Italy and Spain). In other words, the ECB became 'the central counterparty to a banking system that is de facto segmented along national lines' (Gros 2012b).

Under this programme, the ECB lent €489 billion to 523 banks, mainly in Greece, Ireland, Italy, and Spain. Indeed, Italian and Spanish banks took nearly 60 per cent of all new ECB loans, with Spain's overstretched banks taking marginally more than Italy's.[6] Banks used these funds to buy government bonds, effectively easing the debt crisis, at least in the short term—but worsening the sovereign debt–bank loop and increasing bank exposure to fragile sovereigns. In February 2012, following the second Greek bail-out, the ECB held another three-year auction (LTRO 2) of €529 billion to 800 European banks. Although the ECB programme did not specifically target Italy or Spain, these countries benefited from a temporary reduction in borrowing costs. The ECB lent to euro area banks, which in turn lent to euro area governments using the purchased government debt as collateral for even more ECB loans. The ECB refused to commit to extending its bond-buying programme following the 9 December 2011 European Summit agreement on reinforced euro area fiscal policy rules (the Six Pack, see 'Temporary Financial Support to Ailing Countries: The European Financial Stability Facility, below). President Draghi deliberately referenced the Bundesbank in noting that it was necessary to respect 'not just the letter, but the "spirit" of the treaties' on the monetization of debt (*Financial Times*, 9 December 2011).

[6] Reported by the BBC on 14 May 2012 at <http://www.bbc.co.uk/news/business-18058270>.

With the sovereign debt crisis in full swing, several authors—for example, Buiter and Rahbari (2012a, 2012b) De Grauwe (2012), and Wyplosz (2012)—called for LLR in the euro area, not only for the banking sector but also for sovereigns, whereby LLR should stand ready to buy the government bonds of euro area countries hit by the crisis. De Grauwe (2012, 521) pointed out that this new role for the ECB was necessary 'to prevent countries from being pushed into bad equilibria by self-fulfilling fears of liquidity crises in a monetary union' and that the ECB decided to perform this role in 2012. A similar argument about the need for the ECB to act as LLR was also made by Wyplosz (2012, 19), who argued that 'central banks must be lenders of last resort, even when their role is clouded to mitigate moral hazard'. Buiter and Rahbari (2012a, 2012b) maintained that the ECB began acting as LLR for the member states of the euro area when it started the outright purchases of euro area periphery sovereign debt under the SMP in May 2010 (see also De Grauwe 2011; Wyplosz 2011, 2012). Buiter and Rahbari also considered the ECB's LTROs of December 2011 and February 2012 as acting as LLR for Spain and Italy by facilitating the purchase of their debt by domestic banks in the primary issue markets. In so doing, the ECB reduced the (otherwise unsustainable) borrowing costs for these countries on the financial market.

Arguably, the pledge of the ECB's President to do 'whatever it takes to save the euro' by announcing the OMT programme in the summer of 2012 was a further step in the LLR direction. The ECB pledged to stand ready to purchase in the secondary sovereign bond markets, under certain conditions, bonds issued by euro area member state governments experiencing financial difficulties. However, the OMT required beneficiary governments to apply for euro area rescue funds in compliance with strict conditionality in exchange for support. In the autumn and early winter of 2012, Spain was considering whether to apply, but improved access to international funding in the first half of 2013 made this request unnecessary. The ECB's decision was subject to a legal dispute (and extensive legal commentary—see, for example, the special issue of the *German Law Journal* 2014) brought by some German economists and policy-makers before the German constitutional court, which subsequently interrogated the European Court of Justice on certain legal aspects of the case.

The discussion on LLR in the euro area and of the monetary policy of the ECB during the crisis, especially the extraordinary measures adopted by the ECB (Drudi, Durré, and Mongelli 2012; Salines et al. 2012), are intertwined with the discussion of the real-time gross payments system of the euro area—the so-called TARGET 2. Some authors (e.g., Sinn and Wollmershäuser 2012) argue that creditor countries in TARGET 2—namely Finland, the Netherlands, Luxembourg, and Germany—risked 'losing the Target claims of their national central banks should the euro break up' (Sinn 2012). He also linked the imbalances in TARGET 2 to macroeconomic imbalances in the euro area—that is, the imbalances in the current account positions of EMU member states. Other authors (e.g., De Grauwe and Ji 2012) deny the existence of a major risk for creditor central banks (and hence creditor countries) in TARGET 2.[7]

Overall, the ECB was more effective in dealing with the crisis than member state governments operating collectively in the Council of Ministers and the European Council (Yiangou, O'Keeffe, and Glöckler, 2013). This was to be expected during the international financial crisis, when the ECB provided substantial amounts of liquidity to euro area banks; it was less obvious during the sovereign debt crisis. During the latter, the ECB demonstrated its ability to step in to calm financial markets when member state governments were unable to reach agreements that might have enabled them to do so effectively. At the peak of the crisis, on 26 July 2012, at a public speech held in London, the ECB President, Mario Draghi, made clear that 'within its mandate, the ECB will do whatever it takes to save the euro' (ECB 2012b). The ECB repeatedly engaged in a broad interpretation of its treaty-established mandate—focused principally on price stability—but at the same time it was wary of jeopardizing its independence by entering the realm of fiscal policy.

As the sovereign debt crisis unfolded, the crucial stabilizing role of the ECB became clear to all observers as its bond holdings of financially distressed countries increased markedly, either as collateral or as acquisitions on the secondary sovereign debt markets. This ECB performance was possible because the bank was a well-resourced, cohesive institution, with expertise in economic policy, experience in dealing with financial markets, and considerable policy capacity in the areas of its remits (Howarth and Loedel 2005). It was an independent supranational institution, designed to work according to a supranational logic, and relatively insulated from national political pressure. It had considerable firepower, given its financial resources and, ultimately, its ability to print money.

In Banking Union there are several open issues about LLR because whereas the responsibility for banking supervision has been transferred to the supranational/euro area level (the SSM), the responsibility of LLR in the euro area has not (yet?) been re-allocated (Goodhart and Schoenmaker 2014). Furthermore, whereas at the national level the 'fiscal backstop' to LLR is provided by the national treasury and ultimately by taxpayers, there is no equivalent in the euro area. The ESM (which has been designed as the fiscal backstop for resolution) has a limited amount of funding available and its

[7] Sinn (2012) accepts that as long as the euro area survives, this is true.

functioning remains intergovernmental, which might affect its ability to act effectively in crisis situations (Micossi, Carmassi, and Peire 2011). Finally, the accountability of LLR is complicated further in the euro area, feeding into the broader debate on the 'democratic deficit' of the EU and possibly the 'excessive' independence of the ECB, which has no political counterpart (Elgie 2002; Howarth and Loedel 2005; Verdun 1998). At the international level there is no de jure LLR, which also raises a host of problems given the high degree of international financial integration and cross-border finance (see, e.g., Giannini 1999).

Temporary Financial Support to Ailing Countries: The European Financial Stability Facility

The first euro area country to be hit by the sovereign debt crisis was Greece (see also Chapter 2) as a result of a challenging combination of an unsustainable level of public debt (115 per cent in 2009), 80 per cent of which was external, combined with a staggering public deficit of 12.7 per cent of GDP revealed by the new social democratic government after the October 2009 elections in Greece, against the 6 per cent level officially estimated by the previous Conservative government. In November 2012, the EU statistical body, Eurostat, revised the deficit figure to 15.4 per cent of GDP. The announcement of the actual public deficit level prompted unprecedented market speculation against Greek sovereign debt. Borrowing spreads on ten-year German sovereign debt (bunds) jumped to 300 basis points in early 2009 (the highest in the euro area), then receded temporarily before shooting up to prohibitive levels later in the year. Greece was downgraded by the Standard & Poor's credit rating agency to two notches from minimum ECB collateral standards in early 2009—subsequently the ECB changed its rules on collateral rating—and finally downgraded to junk bond status by two credit rating agencies in the spring of 2010, after which the bond spread settled at 700 basis points or above.

In the first months of 2010, an overwhelming majority of market analysts forecast a Greek default. French and German banks were significantly exposed in Greece and would have suffered major losses from a Greek default (see Chapter 3). There were also fears of contagion effects to other countries in the periphery of the euro area, to Belgium and even France, jeopardizing the very survival of the euro. In March 2010, France and Germany brokered an emergency financing mechanism for Greece, following extensive bilateral negotiations.[8] Under the deal, approved subsequently by euro area member

[8] Germany and France financed the majority of bail-out efforts at 27.92 per cent and 20.97 per cent, respectively, according to the ECB capital key.

states, a funding package was created, made up of voluntary bilateral contributions from euro area countries and funding from the IMF. The agreement was dominated by German thinking, while France claimed a reduced IMF role as its negotiating victory.[9] As market prices became prohibitive, in late April 2010 the Greek government accepted an EU/ECB/IMF €110 billion Emergency Financing Mechanism, followed by a rigorous three-year conditionality programme. An Emergency Financing Mechanism was also subsequently set up for Ireland, the second victim of the sovereign debt crisis.

However, the EU–IMF financial aid package was not enough to assuage the markets, and speculation against Greece resumed shortly afterwards. Ireland and (later) Portugal were also hit by the sovereign debt crisis. EU leaders sought to come up with a better solution. Some radical initiatives involving treaty reform and EU support mechanisms were considered but set aside, largely because of opposition from a number of member states, notably Germany and the UK. German policy-makers were explicit in their concern about the potential for moral hazard. They feared that Germany would be the main paymaster of any rescue package and wanted to avoid writing a blank cheque. British policy-makers felt that the sovereign debt crisis was a euro area problem, not an EU (and hence British) problem (Gocaj and Meunier 2013).

Some academic economists (e.g., Gros and Mayer 2010) called for the establishment of a European Monetary Fund (EMF). The German Finance Minister, Wolfgang Schäuble, launched the idea of an EMF in March 2010, attracting the support of Chancellor Angela Merkel and the European Commission, and the opposition of the German central bank and top German officials at the ECB (*The Economist*, 9 March 2010). However, Merkel and Schäuble made clear that a treaty change was required in order to set up an EMF because of the Maastricht Treaty's no-bail-out clause, thus de facto pushing the project far into the future (*Financial Times*, 9 March 2010; see also Ludlow 2010).[10]

The European Commission proposed the establishment of a stabilization fund that would sell bonds backed by guarantees from member states (*The Economist*, 13 May 2010), which was popularized as the Junker's proposal for Euro-bonds (*Der Spiegel*, 8 December 2010). The proposal involved the setting up of a new 'European Debt Agency' issuing Euro-bonds—that is, bonds jointly put on the market by euro area states. In so doing, less creditworthy countries in the euro area (those hit by the crisis) would be able to borrow at lower cost (by being charged lower interest rates). However, for countries with solid creditworthiness, such as Germany, it could mean paying higher rates

[9] <http://www.businessweek.com/globalbiz/content/mar2010/gb20100326_311551.htm>.

[10] On the issue of treaty change required to set up an EMF opinions diverged, see, for example, *The Economist*, 9 March 2010.

(*Der Spiegel*, 8 December 2010), even though Junker subsequently clarified that there would not be a single interest rate because only part of the national debt would be bundled together at the euro area level and the largest portion of the debt would be paid at national interest rates (*Der Spiegel*, 8 December 2010). The proposal remained problematic for Germany because of moral hazard and the existing no bail-out treaty provisions (Gocaj and Meunier 2013). Along similar lines, the Belgian Prime Minister, Yves Leterme, called for a central European debt agency that would issue euro-denominated debt centrally (*The Economist*, 9 March 2010), but the idea was opposed by German policy-makers.

Despite the fact that some innovative proposals were circulated, none was followed up. Only (temporary) incremental solutions were eventually acted upon. In May 2010, the Council of Ministers agreed the EFSM and the EFSF. The EFSM was an emergency funding programme for all EU member states in economic difficulty, subject to conditionality. Funds were raised on the financial markets by the European European Commission and guaranteed by the EU budget. The EFSM could raise up to €60 billion. The EFSM essentially reproduced for the 27 EU member states the mechanics of the existing Balance of Payments Regulation for non-euro area member states. The EFSM programmes were activated for Ireland and Portugal: bonds were issued and funds were disbursed for a total amount up to €48.5 billion—up to €22.5 billion for Ireland and up to €26 billion for Portugal—over three years, from 2011 to 2013.[11]

The EFSF was created by the euro area member states in May 2010 for lending to euro area member states in difficulty, subject to conditionality. The EFSF was, de facto, an intergovernmental Special Purpose Vehicle that could issue bonds for up to €440 billion, guaranteed by all the euro area member states, and intervene in the sovereign debt primary market. It took the form of a Luxembourg-registered company owned by euro area member states, to be liquidated by 2013. Greece, Portugual, and Ireland were the three beneficiaries of EFSF programmes.[12] The total EU/IMF €750 billion financial package—consisting of €440 billion euro area funds (the EFSF), €60 billion European Commission funds (the EFSM), and €250 billion IMF funds provided to avert speculation against other weak peripheral economies—did not succeed in this aim. Financial markets were clearly unimpressed by the measures adopted, and the reactive and reluctant EU policy-making. Within a few weeks of the EFSF's creation, a debate erupted concerning its reform, and specifically the amount of funding available and the interest rate charge on funding provided (Gocaj and Meunier 2013). Germany

[11] <http://ec.europa.eu/economy_finance/eu_borrower/efsm/>.
[12] <http://www.efsf.europa.eu/about/operations/index.htm>.

opposed any major change to the EFSF for the reasons mentioned above, but supported a treaty change to establish a permanent rescue mechanism (*Financial Times*, 15 February 2011). This was to be the ESM.

Establishing the European Stability Mechanism

The Deauville agreement, negotiated in a bilateral meeting between the German Chancellor, Angela Merkel, and the French President, Nicolas Sarkozy, in October 2010, cleared the way to establishing the ESM. However, several important issues remained to be solved before the final agreement on the ESM could be reached. Initially, most of the debate focused on the involvement of private creditors in future debt relief or restructuring (*Financial Times*, 24 October 2010). Germany wanted a clear rule-based system and was keen to impose losses upon private creditors (*Financial Times*, 30 November 2010). It maintained that its readiness to participate in a permanent bail-out mechanism was always conditional on agreement to bind private bondholders into future rescue plans.

The German government wanted provisions added into the ESM treaty that would require private bondholders to participate in any rescheduling of debt for a euro area member and to take a haircut in any outright restructuring (*Financial Times*, 20 May 2011). It argued that without such a requirement, private bondholders would not discriminate between the borrowing of debt-laden countries—such as Greece, Italy, or Belgium—and that of fiscally virtuous countries. The German position was backed by the Netherlands, Austria, and Finland. France led a majority group of the seventeen countries that sought to place all references to private creditors in the political preamble to the treaty, rather than in its legally binding articles (*Financial Times*, 20 May 2011).

The German insistence on burden-sharing unsettled the financial markets as the crisis was still unfolding. Burden-sharing demands were eventually toned down during the negotiations (*Financial Times*, 4 December 2010). In the end, member states agreed that where ESM support was provided to a country deemed by participating member states to be solvent, private sector creditors would be encouraged to maintain their exposure. But if a country was deemed to be insolvent, it would need to agree a restructuring with its creditors as a way to restore its ability to fund itself in the bond markets. The ESM could then provide financial support (*Financial Times*, 30 November 2010). Alinea (l. 12) in the preamble states that 'in exceptional cases an adequate and proportionate form of private sector involvement shall be considered in cases where stability support is provided accompanied by conditionality in the form of a macroeconomic adjustment programme' (ESM 2011).

The second controversial issue was the ability of the ESM to buy bonds on the primary market, which was initially opposed by the three coalition parties in the Bundestag in Germany. The Bundesbank took a similar position in its monthly report. Moreover, 189 German economists wrote a letter to a newspaper denouncing the ESM, calling for immediate bankruptcy proceedings of insolvent euro area states (*Financial Times*, 28 February 2011). The other euro area member states—in particular France, Italy, and Spain—regarded the ability to buy bonds as essential for the ESM. Subsequently, Germany agreed that the ESM could buy bonds on the bond market, but insisted that ESM credits, unlike those of its predecessor, the EFSF, should be superior to those of private investors. The idea was to make default possible from 2013 onwards, with only a moderate risk to the budget of the creditor countries.

However, forward-looking investors correctly assessed the risk of a future default also for existing bonds (*Financial Times*, 14 March 2011). If the ESM's bonds enjoyed preferred status to those of all creditors other than the IMF, that seniority would effectively put ESM bonds at the head of the queue for repayment. This created an unexpected obstacle for Greece, Ireland, and Portugal—which had received bail-outs from the EU and the IMF—as they contemplated a return to private borrowing. Investors worried that any new bonds they bought would be pushed down the credit ladder if one of the three governments was forced to turn to the ESM for funding (*Financial Times*, 20 May 2011).

In the end, Germany agreed to drop from the treaty any reference to the seniority of loans made by the ESM over privately held bonds. However, Clause 13 in the preamble of the ESM treaty states:

> Like the IMF, the ESM will provide stability support to an ESM Member when its regular access to market financing is impaired or is at risk of being impaired. Reflecting this, Heads of State or Government have stated that the ESM loans will enjoy preferred creditor status in a similar fashion to those of the IMF, while accepting preferred creditor status of the IMF over the ESM. This status will be effective as of the date of entry into force of this Treaty. In the event of ESM financial assistance in the form of ESM loans following a European financial assistance programme existing at the time of the signature of this Treaty, the ESM will enjoy the same seniority as all other loans and obligations of the beneficiary ESM Member, with the exception of the IMF loans (ESM 2011: 7).

This addition to the ESM treaty—unveiled by euro area finance ministers at a meeting in Luxembourg in May 2011—was a subtle but potentially important change to the terms of the new mechanism (Hodson 2013). The hope was that it would encourage investors to buy bonds issued by the governments of Greece, Ireland, and Portugal without fear that they could be trumped by new debt in the event of another bail-out or a restructuring (*Financial Times*, 20 May 2011).

The ESM, which was agreed through an international treaty between the seventeen euro area member states, was to assume the role of the EFSF in providing financial assistance to euro area member states after June 2013. The ESM could intervene in the primary debt market. It was set up as an intergovernmental organization, based in Luxembourg, and its shareholders were the seventeen euro area member states. It had a board of governors, which was composed by the Treasury or finance ministers of the participating member states and was chaired by the President of the Eurogroup. The first managing director, appointed by the board of governors for a term of five years, was the previous Managing Director of the EFSF, Klaus Regling, a senior German Ministry of Finance official.[13]

The authorized capital stock was €700 billion (Article 8), divided using the contribution key of the ECB's capital (Article 11): 27 per cent for Germany, 20 per cent for France, 17 per cent for Italy and 12 per cent for Spain. The paid-in capital amounted to €80,000 million. In addition, the ESM disposed of committed callable capital from euro area member states to a total of €620 billion. The ESM was empowered to borrow on capital markets.[14] The most important decisions taken by the board of governors (Article 5)—such as the decision to provide stability support to an ESM member state government; the choice of instruments, conditions and terms of such support; the calling in of authorized unpaid capital; and so on required unanimity. In other areas—such as the terms of accession of a new ESM member; the appointment of the managing director; and so on the board of governors would take decisions by qualified majority, which was defined in the ESM treaty as 80 per cent of the votes cast, with voting rights equal to the number of shares allocated to each country.

According to Article 13 of the ESM treaty, 'An ESM Member may address a request for stability support to the Chairperson of the Board of Governors. Such a request shall indicate the financial assistance instrument(s) to be considered.' The European Commission, in liaison with the ECB, was entrusted to assess the existence of a risk to the financial stability of the euro area as a whole or of its member states; the sustainability of the public debt; and the actual or potential financing needs of the ESM member states concerned. The board of governors could then decide to grant stability support to the ESM member concerned in the form of a financial assistance facility, outlining attached conditionality in an MOU. The ESM could also

[13] The European Commission and the ECB may also appoint one observer each.

[14] Since the EFSF was established, the German Debt Management Office (Bundesrepublik Deutschland—Finanzagentur GmbH) has acted as Issuance Agent and has been responsible for the placement. For the ESM, the German Debt Management Office will initially continue to perform the same role.

grant precautionary financial assistance to member states, accompanied by an MOU detailing conditionality (Article 14).

The ESM was given the power to recapitalize banks directly (Article 15). The request had to be addressed to the Chairperson of the ESM board of governors, indicating, notably, the institutions in distress for which financial assistance was requested, the amount of capital needed, and the type of securities to be used in the recapitalization. The board of governors would then decide whether to grant the loan, following the advice of the European Commission, the ECB, and where possible the relevant ESA, to assess conformity with the eligibility criteria. Conditions would be attached, but unlike the stability support within a macroeconomic adjustment programme, the conditionality would focus only on the financial sector of the member state in question. The policy conditions would be specified in an MOU negotiated by the European Commission in liaison with the ECB and the relevant ESA (either the ECB or the NCA).[15]

The requesting ESM member state would have to be unable to provide financial assistance to the beneficiary bank without very serious effects on its own fiscal sustainability. In addition, ESM financial assistance would have to be considered indispensable to safeguard the financial stability of the euro area as a whole or of its member states. Direct recapitalization by the ESM would be considered after private capital resources had been deployed—that is, after an appropriate level of bail-in in line with EU state-aid rules and the BRRD (discussed in Chapter 6).[16]

The eligibility criteria with respect to the bank requiring recapitalization were that the bank would have to currently be (or be likely to be in the near future) unable to meet the capital requirements established by the ECB in its capacity as supervisor. The bank would also have to be unable to obtain sufficient capital from private sources. Conditionality would be applied to the recapitalized institution and could include rules on the remuneration of management and bonuses. As a general rule, the ESM would acquire common equity shares in the beneficiary institution. The degree of involvement of the ESM in approving the strategy and business model, and appointing senior management of the beneficiary institution, would be considered on a case-by-case basis.[17]

[15] <http://www.esm.europa.eu/pdf/FAQ%20Direct%20Bank%20Recapitalisation%20280620131.pdf>, accessed on 11 September 2015.

[16] This provision is not included in the ESM treaty. However, it is stated clearly on the ESM webpages. See <http://www.esm.europa.eu/pdf/FAQ%20Direct%20Bank%20Recapitalisation%20280620131.pdf>.

[17] <http://www.esm.europa.eu/pdf/FAQ%20Direct%20Bank%20Recapitalisation%20280620131.pdf>.

As acquiring a stake in a bank was considered to be more risky than granting a loan to a member state government, the impact on the ESM's capital and creditworthiness was greater in the case of direct bank recapitalization than for granting loans. For example, because of the different risk profile, €1 for ESM direct bank recapitalization would reduce the ESM's lending capacity by more than €1 in order to maintain the ESM's high creditworthiness. In order to preserve the ESM's lending capacity for other instruments, a limit was to be set on the total amount of ESM resources available for direct recapitalization of banks.[18]

During the Eurogroup meeting held in March 2012, it was decided that the EFSF would continue to fund the existing Facility Agreements for Portugal, Ireland, and Greece. In June 2012, the Spanish government made an official request for financial assistance for its banking system to the Eurogroup for a loan of up to €100 billion. The euro area member states agreed in principle to extend the use of ESM funds to the direct recapitalization of banks—a policy advocated by France, euro area periphery member states, and the European Commission—but this was subject to the creation of the SSM. However, in the summer of 2012, the German government began to backtrack on using ESM funds to directly support ailing banks.

In December 2012, the Spanish government formally requested the disbursement of close to €39.5 billion of funds for the recapitalization of Spain's banking sector. At the December 2012 European Council, euro area member state governments compromised on immediate emergency aid of up to €39 billion for Spanish banks via a specially created Spanish fund, but stated that in the future ESM funds could be used to recapitalize only those banks that developed problems following the creation of the SSM and not those with 'legacy' problems. The emergency aid funds were transferred in the form of ESM notes in December 2012 to the Fondo de Restructuración Ordenada Bancaria, the bank recapitalization fund of the Spanish government. This transfer was accompanied by a pledge by Spain to restructure its financial sector. Subsequently, the ESM granted up to approximately €9 billion of emergency financial assistance to Cyprus, of which €3 billion was disbursed,[19] while the IMF contributed around €1 billion. The ESM has a maximum lending capacity of €500 billion.

Wolfgang Schäuble, the German Finance Minister, insisted that the ESM would not be used for other bank recapitalizations until Banking Union was in full operation (*EUObserver*, 3 December 2012). The European Council agreed that the SSM would allow the ESM to recapitalize banks in difficulties directly,

[18] <http://www.esm.europa.eu/pdf/FAQ%20Direct%20Bank%20Recapitalisation%20280620131.pdf>.
[19] <http://www.esm.europa.eu/pdf/FAQ%20Direct%20Bank%20Recapitalisation%20280620131.pdf>.

subject to 'double majority' voting by both the ECB and the EBA. In June 2013, the euro area member states agreed to allocate up to a total of €60 billion of ESM funds to bank recapitalization if and when required. Upon German insistence, all ESM bail-outs were to be based on strong conditionality and were to be repaid by either the banks or the government of the banks' home member state (*Financial Times*, 15 October 2013; Barker 2013). It is also noteworthy that according to the ESM treaty, only those member states that implemented the Fiscal Compact (see the next section) would be eligible to receive ESM support, with a view to strengthening fiscal discipline and reducing moral hazard.

The EFSF and the ESM were created as a fiscal backstop for euro area member state governments, subject to conditionality and clear funding limits. The ESM's role as LLR for banks remained far from obvious. Most observers have concluded that the ESM is unable to perform the role of LLR because of the strict conditionality rules agreed in June 2013 and clear funding limits: a maximum of €60 billion—not much more than the amounts spent in the 'exceptional' intervention propping up Spain and Cyprus (*Financial Times*, 15 October 2013). Given unanimity rules, the German government enjoyed a veto on any ESM decision to engage in direct bank recapitalization.

In October 2013, the German Finance Minister, Wolfgang Schäuble, insisted that German law would have to be changed for the ESM to take a direct stake in a bank. The German Bundestag would have to vote through direct recapitalization, given the use of German funds, and strong political opposition to the use of taxpayers' money to bail out banks would have to be overcome. The German government—joined by the Dutch and the Finns—insisted that ESM funds could not be used to cover legacy problems, to be revealed by a Comprehensive Assessment of euro area banks by the ECB. Earlier support—as for Spanish banks—was to be 'exceptional' and subject to strict conditionality.

Under the rules established for the direct recapitalization of banks, euro area member state governments agreed that a bank's creditors should absorb 'appropriate' losses—left undefined, initially—before ESM funds could be accessed. In the BRRD, member states agreed that all shareholders—both junior and senior—should lose all their investment prior to direct ESM recapitalization. The concern was that such heavy write-downs would force the closure of a bank prior to the use of ESM funds. ESM rules required a bank's home government to contribute at least 20 per cent of the recapitalization (initially) and then 10 per cent from 2017.

For euro periphery member states, even such small contributions could fundamentally undermine confidence in the sustainability of national debt loads. Furthermore, the ESM could not be used to bolster the capital position of banks failing to meet Basel failing EBA stress tests (see Chapter 5). The 'closely monitored' conditionality that accompanies recapitalization would apply to banks, but also potentially to member state governments, which could have an economic programme imposed upon them through an MOU. The ESM would undertake its own assessment of a bank's balance sheet, including its own stress tests. In the event that a member state government is unable to contribute to a direct bank recapitalization, it might still be required to guarantee the equity stake taken by the ESM.

The Reform of Fiscal Policy Coordination and of the Stability and Growth Pact

From the outset of the crisis, the EU member states and the European Commission sought to develop the 'economic' arm of EMU (see Chapter 2), strengthening fiscal policy coordination and budgetary discipline. These measures—namely the Six Pack, the Fiscal Compact, and the Two Pack—were also designed to reassure Germany (especially its public opinion) about the potential moral hazard arising from ECB action and the provision of euro area financial assistance to member state governments hit by the sovereign debt crisis.

The Six Pack derives its name from the five regulations and one directive agreed in March 2011 (see Chang 2013). It applied to all twenty-seven EU member states, with some specific rules for euro area member states, especially regarding financial sanctions. It covered not only fiscal surveillance but also macroeconomic surveillance under the new Macroeconomic Imbalance Procedure. In the fiscal field, the Six Pack strengthened the SGP by reinforcing the preventive and the corrective arm of the SGP—that is, the Excessive Deficit Procedure (EDP)—which would apply to member states that breached either the deficit or the debt criterion.[20] General government budgets were to be balanced or in surplus, with an annual structural deficit not exceeding 0.5 per cent of GDP (the rule was less strict for countries with government debt significantly below 60 per cent of GDP). Member states were required to introduce legislation to enforce this rule, with the legislation incorporating an automatic mechanism for correcting excessive fiscal deficits.

Member states with public debt in excess of 60 per cent of GDP were required to reduce it by an average annual rate of 5 per cent until they complied with the 60 per cent upper limit. In so doing, the Six Pack operationalized the

[20] According to the SGP, the general government deficit in the member states must not exceed 3 per cent of GDP and public debt must not normally exceed 60 per cent of GDP (or, if in excess, must be dropping towards the 60 per cent threshold).

debt criterion, so that an EDP could be launched not only on the basis of a deficit above 3 per cent of GDP, as had previously been the case. The Six Pack introduced reversed QMV for most sanctions, thereby increasing their likelihood for euro area member states in breach of the rules. This voting mechanism implied that a recommendation or a proposal of the European Commission was adopted in the Council unless a qualified majority of member states voted against it (Chang 2013).[21]

The Treaty on Stability, Coordination and Governance in the Economic and Monetary Union was an intergovernmental agreement signed in March 2012 by all EU member states with the exception of the UK and the Czech Republic. It was to enter into force following ratification by at least twelve euro area member states, but would be non-binding for non-euro area member states. It explicitly stated that EU law had precedence over the treaty (Gros 2012a). The main purpose of the treaty was 'to strengthen the economic pillar of the Economic and Monetary Union by adopting a set of rules intended to foster budgetary discipline through a Fiscal Compact, to strengthen the coordination of economic policies and to improve the governance of the euro area' (Article 1).

The fiscal part of the treaty was publicly referred to as the 'Fiscal Compact' (Gros 2012a). Articles 3 and 4 require governments to bring budgets into balance or in surplus, with the annual structural deficit not to exceed 0.5 per cent of GDP (unless government debt is very low, in which case the structural deficit can be up to 1 per cent); there must be an automatic correction mechanism, triggered if the state deviates from a country-specific medium-term objective, or its adjustment path towards that objective; and if the ratio of general government debt to GDP exceeds 60 per cent, the difference between the actual ratio and 60 per cent should be reduced by an average of a twentieth per year.

The signatory member states were required to place the balanced budget rule into national law, and preferably into constitutional law. The European Court of Justice was given the power to impose financial sanctions (0.1 per cent of GDP) if a country did not properly transpose the new budget rules into national law. In the case of euro area member states, fines would be channelled to the ESM. In the case of non-euro area member states, the funding derived from the fines would be attributed to the EU budget. The treaty set in place a reversed QMV on the European Commission's recommendations issued when a euro area state is in breach of the deficit criterion and subject to the EDP.

[21] 'Six-Pack? Two-Pack? Fiscal Compact? A Short Guide to the New EU Fiscal Governance', European Commission—Brussels: Directorate-General for Economic and Financial Affairs, 2012 <http://ec.europa.eu/economy_finance/articles/governance/2012-03-14_six_pack_en.htm>.

Unless a qualified majority of euro area states does not support the European Commission's recommendation, the latter is adopted. The treaty also established reinforced surveillance and coordination of economic policies, with ex ante coordination of debt issuance.[22] However, Gros (2012a) notes that the real enforcement power for the adoption of fiscal policy rules into national law was to come from the ESM treaty, which stated that only those member states that implemented the fiscal compact would be eligible to receive ESM support. Gros (2012a) argues that the provisions on the Fiscal Compact constitute essentially a political statement, notably in providing 'political cover for the German government in its efforts to sell the euro rescue operations to a sceptical domestic audience' (p. 2).

The UK and the Czech Republic decided not to sign the treaty. In a House of Lords report (2012b), the Minister for Europe explained that the British government sought 'some sort of general safeguard with respect to the integrity of the single market and... something more specific on the issue of financial services'[23] to protect 'the financial services industry in every EU Member State against the risk of discriminatory legislation or protectionist legislation on financial services'.[24] He argued that by refusing to sign the treaty, the UK ensured that the outcome was 'an intergovernmental structure that, whatever else it does or does not do, cannot create obligations on the United Kingdom, cannot form part of the European Union's *acquis* and cannot be a treaty basis for future EU secondary legislation that is binding on us'.

The *Financial Times* (10 December 2011; see also *Daily Telegraph*, 9 December 2011) reported that the UK's demands during the negotiations included a clear statement that euro area integration would preserve the interests of the Single Market and would not undermine the common interest of all twenty-seven member states, and a 'protocol on financial services' in relation to the powers of the new ESAs (including a reassurance that the EBA would remain in London) and including a unanimous vote on any 'user charges' in financial services regulation, which would have given the UK a veto on the financial transaction tax proposal.

[22] <http://ec.europa.eu/economy_finance/articles/governance/2012-03-14_six_pack_en.htm>.

[23] When the new voting weights envisaged in the Lisbon Treaty came into force in 2015, the members of the euro area would have a qualified majority if they voted as a bloc. The British Minister of Europe pointed out that 'clearly there is an inherent risk, just in that arithmetic' (House of Lords 2012b).

[24] The British Minister for Europe, in his evidence before the EP, made reference to the precedents set by the ECB's location policy for central counterparties, which, according to the British government, went against Single Market principles and was designed to protect the interests of the eurozone: <http://www.publications.parliament.uk/pa/ld201012/ldselect/ldeucom/260/26008.htm#a37>, accessed on 1 March 2016.

The Fiscal Compact (which is the fiscal part of the Treaty on Stability, Coordination and Governance) and the Six Pack run in parallel. On the one hand, two provisions included in the treaty mirrored concepts existing in the SGP as reformed by the Six Pack. Some provisions of the treaty were more stringent than the Six Pack—for example, on the application of reverse QMV. To give further impetus to the governance reforms, twenty-three member states, including six outside the euro area (Bulgaria, Denmark, Latvia, Lithuania, Poland, and Romania), signed the Euro Plus Pact in March 2011. This commits signatories to even stronger economic coordination for competitiveness and convergence, also in areas of national competence, with concrete goals agreed on and reviewed on a yearly basis by heads of state or government. The Euro Plus Pact is integrated into the European semester, and the European Commission monitors implementation of the commitments.[25]

Overall, during the sovereign debt crisis and the construction of Banking Union, the development of the economic arm of EMU, particularly concerning fiscal policy, mostly revolved around the efforts made by Germany, the European Commission, and the ECB to force through reforms to ensure fiscal discipline and undermine the likelihood of moral hazard in the future, especially once Banking Union was fully operational. The debate on fiscal policy coordination also highlighted the effects of differentiated integration in the EU (see Schimmelfennig 2016), whereby some (but, interestingly, not all) non-euro area countries that did not join Banking Union refused to sign the Treaty on Stability, Coordination and Governance in the Economic, and Monetary Union was an intergovernmental agreement. Finally, this treaty, like the ESM treaty and the SRF agreement, is a rather atypical instrument in the legislative order to the EU.

Conclusion

This chapter discusses LLR and the fiscal backstop for sovereigns and banks in Banking Union, starting with an examination of the unconventional measures of the ECB that acted de facto as LLR for both banks and sovereigns during the international financial and sovereign debt crises. The analysis then turns to examine the EFSF that was established as an ad hoc temporary emergency measure to deal with the sovereign debt crisis and the permanent ESM created to purchase sovereign debt directly from governments in difficulty and on secondary debt markets. Subject to specific conditions—shown to be particularly strict—the ESM was also assigned the power to engage in direct bank

[25] <http://ec.europa.eu/economy_finance/economic_governance/>.

recapitalization. Finally, the chapter examines the reinforced mechanisms for fiscal policy discipline to limit the potential moral hazard created by the operation of the ECB, the EFSF, and the ESM.

Different member states had different preferences and priorities on both ECB activities, and the creation and operation of European support mechanisms. Some of these national preferences were in line with long-standing preferences on the establishment and operation of EMU, and a comparison with the negotiations on the TEU in 1992 is instructive. French support for ECB extraordinary monetary policy and the creation of the EFSF and the ESM stemmed from a desire to establish a fiscal backstop to the euro area—via LLR-style support for governments and banks. This French position was reminiscent of the (often confused) debate on the 'gouvernement économique' promoted by the French government at the time of the Maastricht Treaty (Howarth 2001). Moreover, France was seen as the next potential target of the sovereign debt crisis if the crisis erupted fullforce in Spain and then spread to Italy.

Euro periphery member states directly hit or directly threatened by the sovereign debt crisis fully supported a fiscal backstop in Banking Union, given the weak state of their national banking systems and public finances. All but Italy had been direct recipients of EU/euro area financial aid. Moreover, Spanish and Italian banks had been heavy recipients of ECB funding (Quaglia and Royo 2015). If one defines sovereign default as the inability of a government to borrow on the market at a sustainable rate, the ECB's action in the summer of 2012 effectively pre-empted Italian default. Although the ECB programme did not target Italy specifically, the country benefited through a temporary reduction of its borrowing costs. The ECB lent to euro area banks, which in turn lent to euro area governments, and then used the government debt they bought as collateral for yet more loans from the ECB.

German governments demonstrated consistent reluctance to accept any LLR role for the ECB beyond limited liquidity support for banks. A number of top German officials consistently expressed their public opposition to ECB support for euro area sovereigns. German governments were also reluctant to accept the construction of a fiscal backstop mechanism for both sovereigns and banks. However, Germany had only a marginal say on ECB policy and only a 'constrained veto power' in negotiations on the EFSF and the ESM. Germany was reticent about the creation of the EFSF and the ESM because it had the least to gain from these mechanisms and, potentially, the most to contribute. However, its veto power was constrained by the fact that the euro area member states (including Germany) needed these mechanisms in order to deal with the sovereign debt crisis, diminish the threat of contagion, and ensure the survival of the euro. In the negotiations on the construction of European support mechanisms, as in the negotiations on

EMU, German policy-makers insisted upon the quid pro quo of tighter euro area fiscal rules. Specifically, the Germans insisted on strict conditionality in exchange for EFSF and ESM financial support for governments and banks, expressing moral hazard concerns that EU-level support would undermine national macroeconomic policy reform and undermine the collective pursuit of more cautious banking.

9

Banking Regulation and the Single Rulebook

This chapter discusses the 'regulatory' element of Banking Union—namely, the Single Rulebook in banking, which was mentioned as the underlying foundation of Banking Union in the Four Presidents' report of June 2012. However, it is important to point out that the Single Rulebook, like all EU regulation, applies to the entire EU, not only to the euro area or Banking Union countries. The term 'Single Rulebook' was coined in 2009 by the European Council in order to refer to 'the aim of a unified regulatory framework for the EU financial sector that would complete the single market in financial services' (EBA 2015a).

In banking, the Single Rulebook was designed to provide a single set of harmonized prudential rules for banks throughout the EU. Despite the fact that banking regulation was well developed at the EU level—the First Banking Directive dated back to 1977 and was followed by several other directives[1]—significant differences in the national implementation of the EU banking legislation remained across the member states, as became clear during the international financial crisis (see, e.g., Padoa-Schioppa 2007). The use of so-called national discretion was facilitated by the fact that most EU banking legislation was based on 'directives' (which need to be transposed by the members states into national legislation) rather than 'regulations' (which, in most cases, are immediately applicable in the member states). Moreover, banking directives were often based on minimum harmonization, and controversial issues were sidestepped or resulted in convoluted compromises. Consequently, when EU legislation was implemented domestically, the member states used the room for manoeuvre (deliberately) left by EU rules to set in place domestic rules that

[1] The most important pieces of pre-crisis EU banking legislation were the Second Banking Directive, issued in 1988, and the CRD of 1993, which was subsequently revised (see Story and Walter 1997).

were less penalizing or more suitable to their national banking systems (Story and Walter 1997; Quaglia 2010a).

Another important feature of EU banking regulation was that it was mostly 'downloaded' from the international level (Quaglia 2014). Therefore, the EU incorporated into successive CRDs the Basel accords, which were international standards that set the capital requirements for large internationally active banks. These international standards were 'soft law' (see Brummer 2012) issued by the BCBS, which brought together national central banks and banking supervisors from selected countries with major banking centres. The provisions of the accords became legally binding only when they were incorporated into the national legislation of the signatories (Zaring 2015), which therefore retained the power de jure not to implement the accords domestically, as the US did with Basel II prior to the crisis (see Herring 2007); or to do so in their own way, in order to take into account national specificities, as the EU did with Basel III, as explained in the following section.[2]

At the start of negotiations on Banking Union, the diversity of national bank regulations and supervisory practice was clear—despite the existence of a significant corpus of EU banking legislation. However, even the adoption of most elements of the Basel III guidelines into EU law through the CRD IV in 2013 ensured ongoing national divergence in transposition and implementation. Furthermore, efforts to achieve bank structural reform—spearheaded by the Likannen Committee, which was created to tackle the problem of 'too-big-too-fail'—would also likely result in continuing to allow very different national practices (European Commission 2012e). The aim of this chapter is to demonstrate that member state government preferences on EU and national banking regulation and supervision continue to reflect significantly the configuration of national banking systems. Despite ECB efforts, starting in 2014, to overcome national discretions, divergence in Banking Union both in the rules to be followed and in the supervisory practice is set to continue for years to come.

The first section of this chapter discusses the main preferences of the EU member states in the negotiations on Basel III, which was the main international regulatory response of the banking sector to the international financial crisis, setting new capital and liquidity rules for internationally active banks. It is argued that in the international negotiations, the UK and the Netherlands mostly sided with the US, calling for higher capital requirements and a stricter definition of capital and liquidity rules. In contrast, the

[2] Several studies show that market pressure and reputational effects limited the ability of jurisdictions not to implement the Basel accords, even for jurisdictions that were not part of the BCBS and that therefore had not negotiated those accords (see Chey 2007; Lyngen 2012).

continental European countries—notably France and Germany, but also Italy and Spain—favoured a broader definition of what counts as capital, lower capital requirements, and flexible liquidity rules. The final Basel III agreement was a compromise between these different positions.

The second section examines the transposition of Basel III into the EU's CRD IV, arguing that some of the compromises on the definition of capital, the leverage ratio, and liquidity rules reached in the Basel III negotiations were reopened in the EU negotiations. Moreover, whereas continental countries favoured legislation based on maximum harmonization, the British authorities opposed it as they wanted to be free to impose higher capital requirements domestically. This section also briefly examines the subsequent activity of the EBA and the SSM in the construction of the Single Rulebook and supervisory convergence. One of the priorities was the reduction (mainly through harmonization) of options and national discretions, which could impinge upon the functioning of the Single Market and the SSM. The third section explains how the configuration of national banking systems—to be precise, systemic patterns in bank capital and liquidity—largely determined national preferences on Basel III and its implementation in the EU through the CRD.

The fourth section examines the recent EU legislation on bank structural reform, arguing that the UK favoured rules on ring-fencing the deposit-taking part of a bank, whereas continental European countries favoured a (much weaker) version of the Volcker Rule, adopted in the US, which mainly prevented deposit-taking banks from engaging in proprietary trading, basically using deposits to fund certain investment banking activities. The penultimate section explains member state preferences on structural reform in terms of the configuration of national banking systems—which also determined the post-crisis separation rules adopted unilaterally in France and Germany. Specifically, a number of EU member state governments came to the defence of the universal banking model and the trading activities of large continental banks which would have been badly affected by strict rules on ring-fencing or provisions similar to those in the Volcker Rule (notably, a ban on proprietary trading) (Hardie and Macartney 2016).

The International Basel III Accord

Capital requirements have traditionally been regarded as the main instruments to ensure the stability of the banking sector and hence financial stability tout court. In 1988, the BCBS issued the Basel I Accord setting minimal capital requirements for banks (Kapstein 1989, 1992; Simmons 2001), which was followed by the Basel II accord in 2004 (King and Sinclair 2003; Tsingou

2008; Underhill and Zhang 2008; Wood 2005). Over time, these 'soft' international rules have been incorporated into (legally binding) national legislation in more than 100 countries. In the EU, this has been done through the CRDs (Underhill 1998; Christopoulos and Quaglia 2009).

After the international financial crisis, the Basel III accord, 'A Global Regulatory Framework for More Resilient Banks and Banking Systems' (2010) set capital requirements and liquidity rules for internationally active banks worldwide. The BCBS put forward concrete proposals on Basel III in December 2009, which were then subject to public consultation. Other documents (e.g., on the countercyclical capital buffer) were issued for consultation throughout 2010. A general agreement was reached in July 2010, and a final agreement was eventually signed in December (BCBS 2010a, b). Compared with the Basel II accord, Basel III was negotiated in record time—less than two years—due to the political salience imparted to it by the international financial crisis. The Basel III rules are to be phased in gradually from January 2013 until 2019.

In the making of the Basel III accord first and in the negotiations on the CRD IV later, the core of the controversy concerned the distributive implications of the regulatory changes proposed. The definition of capital (in particular, the list of financial instruments that count as capital), the level of capital requirements, the definition of liquid assets, and the amount of liquid assets affected different banks and national banking systems in different ways, imposing costs as well as benefits that were not equally distributed. Different banks had different sources of capital; some banks had capital instruments or liquid assets that other banks did not have; some banks were better positioned than others to meet higher capital requirements or liquidity coverage. There were also national banking-system-wide patterns of bank capital and liquidity. EU-headquartered banks and national banking systems thus faced different adjustment costs to the proposed capital rules.

The Basel III accord provided for the first time a common definition of capital, on which there had been no agreement in the past. The main forms of Tier 1 capital were common shares and retained earnings, while subordinated debt could also be included. 'Hybrid capital' instruments—capital which has some features of both debt and equity—were to be phased out (BCBS 2010a: 2). Many EU regulators—in particular, the Germans, Spanish, and Italians—were concerned about the ban on 'hybrid' capital, which would considerably reduce the capital base of many domestic banks (notably alternative banks) that used these and similar non-equity instruments in their calculation of Tier 1 capital (*The Economist*, 23 January 2010).

By contrast, British and US regulators were keen to exclude hybrids from the definition of capital (interviews, US financial regulators, Washington,

5 August 2011). For example, a senior figure from the British FSA noted that 'hybrid capital ... acts like debt as far as the tax man is concerned, and ... like equity as far as the depositor is concerned. This hybrid capital is junior to deposits, but senior to equity' (Huertas 2009: 11). British and US regulators insisted that shareholders should take the losses for hybrids rather than the government having to cover them (Howarth and Quaglia 2015a).

Total regulatory capital, consisting of Tier 1 capital and Tier 2 capital, had to be maintained by banks at a minimum of 8 per cent of risk-weighted assets.[3] Tier 1 had to reach at least 6 per cent of risk-weighted assets, and the Core Tier 1, which comprised common equities, had to reach at least 4.5 per cent of risk-weighted assets (BCBS 2010a: 12). The original proposals for higher capital requirements were watered down in a search for a compromise between the UK, the US, and Switzerland—which were keen to set higher requirements—and several continental regulators, which resisted them and asked for longer transition periods (*Financial Times*, 22 October 2010).

Basel III introduced a 'capital conservation buffer' of 2.5 per cent, comprising common equities, above the regulatory minimum.[4] Capital distribution constraints were to be imposed on a bank when capital levels fell within this range (BCBS 2010a: 55). On Core Tier 1, therefore, Basel III set risk-weighted capital requirements of 4.5 per cent compared with a pre-existing (Basel II) level of 2 per cent, plus a new buffer of 2.5 per cent, establishing a new effective floor at 7 per cent. National countercyclical buffers, designed to take into account the macro-financial environment in which banks operate, were also to be introduced (BCBS 2010a: 57). These buffer requirements, to be decided by national jurisdictions, could vary between 0 and 2.5 per cent of risk-weighted assets. Bank specific countercyclical buffers could also be imposed (BCBS 2010a: 58). Capital buffers were to be phased in between 2016 and 2019. Basel III also envisaged a capital surcharge to mitigate the risk of systemic banks, to be agreed subsequently.

Basel III introduced a 'leverage ratio', which was a non-risk-based ratio calibrated to act as a supplementary measure to the risk-based capital requirements. The BCBS would test a minimum Tier 1 leverage ratio of 3 per cent during the trial-run period from 1 January 2013 to 1 January 2017 (BCBS 2010a: 61). This regulatory instrument was already in use in the US, but its introduction into Basel III was resisted by most continental European regulators, who argued that the riskiness of the activities of their traditional

[3] Tier 2, or supplementary capital, consists of undisclosed reserves, revaluation reserves, general provisions, and subordinated term debt.

[4] This buffer is intended to promote the conservation of capital and the build-up of adequate buffers above the minimum that can be drawn down in periods of stress.

universal banks was lower than that of (largely Anglo-Saxon) investment banks, and that this feature would not be captured by a crude leverage ratio (*Financial Times*, 26 October 2010; interview, French regulator, Paris, 7 July 2011). Having failed to prevent the inclusion of the leverage ratio in the Basel III rules, continental regulators lobbied hard for it not to be included in the European Commission's proposed legislation implementing Basel III, as explained in the following section.

Basel III established internationally harmonized minimum liquidity standards to address short-term mismatches (through the 'liquidity coverage ratio') and long-term liquidity mismatches (through the 'net stable funding ratio' [NSFR]). After an observation period, the liquidity coverage ratio would be implemented in 2015, and the NSFR in 2018 (BCBS 2010b: 8–9). Here the main disagreement within the BCBS concerned which categories of financial instrument should be considered as liquid (Cotterill 2010; interview, Bank of France officials, 6 December 2010)—that is, the composition of liquidity cushions. British policy-makers as well as policy-makers from some other member states wanted to restrict the definition of liquid instruments to government debt, deposits with central banks, and the like. The French opposed this (Noyer 2012; Schmitz 2012; interview, Bank of France officials, 6 December 2010). Eventually, Basel III allowed high-grade corporate bonds to be considered as liquid instruments.

If one considers the evolution of the negotiations, in its draft issued in December 2009, the BCBS took a surprisingly hard-line approach on capital and liquidity requirements, pushing for a higher adequacy threshold and a restriction on hybrids, with minimum capital to be composed of predominantly equity capital. Given the similarity of preferences of British and US regulators, their remarkable financial expertise, the large size of their financial sectors, and their chairmanship of key working groups,[5] they were able to leave a strong imprint on the initial Basel III draft of December 2009 (Howarth and Quaglia 2015a).

However, the final December 2010 version was less strict: in particular, it contained longer transition periods. This relaxation was due in part to the extensive lobbying from banks and bank associations, but also largely to the resistance of continental European and Japanese regulators to some of the most draconian provisions. Indeed, at the crucial meeting of the BCBS in September 2010, three months prior to the final agreement, German regulators refused to endorse the document prepared by the BCBS, asking for (and subsequently obtaining) important revisions, notably on transition periods (*Financial Times*,

[5] For example, the working group on liquidity was chaired by Nigel Jenkinson of the Bank of England; the working group on the trading book was chaired by Alan Adkins of the British FSA.

9 September 2010; interview, German financial industry representative, Frankfurt, 18 April 2012).

The preferences of national regulators were not monolithic, and different internal views tended to emerge once the accord had been agreed internationally, which then had to be implemented domestically. The most notable case was in the UK, where Andy Haldane, the Bank of England's Executive Director for Financial Stability, criticized Basel III, which was defended by the then Governor, Mervyn King. Haldane argued that the Basel III rules were too complex. He was a keen supporter of a simple leverage ratio, rather than risk-weighted assets. Deputy Governor Paul Tucker, parting ways with both Haldane and King, refused to highlight the 'too big to fail' problem and the need to break up big banks (*The Telegraph*, 27 November 2012).

The Capital Requirements Directive IV 'Package'

EU institutions followed closely the negotiations on Basel III by the BCBS, in which the European Commission and the ECB had observer status (after the establishment of the SSM, the ECB and the SSM became a full two-seat member of the BCBS). The incorporation of Basel III into EU law, however, met with considerable member state and EU institutional reticence. The EU directive and regulation (referred to collectively as the CRD IV), eventually adopted in 2013, qualified (critics would argue that they watered down) the application of the Basel III capital requirements in the EU. Some of the issues that had been papered over in the making of the Basel III accord resurfaced, and so did disagreement among the member states and EU institutions.

In July 2011, after extensive consultations conducted in parallel with the work of the BCBS, the EU Commission adopted the CRD IV legislative package designed to replace the CRD III with a directive that governed the access to deposit-taking activities and a regulation that established prudential requirements for credit institutions. The decision to issue a regulation, in addition to a directive, which had been used as a legislative instrument for capital requirements in the past, was a deliberate attempt to foster the Single Rulebook in banking and to eliminate a key source of national divergence. In the CRD III, more than 100 national discretions (differences in national legislation transposing the EU directive) remained. Moreover, the Commission's draft regulation also proposed a maximum capital ratio, whereas the Basel accords set minimum capital requirements. This maximum harmonization approach was opposed by those who argued in favour of EU standards that exceeded the Basel minimum because of prevailing balance-sheet uncertainties in the EU, the lack of EU-wide resolution arrangements, and a fully unified fiscal backstop.

The directive contained rules concerning the establishment and pursuit of banking operations: the conditions for the freedom of establishment and the freedom to provide services; the supervisory review process; and the definition of competent authorities. The directive also incorporated two elements of the Basel III accord, namely the introduction of two capital buffers in addition to the minimum capital requirements: the capital conservation buffer (identical for all banks in the EU), and the countercyclical capital buffer (to be determined at national level). After its approval, the directive had to be transposed by the member states in a way suitable to their own national environment. The regulation contained prudential requirements for credit institutions and investment firms. It covered the definition of capital, increasing the amount of their own funds that banks need to hold as well as the quality of those funds; it introduced the liquidity coverage ratio—the exact composition and calibration of which was to be determined after an observation and review period in 2015; and it outlined the need to consider a leverage ratio, subject to supervisory review.

The Commission's CRD IV draft, as initially proposed, watered down or modified the Basel III guidelines, attracting the criticism of a range of national regulators and the IMF (2011a). Speaking at a meeting of the economic and finance ministers held to discuss the CRD IV, the British Treasury minister complained that '[w]e are not implementing the Basel agreement, as anyone who will look at this text will be able to tell you' (*Financial Times*, 2 May 2012).

The Commission 'softened' its definition of Core Tier I capital relative to the Basel III recommendations in some areas. Notably, the Commission draft includes as Core Tier 1 'silent participations'—that is, long-term loans from government that make up a significant part of the capital of many EU banks, including the publicly owned German Landesbanken (Howarth and Quaglia 2013b). Moreover, the Commission's draft regulation, where capital was defined, contained specific provisions concerning 'capital instruments of mutuals, cooperative societies, savings institutions or similar institutions in Common Equity Tier 1', which were important for EU member states, such as Germany, Italy, and Spain, which had a significant presence of alternative banks (Howarth and Quaglia 2013b).

The Commission's draft also limited the role of the leverage ratio designed to limit risk-taking at banks. The almost unique reliance on the risk-weighted Core Tier 1 ratio in the Commission's draft CRD IV, which was in line with what agreed in Basel III, was criticized for inadequately representing the health of the European banking sector (*Financial Times*, 30 January 2012) (Howarth and Quaglia 2013b).[6] On liquidity, the Commission adopted the

[6] There were wider questions being asked about the Basel focus on risk-weighted assets; hence, the desire for the leverage ratio, which looks at overall assets.

less prescriptive definition of liquid assets—namely, for the liquid capital ratio (LCR) to include 'transferable assets that are of extremely high liquidity and credit quality' and 'transferable assets that are of high liquidity and credit quality'. The Commission's draft lacked a firm commitment to implement the NSFR by 2018 called for in Basel III. The Commission's proposed regulation also set higher capital requirements for over-the-counter derivatives that were not cleared though Central Counterparties.

Following the agreement on Basel III and during the intra-EU negotiations on the CRD IV, some of the compromises reached in the BCBS unravelled. Several EU member states, the EP, and even the Commission itself called for the taking into account of 'European specificities' in incorporating the Basel III rules into the CRD IV, reopening some of the issues that had caused friction within the BCBS. Basel III applied to internationally active banks, whereas EU legislation was to apply to all banks, making some Basel III provisions—notably the calculation of Tier 1—impossible to apply in EU member states without a massive shift in the structure and operations of a large range of banks (Howarth and Quaglia 2013b).

The Commission justified its decision to apply Basel III rules, as with Basel I and Basel II, to all EU banks on both stability grounds and reasons linked to the application of EU competition policy. Both the Commission and the EP also emphasized competition concerns and the need to ensure an 'international level playing field'. Of particular concern was that in the US, the Basel III accord would be applied only to financial institutions with over (US)$50 billion in assets, whereas the new rules would be applied to all banks in the EU, as in the case of Basel I and Basel II (EP 2010, 2011).

The assessment carried out by the BCBS on the EU CRD IV packages and the accompanying EBA standards and guidelines (discussed in the following section) highlighted several differences between Basel III and EU prudential rules.[7] The 'important divergences' between Basel III and EU legislation identified by the report were as follows:

> Overall, eight of the 14 components assessed are compliant with the Basel framework, and four components (definition of capital and calculation of minimum requirements, Standardised Approach for credit risk, credit risk (securitisation framework) and Standardised Measurement Method for market risk) are largely compliant; one component (Internal Ratings-Based (IRB) approach for credit risk) is materially non-compliant; while the counterparty credit risk

[7] The report was prepared by the Basel Committee's Regulatory Consistency Assessment Programme, which was tasked with promoting the full, timely, and consistent implementation of Basel III regulatory standards by the committee's members. The BCBS assessment was carried out for all the members of the committee. The approach taken in the report was to ascertain whether the EU banking prudential framework incorporated 'Basel minimum standards in both letter and spirit'.

> component is non-compliant. In view of this, the prudential regulatory framework in the EU and the nine Member States was evaluated to be materially non-compliant with the minimum standards prescribed under the Basel framework (BCBS 2012: 4).

Once the CRD IV/Capital Requirements Regulation (CRR) package was agreed by the Council and the EP, the EBA was mandated to produce technical standards, guidelines, and reports on its implementation. 'Technical standards' are binding legal acts that elaborate upon particular aspects of EU legislation (directive or regulation) with a view to promoting harmonization across the member states. These standards are then adopted by the European Commission by means of regulations or decisions. 'Guidelines', which are not legally binding, foster the convergence of supervisory practices across the EU. They operate according to the principle of comply or explain, whereby NCAs have to inform the EBA about their compliance (or otherwise) with the guidelines and explain the reasons for an eventual non-compliance.

Around 155 options were allowed under the CRD IV/CRR.[8] Some options were 'general'—that is, applicable to all banks (e.g., large exposures options or compulsory use of International Financial Reporting Standards)—so they were linked to entire national banking systems. Others were 'case-by-case' options—that is, applicable to individual institutions, such as waivers. Approximately thirty options were created for specific member states. The remainder applied to NCAs. The use of these options was particularly important in the context of the SSM, with reference to both significant credit institutions directly supervised by the ECB and less significant ones, which were directly supervised by NCAs. Whereas the exercise of the specific member state options could not be easily harmonized—because the ECB was not the addressee and national legislative changes would be necessary—NCA options could be harmonized by the ECB. With reference to significant banks directly supervised by the ECB, the ECB/SSB had the power to draft 'regulations' for general options and national discretion as well as 'policy statements' for case-by-case options and national discretion. Public consultations on these documents were launched in late 2015.

The SSB was to proceed to harmonize options and national discretions concerning less significant institutions once the process regarding significant institutions was completed. In the majority of cases the same measures were to apply to significant and less significant banks in the SSM for reasons of

[8] 'Option' refers to a choice on how to comply with a given provision selected from alternatives set out in the CRD IV/CRR package. 'Discretion' illustrates a choice as to whether to apply a given provision at all.

consistency of supervisory approach across the SSM and ensuring a level playing field. It should also be noted that according to recital 34 of the SSM regulation, 'where the relevant Union law is composed of Regulations and in areas where, on the date of entry into force of this Regulation, those Regulations explicitly grant options for Member States, the ECB should also apply the national legislation exercising such options' (Council 2013)—meaning that the ECB was unable to regulate on and force changes to member state options.

Furthermore, the EBA was assigned the task of promoting the convergence of supervisory practices, which was seen as essential to achieve consistent outcomes, avoid supervisory arbitrage (by NCAs and banks), and achieve a level playing field in the Single European Market. The EBA's activities included issuing guidelines and best practice information, active participation in colleges of supervisors, dedicated training, and peer review. Following the establishment of the SSM, the EBA was assigned the responsibility of issuing a European supervisory handbook (not legally binding), which was to identify best practices across the EU concerning supervisory methodologies and processes. In 2014, the EBA issued the first two chapters of the handbook (EBA 2015a).

From 2013, the SSM NCAs began working on the Single Supervisory Manual, which covers the processes and procedures as well as the methodology for the supervision of significant and less significant institutions in the Banking Union member states. The manual, which was described as 'a living document intended for SSM staff' (ECB 2014a), was issued in November 2014 and continued to be updated afterwards. It is expected to conform to the EBA's guidelines. The working of the EBA and the SSM on these interrelated issues potentially created tensions among EU member states and NCAs in and out of the euro area. Notably, euro area/Banking Union NCAs could present a unified position in the EBA discussions, dictating the outcome of the EBA's work, despite the reform of EBA voting requiring a double majority. Also, real tensions have been reported in the EBA because ECB officials, with only observer status in the EBA, came to perform a more vocal role in discussions (interview, Bank of England official, London, 2 June 2014).

Explaining National Preferences on Capital and Liquidity Rules in the EU

Member state preferences on Basel III and the CRD IV were shaped by the configuration of national banking systems, specifically the capital base, leverage, and the liquidity position of national banks.

Diverging Capital Positions

A perusal of the equity and other Tier 1 capital held by banks in the six country cases shows that, on average, British banks would have the least difficulty in meeting the Basel III standards (of 6 per cent by 2015 and 8.5 per cent, with the capital conservation buffer by 2019) (see Tables 13, 14, and 15 in Chapter 4). The relative confidence of British banks is reflected in Barclays' response to the BCBS consultation (2010a: 2): 'we... have pre-empted the anticipated change by increasing our capital ratios in 2008–9... whilst also lowering our leverage and improving our liquidity positions' (see Figure 9). With an eye to profitability and competitiveness, one senior British bank representative indicated that British banks would have preferred lower capital requirements, but also that 'they could live with the new levels set in Basel III' (interview, London, 15 March 2012). The main British bank-lobbying group, the British Bankers' Association (BBA), nonetheless expressed its concern about the tightening of capital requirements.

The BBA expressed much stronger concerns in its documentation and official statements on Basel III. While tighter capital rules potentially strengthened the position of British banks in relation to undercapitalized European competitors, more stringent Basel guidelines, if adopted into EU legislation, could put British international bank champions at a competitive disadvantage in relation to non-European banks with headquarters in jurisdictions that either did not implement Basel III or did so only in part—notably the US and China (Knight 2010). The BBA called for a long transition period because of deleveraging pressures and the impact upon investor confidence in the event that banks retained earnings and cut dividends to shareholders to improve their capital position (*Financial Times*, 28 June 2011).

Only marginally less capitalized on average than their British competitors,[9] the four largest Dutch banks demonstrated similar sangfroid with regard to Basel III, insisting in their 2010 annual reports upon their optimism in being able to meet the new requirements (Stegeman and van den Meer 2012). Adopting a typical stance, the part-cooperative Rabobank entitled its early 2011 report on the new capital requirements *Basel III: Tough but Realistic* (Rabobank 2011). Concerns remained—notably with regard to the use of hybrids and the double counting of insurance subsidiary capital for some banks, including Rabobank—but these did not prompt bank opposition (Stegeman and van den Meer 2012).

However, large French, German, Spanish, and Italian banks had more pressing concerns regarding the ban on the double counting of insurance subsidiaries and the use of hybrid capital. The data on French banks suggest their strong position,

[9] Core Tier 1 ratios for Dutch banks at the end of 2011—albeit based on Basel II calculations—were ABN AMRO Bank, 11.4 per cent; ING Bank, 9.4 per cent; Rabobank, 12.7 per cent; and SNS Bank, 8.4 per cent.

but the double counting of capital in the banks' insurance subsidiaries—to be banned under Basel III but allowed in the EU legislation implementing Basel III—inflated the figures significantly. The IMF estimated that a ban on double counting would result in French banks losing a total of 28.9 per cent of their Tier 1 capital, preventing several from meeting the 6 per cent threshold and all from meeting the 8.5 per cent threshold (with the capital conservation buffer to be in place from 2019) (IMF 2011b). A ban would hit the three large French commercial banks particularly hard because of *bancassurance*. The French Banking Federation (FBF) considered the BCBS proposal to exclude insurance subsidiary capital from Tier 1 capital as 'completely unacceptable' (FBF 2010: 5), and the French authorities fought a pitched battle against the inclusion of the ban in EU capital requirements legislation.

The *bancassurance* system predominated in a number of other EU member states, including Italy, Spain, and Austria. At least one British bank, the part-state-owned Lloyds-TSB, was also potentially exposed as it is one of the UK's largest insurance providers. The ABI noted that the ban on double counting 'would be particularly penalizing and would also lead to distortive effects on the competition' between the country's two major financial conglomerates, Unicredit and Banca Intesa, given their large insurance components (ABI 2010: 3). Indeed, Unicredit pointed out that, 'In addition, the deduction of the insurance shareholdings breaks the principle of equal competition within the European Community between banks and insurance companies. In fact, financial conglomerates are subject to an additional supervision which avoid the phenomenon of double counting and ensures a wider transparency' (Unicredit 2010: 4). EU implementing legislation of the two previous Basel accords applied the rules to all EU-headquartered banks—not just large entities with cross-border operations—on the grounds of fair competition in the EU internal market.

Therefore, without significant dilution, Basel III would force major changes to national banking systems, especially the three-pillar German banking system. The implications of the new capital rules were potentially greatest for the many non-listed public sector, cooperative, and mutual banks (a much more significant element of the German, French, Italian, Spanish, and even Dutch banking systems than in the UK; see Chapter 4), which did not use equity, relying on other forms of capital to meet capital requirements in the past, including hybrids—notably 'silent participations' (*Financial Times*, 10 September 2010). Basel III menaced a significant overhaul of the capital structure and legal status of internationally active publicly owned banks and mutuals—although exceptions could have been allowed which did not apply to commercial banks with listed equity. Proportionately, the ban on hybrids would hit the German banking system the most, where many public and commercial banks relied on 'silent participations'.

The ABI (2010: 3) argued for the need to 'take into account the national specificities and the various legal categories of banking intermediaries', stressing Basel III's inadequate consideration of 'the legal and operating singularities of the cooperative banks and their network organization'. It (2010: 3) also warned against penalizing capital instruments, 'which in the Italian context can essentially be placed on the same footing as [other instruments recognized in Basel III as Tier 1, including] savings shares, privileged shares and the shares of co-operative banks'. The Spanish Banking Association (2010) similarly argued that 'the process does not take sufficiently into account the plurality existing in the banking sector, especially the different legal forms of entities', and that 'it is noteworthy that the preference shares of many Spanish entities have characteristics could exclude them from being counted as Tier I as defined by the new [Basel III] approach'.

Given the capital position of German banks, it is little wonder that the German bank peak association asked for a grandfathering clause on Basel III capital rules of 'at least 30 years' (Zentraler Kreditausschuss 2010: 3) and the German government demanded the inclusion of 'silent participations' as acceptable Tier 1 capital in the EU capital requirements legislation (see also Deutsche Bank 2010). The Italian and Spanish banking associations also asked for a 'grandfathering period for capital instruments and a reasonable and realistic phase-in period for the new capital standards' (Spanish Banking association 2010: 4).

Leverage Ratio of National Banks in the European Union

The strong opposition of French and German regulators to the use of a leverage ratio reflected the higher ratios of their large commercial banks (compared with the UK) and, in particular, the difficult situation facing German Landesbanks and savings banks, and French mutual banks, given the lack of equity capital (see Table 9).[10] Basel III was written with banks funded by equity finance in mind (hence the emphasis on common equities in Core Tier 1 capital), whereas the external funding of many EU-based banks came from other sources. While the leverage ratio of British banks increased significantly in the two years prior to the outbreak of the international financial crisis, they were historically positioned among the least leveraged in the EU, holding on average over a third more equity as a percentage of assets than German banks (ECB Statistical data warehouse).

[10] For example, the Zentraler Kreditausschuss rejected the concept of the leverage ratio (2010: 30), and the Fédération Bancaire Française wanted to limit the use of the leverage ratio to Basel Pillar II (2010: 2).

On first examination, the figures for French banks appear similarly low. In both countries, average figures for systemically important banks were well below the Basel III recommended assets-to-equity threshold of 33 (or equity-to-asset ratio of 3 per cent). However, the Basel III ban on the double counting insurance subsidiary capital would lower the leverage ratios of the three largest French commercial banks.[11] The opposition of French and German banks and their regulators to the use of a simple leverage rule, as opposed to risk-weighted assets, is also due in large part to the relative importance of trade financing in their operations. Trade financing is high in terms of overall assets but low in terms of risk-weighted assets. Italian and Spanish banks were also critical of the leverage ratio (ABI 2010; Spanish Banking Association 2010). Dutch banks also preferred the optional character of the Basel III guidelines on leverage, especially given the potential impact upon Dutch mortgage banks and public-sector banks (Stegeman and van den Meer 2012). The largest Dutch bank, ING, stressed that 'the concept of the leverage ratio is inherently inconsistent with the liquidity proposals; namely, a narrow buffer for eligible assets would require banks to buy eligible securities, thereby automatically increasing their leverage' (ING 2010: 3).

The Liquidity Position of National Banks Across the European Union

By discouraging reliance on short-term wholesale funding, Basel III liquidity rules affected EU member states differently (see Table 13). French banks are set to be more severely constrained by new liquidity rules because a larger percentage of their wholesale funding is short term (less than one year) than for banks in other EU member states: 28.3 per cent of French debt had maturity of up to a year at the end of 2010. The FBF (2010: 2) called for 'much more realistic liquidity ratios', and BNP Paribas argued that the 'objectives and assumption of the NSFR must be totally reconsidered' (2010: 2).

In Germany, bank debt was issued principally in the form of longer maturity covered bonds; at the end of 2010, only 2.6 per cent had a maturity of less than a year.[12] The adoption of a prolonged phase-in period for the liquidity coverage ratio (to 2015) and the NSFR (2018) can be explained by concerns about the potential impact of these measures on lending, in particular in bank-based continental financial systems, where banks are the

[11] The largest French bank, BNP Paribas, argued that the 'leverage ratio... has proven failures [*sic*] or flawed definitions wherever it has been applied, in particular in the US. Application should be based at most on a pillar 2 approach' (2010: 2).

[12] French and German short-term debt figures reached a peak of 36.6 per cent and 3.8 per cent of the total, respectively, in late 2007. ECB figures: <http://www.ecb.int/stats/money/aggregates/bsheets/html/outstanding_amounts_2010-12.en.html>, accessed on 17 November 2010.

main source of finance for firms, especially for SMEs (*Financial Times*, 26 October 2010; interviews).

The ABI (2010) argued in favour of the inclusion of other 'types of assets—such as corporate bonds, covered bonds, securities included in share indexes, bank shares, non-subordinate bank debt securities and certain sovereign securities' in the Basel III definition of liquid assets. It also argued:

> liquidity requirements do not take into account the operating features of the network systems such as that of the co-operatives.... Given the structure of multi-purpose groups which characterizes the Italian banking system, the Italian banks are led to request... the application [of Basel III liquidity rules] at only the consolidated level and not also at the individual bank level.

The Spanish Banking Association (2010) noted that 'the limited scope of eligible liquid assets [in domestic banks] could also lead to reduced liquidity, particularly during periods of stress'. The largest Dutch bank, ING, criticized 'the proposed, narrow definition of liquid assets', noting that 'calibration does not properly reflect reality in such severe stress scenarios as proposed' and calling for the 'inclusion of a wide variety of assets, including central bank eligible collateral and marketable securities' (ING 2010; see also Stegeman and van der Meer 2012). The Dutch Rabobank focused its entire response to the BCBS consultation on liquidity rules, drawing attention to the 'peculiarities of the financial markets in the Netherlands' and pointing out that 'a too narrow definition of liquid assets will lead to a new concentration risk in the banks' balance sheets, and even this asset class can become illiquid during a market wide crisis' (Rabobank 2010: 2).

The more reticent position of several continental European countries became clear through an examination of the subsequent EU Commission's legislative draft of these liquidity ratios and the provisions ultimately adopted in the EU's CRD IV. The CRD IV fails to include a commitment to implementing the NSFR by 2015 as recommended in Basel III, and rather calls for an observation and review period, with possible adoption after 2018. The CRD IV also includes less prescriptive language than Basel III on what counts as an eligible liquid asset under the LCR: liquid assets would include 'transferable assets that are of extremely high liquidity and credit quality', and 'transferable assets that are of high liquidity and credit quality'.

The crucial explanation of different national positions on Basel III liquidity rules is that the various countries reduced their reliance on short-term wholesale markets at different rates since the height of the financial crisis in 2008 (see Table 8). British banks went the furthest by far to reduce their reliance and increase the resilience of their funding positions, and thus they and the British authorities were most comfortable with the liquidity rules and ambitious phase-in dates. This was due in large part to the early introduction in 2009 of restrictive liquidity rules in the UK, which gave British banks a head start on liquidity. The largest British bank, the HSBC, in its response to the BCBS, welcomed Basel III liquidity rules, arguing that the LCR and the NSFR were similar to those already applied throughout the HSBC group (2010: 1; see also Barclays 2010).

The European Union's Regulation on Structural Measures Improving the Resilience of Credit Institutions

In February 2012, the European Commission appointed a High-Level Expert Group (HLEG), headed by Erkki Liikanen (former Governor of the Central Bank of Finland), to examine structural reforms that would directly affect the structure of individual banks and the market as a whole. The report (HLEG 2012), which was issued in October 2012, did not put forward proposals similar to those of the Independent Banking Commission in the UK (discussed later in this section). Rather, it preferred something more similar to the Volcker Rule in the US, whereby proprietary trading and other high-risk trading activities should be assigned to a separate legal entity if the activities to be separated amounted to a significant share of a bank's business and were above a certain threshold. This would leave unchanged the long-standing universal banking model in Europe, where banks provided a wide range of financial services to their customers.

On 29 January 2014, the European Commission presented a draft regulation on structural measures to improve the resilience of EU credit institutions (European Commission 2014b). The proposal contained a ban on proprietary trading of financial instruments and commodities.[13] Exemptions were provided for financial instruments issued by sovereigns, multilateral development banks, and certain international organizations. The Commission adopted a narrower definition of proprietary trading than that used in the Volcker Rule. Moreover, according to the Commission's proposal, trading on behalf of clients was to be ring-fenced from banks' other activities. On the one hand, the proposal significantly eased the recommendations of the 2012 Liikanen Report on bank structures, so that banks were not automatically required to split their lending operations from risky trading activities. On the other hand, the proposal, if adopted, would have forced a significant restructuring of big banks, such as Deutsche Bank and BNP Paribas (*The Economist*, 1 February 2014).

[13] It is, however, difficult to ascertain whether banks are involved in pure speculation or are engaged in market-making—that is, holding stocks of securities that their clients might want to buy.

According to the Commission's proposal, bank supervisors were to be empowered to require the transfer of other high-risk trading activities (e.g., market-making,[14] complex derivatives, and securitization operations) to separate legal trading entities within the group. This judgement would be based on 'metrics' set by the EBA (*Financial Times*, 29 January 2014). Banks would have the possibility of not separating activities if they could show to their supervisor that the risks generated were mitigated by other means. Exemptions would be allowed if a national supervisor introduced special measures to ensure the effective separation of certain activities to prevent financial instability (*Reuters*, 6 January 2013). The Commission's proposal set out 'derogations' or exemptions from an automatic proprietary trading ban. Article 21 provided a possible derogation from the trading activities separation requirements where a bank was to be subject to national primary legislation adopted before 29 January 2014.[15] The Commission's proposal also sought to prevent banks from holding stakes in hedge funds that could take trading bets on their behalf.

The proposed legislation was to apply only to Europe's thirty biggest banks, albeit holding over 65 per cent of total EU banking assets. According to Commissioner Michel Barnier, the legislation dealt with 'the small number of very large banks which otherwise might still be too-big-to-fail, too-costly-to save, too-complex-to-resolve' (press release, 29 January 2014).[16] Among the criteria whereby a bank would fall under the scope of application of the regulation was its designation as a global systemically important institution under the EU's CRD IV, or if, for a period of three consecutive years, an entity maintained total assets of at least €30 billion and trading activities of at least €70 billion, or 10 per cent of total assets. This made the scope of the prohibition more limited than the Volcker Rule, which also applied to mid-tier, small, and community banks.

The Commission's proposal would also apply to the European subsidiaries of big foreign banks, if they were deemed to be systemically important in the EU. European Union branches of non-EU entities would also fall under the regulation if they met the established thresholds (the asset/trading activity test likely centred on the EU branch, not the larger entity). The proposed regulation provided for a third country-equivalence regime whereby, pursuant to Article 4, foreign subsidiaries of EU banks and EU branches of foreign banks might be exempted if they were subject to equivalent separation rules. The US Volcker Rule, by contrast, applied to the US branches and subsidiaries of

[14] A market-maker in this context is a broker-dealer firm that accepts the risk of holding a certain number of shares of a particular security in order to facilitate trading in that security. Market-making is aimed at securing liquidity in securities that are not frequently traded.

[15] <http://eur-lex.europa.eu/legal-content/EN/TXT/HTML/?uri=CELEX:52014PC0043&from=EN>.

[16] <http://europa.eu/rapid/press-release_IP-14-85_en.htm>.

EU and other non-US banks with a US banking presence. Additionally, application of the Volcker Rule was not limited by a bank's systemic importance. Only a handful of non-EU bans were likely to be affected by the new proposed EU regulation, among them UBS and JP Morgan Chase (*The Economist*, 1 February 2014).

Some described the Commission's proposal as a 'cop-out compromise' (*Financial Times*, 29 January 2014), whereby the Commission sought 'a compromise with everyone... between Volcker and Vickers, between the lobbying of the consumer associations and the financial sector, and between the positions of the UK on one hand and France and Germany on the other' (*Reuters*, 6 January 2014). The Commission's proposal gave countries such as France and Germany leeway to avoid splitting up their big universal banks into separate deposit-taking and more risky investment banking operations. In several EU member states there was political unease over breaking up big banks and giving a competitive advantage to large non-EU rivals (*Reuters*, 6 January 2014).

One peculiarity of the proposed legislation was the reference to 29 January 2014 as a 'cut-off date' whereby a possible derogation from the trading activities separation requirements was provided if a bank was subject to national primary legislation adopted before that date. Indeed, only the UK, France, Germany, and Belgium had adopted legislation on this matter prior to January 2014. Pierre Moscovici, France's Finance Minister, was at pains to point out that the existing laws in France and Germany were 'in complete conformity with the spirit of the Liikanen report' and that EU legislation 'should take into account what has already been legislated in the two countries' (*Financial Times*, 29 January 2014).

Other countries, such as Italy, Spain, and the Netherlands, had deliberately not adopted national legislation on this matter, waiting for EU legislation. When the Commission presented its draft legislation, these countries felt penalized: their banks would not be able to benefit from the possible derogation from the trading activities separation requirements mentioned above because they were not subject to national primary legislation adopted before the Commission's proposal. For example, the ABI, in its response to consultation, strongly supported 'the principle that the regulation affecting the actors of the single EU market should be issued at the EU level, applied and sanctioned in the same way across the EU. No gold-plating or divergent national regulations should therefore in principle be permitted.' Similarly, the Dutch authorities, which had not implemented a national reform, argued that 'it is desirable that structural reform measures take place at the EU level'. Hence, these countries resisted certain elements of the proposal in the Council, joining the already heated debate among the first movers—that is France, Germany, and the UK (interview, Italian official, Luxembourg, June 2015).

The text eventually agreed in the Council watered down the official Commission's proposal in order to accommodate existing national legislation. According to the Council's text, excessive risk stemming from trading activities could be addressed in two ways: either through national legislation requiring core retail activities to be ring-fenced, or through measures imposed by competent authorities in accordance with the regulation.[17] While the possibility of separating excessively risky activities remained, supervisors could also opt to increase capital requirements, as well as other prudential measures. Furthermore, instead of a ban on proprietary trading, as proposed originally by the Commission, the Council approach opted for a mandatory separation of proprietary trading activity.

National Preferences on Bank Structural Reform

National preferences on EU bank structural reforms stem largely from the configuration of national banking systems. First, the universal banking model in many EU member states and the high-risk activities undertaken by most of the EU's largest banks made certain proposals for reform both very expensive for the banks and, ultimately, politically unfeasible. Second, France, Germany, and the UK were the first movers in reforming national legislation on this matter, partly as a way to push the EU policy debate in the direction they favoured. To be sure, this was more the deliberate intention of France and Germany rather than the UK, but the effects were similar: the national measures adopted restricted the win set of the main participants in EU negotiations. In turn, the national measures adopted prior to EU legislation were those that did not significantly constrain the operations of national banks. These points are elaborated in turn.

According to Hardie and Macartney (2016), the 'market-based banking' of the largest universal banks in France and Germany, and their holding of large volumes of trading (risky) assets, explain why the regulatory reforms implemented in these countries were of limited impact and why the French and German authorities sought to water down (with some success) the Commission's legislative proposal. The more the deposit-taking bank was prevented from supporting the trading bank, the higher the financing costs of the trading bank, limiting its profitability. Consequently, larger universal banks would have had to reduce their trading activities to the advantage of foreign trading institutions (Hardie and Macartney 2016). Hence, regulatory arbitrage and bank competition across jurisdictions were at stake (as

[17] <http://www.consilium.europa.eu/en/press/press-releases/2015/06/19-restructuring-risky-banks-council-agrees-negotiating-stances/>, accessed on 7 December 2015.

pointed out, for example, by the Dutch authorities in their response to the Commission's consultation [Netherlands Government 2015]. Moreover, national governments had a further incentive to protect their big national banks. As argued by Christian Noyer, former Governor of the Bank of France, 'the French state would have found itself with only the big Wall Street banks to place its debt. Companies would have only found Wall Street banks to finance their operations' (*Financial Times*, 19 December 2012, cited by Hardie and Macartney 2016).

Given the political sensitivity of bank structural reforms, the British, French, and German authorities decided to move in earnest. The UK was the first mover. The so-called Vickers Report, named after the chairman of the Independent Banking Commission that produced the report, was commissioned by the then newly elected Conservative-Liberal government in 2010. The main proposal in the report was the ring-fencing of banks, whereby the Commission recommended that domestic retail banking services should be separated (i.e., ring-fenced) from global wholesale/investment banking. The ring-fenced part of the bank would be legally and operationally separate from the parent bank and would be subject to higher capital requirements (James 2016). The UK Financial Services Act (Banking Reform Act) in 2013 put into law some of these recommendations. The scope of the national legislation covered banks with more than a specific amount of deposits from SMEs and individuals, and the retail ring fence including SME and individual deposits was established. Ring-fenced entities were prohibited from conducting proprietary trading, with some exemptions (e.g., simple securitizations, debt-equity swaps, and ancillary services). Non-ring-fenced entities were not allowed to accept deposits from individuals or SMEs (see Deloitte 2014: table 1).

In France and Germany, the scope of national structural reforms was limited to the largest banks (by assets). No propriety trading outside the ring fence was explicitly prohibited, although trading was defined in a 'reductive' way so as to include only a limited number of trading activities and certain unsecured transactions with hedge funds. Market-making activities were allowed, but if they exceeded a certain threshold (in the French legislation), or at the discretion of national supervisors (in the German legislation), they could be ring fenced (France) or banned (Germany). There were some limited restrictions on ring-fenced entities: for example, concerning the trading of derivatives of agricultural commodities in France or the provision of payment services in Germany. Non-ring-fenced retail entities could not engage in ring-fenced trading activities or have a relationship with hedge funds (see Deloitte 2014: table 1).

In their joint response to the Commission's legislative proposal, the French and German authorities argued that 'the established and proven *European universal banking model should not be jeopardized* but further improved by separating speculative activities of certain banks on a functional basis' (French and German Governments 2013; emphasis added). The French and German governments (2013) also pointed out their concerns as to the effects of the proposed rules on the real economy:

> It is of vital importance to secure that no activities have to be separated that serve the *financing needs of the economy*. Mandatory separation of a broad range of capital market activities, including market making which is a natural complement to securities underwriting, might significantly hurt the financing of the economy and the functioning of capital markets through a decrease in liquidity (emphasis added).

Finally, the French and German governments (2013) concluded that '[a]ny structural banking reform must respect the *diversity of the European banking system*, including the business model of the savings banks as well as the mutual and cooperative banks' (emphasis added). This point was also made by the Italian, Spanish, and Netherlands governments in their consultation documents (Italian Government 2013; Spanish Government 2013; Netherlands Government 2013a)—while the British did not highlight this concern.

For the UK, the prohibition of proprietary trading by ring-fenced entities in the Commission draft legislation was at variance with the UK Banking Reform Act 2013. However, this variance was unlikely to impair legitimate market-making services or significantly impact upon British banks, notably thanks to a derogation in the Commission draft allowing firms to implement British measures without having to implement proposed EU rules as well—thus removing the risk of a duplicated compliance burden (House of Lords 2014b).

The very large majority of banks in the UK, France, and Germany supported the broad thrust of the regulatory reforms implemented in their respective jurisdictions, as suggested by their responses to consultation. However, most banks expressed a range of concerns, notably with regard to the impact of national legislation upon those market-making activities which they claimed directly supported the financing of the real economy and/or provided useful risk management services to clients. For example, one of the largest French banks, Crédit Agricole, called 'for a more balanced consideration of [such] market-making activities' and argued that 'there is no convincing evidence that structural reform measures would have a direct influence on systemic risk, or for that matter, that large banking structures relying on a combination of different banking activities (so-called "universal banks") are a major risk factor'. The Head of the French Banking Federation, Marie-Anne Barbat-Layani, argued that the adoption of the Commission's proposed regulation would seriously undermine the ability of French banks to serve the European market. Barbat-Layani argued that the adoption of the text would amount to 'one of the most shocking financial scandals in European history' (*Financial Times*, 19 June 2015).

Furthermore, Deutsche Bank (2010: 23) argued that it was not 'necessary to have legal and organizational separation from other activities in order to achieve the desired protection'. The German Banking Industry Committee—a joint committee operated by the different peak associations of banks in Germany[18]—pointed out that 'the symbiotic relations between the banking sector and the real economy... mixed funding from both deposits and the capital market benefits... banking business as a whole' (German Banking Industry Committee 2010: 2). While structural reform would most significantly affect the EU's largest banks, smaller institutions were also concerned. The European Association of Cooperative Banks stated that 'a radical reform of the banking sector would run the risk of: disrupting the market in a fragile economic context; driving costs upwards; rising uncertainty among clients and investors; and hampering efforts towards economic growth' (EACB 2013b: 3).

The ABI (2013: 2) argued:

> [structural] reform should not be aimed at reducing the complexity, interconnectedness and size of all the large and complex banking groups in the EU: on the contrary... an optimal degree of discretion should be granted to the EU supervisory authority in order to identify those banking groups which [should be addressed].

The biggest Italian bank, Unicredit, argued: 'We do not share the Commission's view that the problems experienced during the crisis have a clear link with the way some large banking groups are structured.... On the contrary, the universal banking model increases financial system stability' (Unicredit 2013). Like other banks, Unicredit argued that 'drawing up a line between different activities creates a competitive disadvantage for the EU banking sector and especially for that part primarily focused on serving the real economy'.

On 19 June 2015, EU member states finally reached a common position on a watered-down version of the Commission's proposed structural reform regulation following an Anglo-French compromise (*Financial Times*, 19 June 2015; Council 2015). The deal would apply structural reform only to banks that were deemed either to be of global systemic importance or to exceed certain thresholds in terms of trading activity or absolute size. The deal notably allowed

[18] These associations are the Bundesverband der Deutschen Volksbanken und Raiffeisenbanken for the cooperative banks, the Bundesverband deutscher Banken for the private commercial banks, the Bundesverband Öffentlicher Banken Deutschlands for the public-sector banks, the Deutscher Sparkassen- und Giroverband for the savings banks finance group, and the Verband deutscher Pfandbriefbanken for the Pfandbrief banks; collectively, they represent more than 2,000 banks.

the British authorities to implement stricter Vickers measures—although the exemption applied to all member states. Several observers noted their concerns that the text might lead to fragmentation of the Single Market (see, e.g., ECB executive board member, Benoît Cœuré, quoted in *Financial Times*, 19 June 2015) and a lack of uniformity, which would make it more difficult for the ECB/SSM to enforce rules consistently. Cœuré also complained that the text provided for ill-conceived 'overlapping supervisory powers' (*Financial Times*, 19 June 2015).

Some French concerns were addressed in the compromise deal, including greater reassurance on the common application of 'large exposure rules' that would limit business between different units of a separated bank. However, a number of French and German concerns remained. They argued that British exemption would in effect create a competitive advantage for the British banking system. Notably, they were concerned that non-EU investment banks with large subsidiaries in London would largely be excluded from the regulation. However, the German and French authorities enjoyed their own exemptions. There remained widespread concern that other euro area member states would opt in favour of exemptions which would further undermine the application of a Single Rulebook in Banking Union (*Financial Times*, 19 June 2015).

Conclusion

This chapter has examined intergovernmental negotiations and national preference formation on EU banking regulation with a view to explaining the difficulties in the establishment of the Single Rulebook—which was seen as a core component of Banking Union, even though it applied to the entire EU—as well as the ongoing diversity in member state transposition and implementation (supervision) of the rules. It is argued that the configuration of the national banking system has considerable explanatory power in accounting for member state preferences on both national and EU bank regulation and supervisory practices. In turn, divergent national preferences complicated the negotiations concerning the Single Rulebook.

British policy-makers (joined by the Americans) called for tighter bank capital rules—which was unexpected, given their positioning on financial regulation prior to the financial crisis. The financial crisis hit the UK more severely than most other EU member states, highlighting the growing reliance of British economic growth upon the financial sector prior to 2008 and the massive liability that 'international champions' deemed 'too big to fail' posed for taxpayers. Clearly, early recapitalization (both public and private from

2007 to 2009) improved the capital position of British banks, giving them a massive leg-up in their ability to meet the Basel III rules.

In France, 'national bank champions' had a comparatively weak capital position, given the reliance of most on the 'double counting' of insurance subsidiary capital to meet international capital guidelines. In Germany, the main problem was the even weaker capital position of the 'local champions'. The particularly heavy reliance of the German Mittelstand (SMEs) on bank credit for their external funding reinforced German government concerns about the impact of applying Basel III rules undiluted to the capital and that funding of savings and cooperative banks would squeeze the Mittelstand just when these smaller banks had come to the rescue of this sector in the wake of the financial crisis (see Hardie and Howarth 2013). Italian and Spanish policy-makers were similarly concerned about the impact of higher and tighter capital requirements on both the competitiveness of undercapitalized national banks (especially domestic alternative banks) and financing the real economy, given traditionally underdeveloped equity and corporate bond markets in these two countries.

In the case of the new rules concerning bank structural reform, the configuration of national banking systems and bank models also go a long way to explaining the preferences of the main member states. The UK was the first-mover to propose national legislation on ring-fencing, which was somewhat watered down compared with the initial proposal, following intense lobbying from the banking industry—but nonetheless more restrictive than the EU legislation agreed by the member states in June 2015. Continental countries, first and foremost France and Germany, were worried about the impact of EU structural reform on their universal banks, in particular the large ones, heavily involved in proprietary trading and other risky activities. To this end, they enacted weak national legislation prior to the formulation of EU rules with a view to influencing the EU regulatory debate on this issue (Hardie and Macartney 2016).

If the preferences of the main member states based on the configuration of their national banking systems were significantly different and potentially incompatible, EU legislation reflected convoluted compromises that either kept the EU rules non-intrusive or left some national discretion. The regulation on bank structural reform (agreed by the member states in June 2015, but still needing EP approval as of March 2016) is a clear example of non-intrusive EU rules. The CRD IV, which was based on detailed international standards (totalling more than 200 pages), contained several important differences compared with Basel III, as well as some national discretion. This was the result of intra-EU negotiations, in the context of which member state governments defended preferences which largely reflected the configuration of national banking systems. From 2014, the ECB devoted considerable effort to further harmonization and the reduction of NCA discretion within the SSM. Nonetheless, the claim that 'Banking Union will start out with capital rules that are more like Emmental cheese than a single rule book' (Lannoo 2013: 1) is highly appropriate.

10

Conclusion

This book set out to address two interconnected questions concerning the rationale and the shape of Banking Union: why and why this form of Banking Union? The 'official' rationale for Banking Union was the 'completion' of EMU. The economic rationale was to address the financial trilemma between financial stability, financial market integration and national regulation; supervision; and resolution—this trilemma was made particularly acute by the single currency, and it became untenable in the euro area. The timing of Banking Union was determined by the sovereign debt crisis that followed the international financial crisis and which created a doom loop between banks and sovereigns. Ultimately, the choice for euro area member states was to break up the single currency (with all the dire consequences that would follow from it) or to move forward towards the announced 'completion' of EMU, whereby Banking Union was the first and most urgent step designed to break the doom loop and restore financial stability (one of the elements of the trilemma). In order to reconcile the trilemma, national banking policies (regulation, supervision, and resolution) had to be moved to the supranational euro area level.

National preferences on Banking Union were determined by two main factors: the configuration of national banking systems; and varying national preoccupation with moral hazard. The outcome of the intergovernmental negotiations on Banking Union reflect these different national preferences and the asymmetric bargaining power of the member states, particularly the constrained veto power of Germany, and the 'demanders'—that is, euro area periphery countries hit hardest by the sovereign debt crisis and in greatest need of a deal to bolster confidence (even if this contradicted national preferences).

The most important factor shaping national preferences on Banking Union was the configuration of the national banking system. In our study we have demonstrated the importance of internationalization (measured in different ways), and specifically the domestic reach of internationalization, to explain both interest in Banking Union and, more specifically, national preference on the threshold of ECB supervision (see also Howarth and Quaglia 2016). In the case of the SRM and the DGS, the degree and reach of internationalization as well as the health of national banking systems shaped national preferences. For the DGS, the presence of distinctive domestic DGSs, which in turn reflected national banking system configuration, also shaped the preferences of national policy-makers. Lastly, in the case of the common fiscal backstop, the relative health of national banking systems was a crucial factor in shaping national preferences.

Moral hazard was a concern first and foremost for German policy-makers (see Dyson 2014), and more generally for other northern 'core' euro area member state authorities. These countries were least likely to need Banking Union's fiscal, resolution, and deposit guarantee support mechanisms. They had comparatively healthier banking systems and more sustainable public finances—or, at the very least, they had sufficient financial resources to deal with real and potential bank losses (see Hall 2014). These 'core' countries agreed to Banking Union insofar as it was necessary to bolster confidence in the survival of the euro and avoid the unpredictable economic and political consequences that would follow from the departure of individual member states or collapse. However, they sought to limit their financial commitments to the project and to discourage risky behaviour by banks and sovereigns that could potentially ensue from a financial support mechanisms. France was in between the 'core' and periphery member states. With a large and rapidly rising debt load, one of Europe's largest banking systems, at least two 'too big to fail' banks, and the highest exposure to the euro periphery by most measures, the French had a strong interest in tackling the sovereign debt crisis and downplaying moral hazard concerns. Although the French banking system was in comparatively good health, it was—given the double counting of insurance subsidiary capital—effectively undercapitalized.

Periphery euro area member states had less healthy banking systems and less sustainable fiscal positions, and they were most reliant upon external financial assistance. The authorities of these countries were the least preoccupied with moral hazard; rather, they played up the need to pool bank risk and were broadly supportive of Banking Union. Some euro periphery countries—Spain, Ireland, and Cyprus—had sound public finances prior to the crisis. However, the rescue of national banks resulted in massive deficits and a rapidly rising debt burden, calling into question fiscal sustainability—one side of the doom loop (see, e.g., Quaglia and Royo 2015). Other countries—such as Greece and Portugal—had run unsound fiscal policies for many years prior to the financial crisis. Once financial markets began to challenge the sustainability of national public finances, bond yields increased, and so did

Table 17. National preferences on the components of Banking Union

	ECB supervision	SRM scope	SRF	Calculation of bank contributions to SRF	European Commission power to resolve banks	CDGS	Fiscal backstop	Capital rules—CRD IV/CRR
Germany	Largest systemically important banks only and banks receiving ESM support	Only banks under direct ECB supervision	National funds—until later treaty change/moral hazard concerns	Systemically important institutions should contribute more than others	No	Strongly opposed	Limited and subject to strict conditionality	Qualify Basel III
France	All banks	All banks	Single fund	According to bank's risk profile	Yes	Strongly in favour	Yes: massive	Qualify Basel III
Netherlands	All banks	All banks	National funds—until later treaty change/moral hazard concerns	According to bank's risk profile	No	Moderately opposed/ moral hazard concerns	Limited and subject to strict conditionality	Apply Basel III in full
Italy	Formal 'delegation' to national supervisors for non-systemic banks	All banks	Single fund	According to bank's risk profile	Yes	In favour but keen to preserve national DGS structure	Yes: massive	Qualify Basel III
Spain	Neutral	All banks	Single fund	According to bank's risk profile	Yes	Strongly in favour	Yes: massive	Qualify Basel III

Source: This table was inspired by a table in Schild (2015: table 3) covering European Commission, French, and German preferences on the components of Banking Union.

the cost of government funding, worsening the state of public finances (see, e.g., Pagoulatos and Quaglia 2013). With the downgrading of sovereign debt, banks in the respective countries experienced prohibitive funding costs and depreciating assets, first and foremost the national sovereign debt held in large quantities on their balance sheets—the other side of the doom loop. Italy was in between the two euro periphery sub-groups because it faced a comparatively small balance of payments deficit and a manageable deficit (including a primary surplus), but also a large public debt load and a banking system that proved to be less sound than previously thought.

Finally, the configuration of the national banking system and the 'manageability' of real and potential bank losses contributed to the asymmetric bargaining power in the negotiations on the Banking Union components (see, e.g., Schimmelfennig 2015). Euro area periphery member states were 'demanders', which means that they had limited bargaining power because they needed a deal to help stabilize their banking sectors and reduce government bond yields. There was no 'best alternative' to non-agreement. However, on issues that were crucial for euro periphery member states, such as the resolution fund, they bargained hard, and with some success.

'Core' euro area member states, first and foremost Germany—which was also the largest economy in the EU, the largest banking sector in the euro area, and the main contributor to the EU budget—had the greatest bargaining power, even though the 'best alternative' to non-agreement was unpalatable and fraught with uncertainties for German policy-makers. For these reasons, Germany had constrained veto power (Bulmer and Paterson 2013). Moreover, not all 'core' euro area member states had the same 'win set'. The Netherlands sided with Germany on some matters (e.g., the exclusion of 'legacy' losses from ESM coverage), while on other issues (e.g., the threshold for direct ECB supervision and the mutualization of resolution funds), the Dutch authorities forwarded a distinctive position. Last but not least, countries were sometimes internally divided, in that policy-makers and interest groups had different preferences and priorities—Germany, with its federal political system and three-pillar banking system, was the most notable case. We understand national preferences as the result of domestic political compromises. National preferences on the different elements of Banking Union are summarized in Table 17.

Contributions to the Literature and Proposals for Further Research

This study makes theoretical and empirical contributions to the literature in several sub-disciplines: notably, comparative political economy and European integration studies. Theoretically, we develop the concept of the financial trilemma (Schoenmaker 2011, 2013), explaining why it was so acute in the euro area and how it resulted in the sovereign debt–bank doom loop. This study also contributes to the literature on national banking systems (see, e.g., Hardie and Howarth 2013) by teasing out key features that are relevant to explaining national preferences on Banking Union and its components. We link the discussion of moral hazard to the health of national banking systems and the fiscal position of governments, which in turn affected their bargaining power during the negotiations on Banking Union. Empirically, it examines the key issues in the negotiations on the components of Banking Union, and the Single Rulebook, discussing national preferences and outlining the final deal eventually reached (the burgeoning literature on Banking Union was discussed in Chapter 2). We also 'map' a range of relevant features of six national banking systems.

Our analysis suffers from several limitations, which, however, provide interesting directions for further research. First, in terms of country coverage, we do not examine all EU or even all euro area countries; we focus instead on the preferences of the governments of the six countries with the largest EU banking systems, which provide a balanced mix of core and periphery, with one euro area outsider. As the largest national economies/banking systems, the five selected had considerable clout in EU/euro area negotiations—albeit with the caveat mentioned above about periphery states. The countries selected also embodied different varieties of capitalism, with differing pre- and post-crisis preferences on financial (banking) regulation. Further research could extend the analysis to other countries, most notably the CEECs (see, e.g., Mero and Piroska 2016), or to a selected mix of smaller countries—both groups received limited attention here. Although, for reasons of space and scope, we do not delve into the domestic politics of the various member states, in-depth country studies (possibly with a comparative perspective) would also be welcome.[1]

A second limitation of our study is that it does not investigate the potential or actual operation of the various components of Banking Union, which were being set up while this book was being researched and written—the SSM being the main exception.[2] Research can now investigate, inter alia, the operation of the SSM, cooperation among national and ECB supervisors, and even the convergence of national supervisory practice; the political and financial difficulties linked to the implementation of the BRRD and the construction of the SRM; the convergence of national DGSs; and ongoing divergence in the

[1] See, for example, the special issue focused on the creation of the SSM in *West European Politics* (2016), guest edited by David Howarth and Huw Macartney.

[2] For an analysis of the first Banking Union-wide comprehensive assessment undertaken by the ECB in 2014, see Gren, Howarth, and Quaglia (2015).

application of the supposed Single Rulebook because of national discretions. Of particular interest are the relations between the 'supranational' parts of the Banking Union mechanism (e.g., the ECB in the SSM) and the national elements (e.g., the NCAs in the SSM) (see Gren, Howarth, and Quaglia 2015). Another potentially fruitful avenue of research would be to explore which national authorities adapted better to the new mechanisms or were better able to 'upload' their tools and practices to them.

A third limitation of our study is that it does not consider the implications of Banking Union for the participating countries, for the EU as a whole, and for the relations between the participating and non-participating countries. The expected impact of Banking Union on the participating countries will mainly concern their banking systems, and it is likely to be greatest in countries with large 'alternative' banking sectors (for an in-depth discussion of this issue, see Deeg and Donnelly 2016; Howarth and Quaglia 2016). For the EU as a whole, the expectation is that Banking Union will lead to further economic and political integration in the euro area, as already made clear in the Five Presidents' Report (discussed in the next section). In turn, this is likely to have an impact on EU economic governance and the operation of the Single Market, reinforcing differentiated integration (see Schimmelfennig 2015).

The Never-Ending 'Completion' of Economic and Monetary Union

In October 2015, the President of the European Commission, in close cooperation with the President of the Council, the President of the Eurogroup, the President of the ECB, and the President of the Bourchier, produced what became known as the 'Five Presidents' Report' entitled *Completing Europe's Economic and Monetary Union* (Juncker 2015). This built on *Towards a Genuine Economic and Monetary Union* (the so-called 'Four Presidents' Report') of December 2012, the Commission's *A Blueprint for a Deep and Genuine Economic and Monetary Union* of November 2012, and the Analytical Note 'Preparing for Next Steps on Better Economic Governance in the Euro Area' of February 2015. The 'Five Presidents' Report' stated the objectives of a 'genuine Economic Union', a 'Financial Union', a 'Fiscal Union', and a 'Political Union', arguing that these four unions depended on each other, and should therefore be developed in parallel and with the participation of all euro area member states.

Financial union—meaning a 'single banking system' that would be 'the mirror image of a single money'—was to be completed through the construction of a common DGS (now officially labelled the European Deposit Insurance Scheme—EDIS) and through CMU. The EDIS was justified on the basis that 'the vast majority of money is bank deposits, [hence] money can only be truly single if confidence in the safety of bank deposits is the same irrespective of the Member State in which a bank operates' (p. 11). The 'Five Presidents' Report' also called for a prompt agreement on an 'adequate bridge financing mechanism' to ensure additional funding for bank resolution if the SRF was not enough. Hence, a credit line from the ESM to the SRF was proposed, making clear that 'this backstop should be fiscally neutral over the medium term by ensuring that public assistance [was] recouped by means of *ex post* levies on the financial industry' (p. 8). The report also proposed a review of the ESM's direct bank recapitalization instrument, given the restrictive eligibility criteria attached to it.

The Five Presidents (Juncker 2015) presented CMU as a necessary complement to Banking Union to 'strengthen cross-border risk-sharing through deepening integration of bond and equity markets, the latter of which [was seen as] a key shock absorber' (p. 12). They argued that 'truly integrated capital markets would also provide a buffer against systemic shocks in the financial sector and strengthen private sector risk-sharing across countries. This in turn reduces the amount of risk-sharing that needs to be achieved through financial means (public risk-sharing)' (2015: 12). The Five Presidents saw CMU as ultimately leading to 'a single European capital markets supervisor'. Although CMU was presented as complementary to Banking Union, there were very few similarities and several differences between these two projects. The main intersection between Banking Union and CMU was that the transfer of supervision to the ECB and pressures to converge national supervisory practices would likely increase pressure for policy integration in related areas, such as accounting and audit policies, which fell under the remit of CMU (Véron 2014). The most obvious difference was that Banking Union applied to euro area member states and EU member states that decided to opt in, while CMU applied to all EU member states.

A second difference was that the use of the term 'union' in CMU was somewhat misleading because the Commission presented CMU as 'an incremental improvement of the existing regulatory framework governing the integration of the different, national capital markets' in the EU (Ringe: 6). Third, the logic behind the two 'unions' differed significantly. Banking Union was the direct response to the sovereign debt crisis and the sovereign debt–bank doom loop. Banking Union was designed to address the fragmentation of banking markets and the impact this had on the transmission mechanism of the monetary policy of the ECB. CMU was an indirect response to the sovereign debt crisis and to the decreased funding made available by banks in a number of EU member states to the real economy. The aim of CMU was to build up alternative ways of funding the economy that were underdeveloped in most EU member states.

Fourth, Banking Union centralized the significant elements of the banking policy framework for participating countries, transferring supervision, resolution, and potential support to the Banking Union level. In CMU, centralization was not the main objective. On the contrary, Commissioner Jonathan Hill pointed out that 'the direction we need to take is clear: to build a Single Market for capital from the bottom up, identifying barriers and knocking them down one by one', over a period of several years (Hill 2015). However, some 'centralization' or harmonization through EU reregulation would be needed in CMU, as in the case of previous initiatives designed to promote financial market integration in the EU. Indeed, most of the measures proposed in Hill's Green Paper were not bottom up; they involved top-down EU legislation concerning the harmonization of certain EU capital market rules (Ringe 2015).

In keeping with the analysis presented in this book, EU member states approached CMU in different ways, adopting perspectives that largely conformed to national financial systems. The UK government, pursuing the interests of the largest and most diverse financial centre in the EU, was strongly in favour of opening national capital markets, although it baulked at further supranational institutional developments, thus limiting the Commission's margin of manoeuvre (Véron 2014). In several continental European countries the project did not chime well with a 'traditional' suspicion of capital markets—notably in Germany. In a July 2015 joint letter to Commissioner Hill, the finance ministers of Germany and France, Wolfgang Schäuble and Michel Sapin, expressed some scepticism about copying the financial model of the US:

> Since different economic conditions, legal frameworks and cultural roots constitute Europe's current financial landscape, we will have to find a specifically European solution and should refrain from bluntly reproducing the US financial system. [CMU must be] framed appropriately so as to preserve financial stability and to ensure a level playing field between the various capital and bank based financial instruments... We therefore deem it essential to keep a clear focus on financing business especially SMEs and medium sized companies and infrastructure projects. At the same time this points out that banks should be an integral part of consideration in this respect.[3]

Whereas in most member states, non-financial enterprises would unambiguously benefit from better access to finance, some have argued that 'the impact on the domestic financial sector could be neutral or even negative given the additional competitive pressure' (Véron 2015). For this reason, domestic banks and protected financial 'national champion' market infrastructure firms

[3] <http://www.economie.gouv.fr/files/files/PDF/2015-07-06_letter-about_capital-markets-union_6-july-2015.pdf>.

in some member states, which disliked the prospect of competition from alternative financing channels, were the main foot-draggers on CMU (Véron 2014). Since bank lending had a dominant position in Europe, CMU put savings and retail banks on the defensive. For example, a senior German banker warned that the EU's efforts to build a CMU should not be seen as a way of reducing the role of banks (*Financial Times*, 23 August 2015). Caroline Gourisse of the European Savings and Retail Banking Group argued that 'capital markets funding is in the limelight [at] the moment but bank lending should not be simply harmed because of some financial requirements'.[4] For savings and retail banks the top priority was to loosen the conditions that had been imposed on banks after the crisis, and notably reducing capital requirements.[5]

It is revealing of the bank-centred focus of most EU financial systems that the first building block of CMU—that is, the first legislative proposal officially put forward by the Commission in September 2015—was a package of two legislative proposals: a Securitisation Regulation that set out criteria for Simple, Transparent, and Standardised Securitisations; and a proposal to amend the CRR to make the capital treatment of securitizations for banks and investment firms more risk-sensitive (basically, to reduce those requirements). This focus corresponded to ongoing efforts to rebuild confidence shattered by the financial crisis in securitization markets, thus enabling banks to lend more to the real economy (and specifically to SMEs). While of potential benefit to all EU member state economies, it is clear that the UK's financial sector had a particular interest in reviving securitization—the UK accounted for 22 per cent of European securitization issuance and 46 per cent of the investor base in 2014 (UK Government 2014).

Conclusion

In the first decade of EMU, the single currency contributed to financial integration in the euro area and, more widely, the relaunch of the single financial market spurred financial integration throughout the EU. Hence, EMU and the single financial market proceeded almost in parallel, despite differentiated membership. The incomplete EMU coupled with financial integration eventually resulted in the sovereign debt crisis in the euro area, which most euro area member states and EU institutions hoped to tackle with the establishment of

[4] <http://www.politico.eu/article/moving-money-a-capital-markets-union-primer/>, accessed on 24 October 2015.

[5] <http://www.politico.eu/article/moving-money-a-capital-markets-union-primer//>, accessed on 24 October 2015.

Banking Union. However, Banking Union may have significant implications for the 'singleness' of the single financial market, for which CMU will only partly compensate.

First, Banking Union may skew future financial integration in the euro area. Second, over time, Banking Union may promote the formation of a coalition of member states with similar interests concerning EU banking regulation and supervision, and this coalition may have sufficient bargaining power to tip the balance in EU decision-making on these matters. This concern should not be overstated: national banking systems in Banking Union are structurally different and will retain their distinctive characteristics for the foreseeable future. Nonetheless, the creation of a euro area coalition has been a major concern for the UK (see House of Lords 2014a), home to the EU's largest financial sector, and other EU member states that remain out of the euro area. This concern drove British policy-makers to insist on a reform of decision-making in the EBA (double majority voting) in order to agree to Banking Union. However, this 'safeguard' does not exist in the Council, where euro outsiders can be outvoted. Third, there is a potentially uneasy relationship between the EBA and the SSM. The EBA is responsible for developing the so-called Binding Technical Standards for bank regulation for the entire EU, which are legal acts that specify particular aspects of an EU legislative text (directive or regulation), and for issuing guidelines or recommendations concerning banking supervision across the entire EU. The SSM, with the ECB at its centre, also has regulatory and supervisory powers. Thus, for example, the supervisory manual of the SSM must follow EBA guidelines (in theory), but the ECB and Banking Union NCAs can seek to influence these guidelines (Ferran 2014; Gren 2015). There remains, however, a potential danger of creating inconsistent regulatory and supervisory regimes for banks operating in the EU (Lastra 2013).

References

Acharya, V., and Steffen, S. (2014). 'Making Sense of the Comprehensive Assessment'. *SAFE Policy Letter*, 32, <http://nbn-resolving.de/urn:nbn:de:hebis:30:3-350190>, accessed on 13 April 2015.

Adam, S., and Parras, F. J. M. (2013). 'The European Stability Mechanism through the Legal Meanderings of the Union's Constitutionalism: Comment on Pringle'. *European Law Review*, 2013, 38 (6): 848–65.

Agence France Trésor (2013). *Rapport d'activité de l'Agence France Trésor*. <http://www.economie.gouv.fr/rapport-activite-2012-aft>, accessed on 13 October 2015.

Alexander, K. (2015). 'European Banking Union: A Legal and Institutional Analysis of the Single Supervisory Mechanism and the Single Resolution Mechanism'. *European Law Review*, 40 (2): 154–87.

Alford, D. (2010). 'Supervisory Colleges: The Global Financial Crisis and Improving International Supervisory Coordination', *Emory International Law Review*, 24: 57–82.

Allen, F., Beck, T., Carletti, E., Lane, P., Schoenmaker, D., and Wagner, W. (2011). *Cross-Border Banking in Europe: Implications for Financial Stability and Macroeconomic Policies*. London: CEPR.

Allen, F., Carletti, E., and Gray, J. (2013). *Political, Fiscal and Banking Union in the Eurozone?* Philadelphia: FIC Press.

Allen, F., and Gale, D. (2000). *Comparing Financial Systems*. Cambridge, MA: MIT Press.

Armingeon, K., and Baccaro, L. (2012). 'Political Economy of the Sovereign Debt Crisis: The Limits of Internal Devaluation'. *Industrial Law Journal*, 41 (3): 254–75.

Ayadi, R., and Lastra, R. M. (2010). 'Proposals for Reforming Deposit Guarantee Schemes in Europe'. *Journal of Banking Regulation*, 11 (3): 210–22.

Ayadi, R., Schmidt, R. H., Carbo Valverde, S., Fernandez, F. R., and Arbak, E. (2009). *Investigating Diversity in the Banking Sector in Europe: The Performance and Role of Savings Banks*. Brussels: CEPS Paperbacks, June.

Bank for International Settlements (BIS) (2011). 'The Impact of Sovereign Credit Risk on Bank Funding Conditions'. *Committee on the Global Financial System Paper*, 43. Basel: BIS.

Bank of England (several years, from 2009). 'Trends in Lending'. <http://www.bankofengland.co.uk/publications/Documents/other/monetary/TrendsNovember09.pdf>, accessed on 3 October 2015.

Bank of England (2014). *The Bank of England's Approach to Resolution*, October. <http://www.bankofengland.co.uk/financialstability/Documents/resolution/apr231014.pdf>, accessed on 24 September 2015.

Barclays (2010). *Response to the Consultative Document of the BCBS 'Strengthening the Resilience of the Banking Sector'*. 16 April. <http://www.bis.org/publ/bcbs165/cacomments.htm>, accessed on 21 December 2012.

Barker, A. (2013). 'An Unusable Backstop: 10 Reasons Why the ESM Might Never Take a Stake in a Bank'. *Financial Times*, 13 October.

Barra, C., Destefanis, S., and Lubrano Lavadera, G. (2011). 'Risk and Regulation: The Efficiency of Italian Cooperative Banks'. Centre for Studies in Economics and Finance, University of Naples, Working Paper no. 290.

Basel Committee on Banking Supervision (BCBS) (2010a). *Basel III: A Global Regulatory Framework for More Resilient Banks and Banking Systems*, December. Basel: BCBS. <http://www.bis.org/publ/bcbs189_dec2010.htm>, accessed on 20 September 2015.

Basel Committee on Banking Supervision (BCBS) (2010b). *Basel III: International Framework for Liquidity Risk Measurement, Standards and Monitoring*, December. Basel: BCBS. <http://www.bis.org/publ/bcbs188.htm>, accessed on 20 September 2015.

Basel Committee on Banking Supervision (BCBS) (2010c). *Report and Recommendations of the Cross-Border Bank Resolution Group: Final Paper*, March. Basel: BCBS. <http://www.bis.org/publ/bcbs169.pdf>, accessed on 2 June 2013.

Basel Committee on Banking Supervision (BCBS) (2012). *Basel III Regulatory Consistency Assessment (Level 2) Preliminary Report: European Union*, Basel, <http://www.bis.org/bcbs/implementation/l2_eu.pdf>, accessed on 6 January 2016.

Basel Committee on Banking Supervision (BCBS) (2014). 'Regulatory Consistency Assessment Programme (RCAP) Assessment of Basel III Regulations—European Union', December, <http://www.bis.org/bcbs/publ/d300.pdf>.

Beck, T., (ed.) (2012). *Banking Union for Europe Risks and Challenges*. London: CEPR.

Begg, D., De Grauwe, P., Giavazzi, F., Uhlig, H., and Wyplosz, C. (1998). *The ECB: Safe at Any Speed? Monitoring the European Central Bank*, 1. London: CEPR.

Begg, I. (2012). 'Banking Union: Inevitable, but Profoundly Challenging?'. *CESifo Forum*, 13 (4): 15–20.

Bernanke, B. (2005). *The Global Saving Glut and the U.S. Current Account Deficit*. Speech at the Sandridge Lecture, Richmond, 10 March. <http://www.federalreserve.gov/boardDocs/Speeches/2005/200503102/default.htm>, accessed on 2 February 2013.

Bernet, B., and Walter, S. (2009). 'Design, Structure and Implementation of a Modern Deposit Insurance Scheme', *SUERF Paper*, 5.

Bindseil, P., and König, J. (2012). 'TARGET2 and the European Sovereign Debt Crisis'. *Kredit und Kapital*, 45 (2): 135–74.

Bini Smaghi, L. (1992). 'Waiting for EMU: Living with Monetary Policy Asymmetries in the EMS'. *Temi di Discussione del Servizio Studi della Banca d'Italia*, no. 168.

Bini Smaghi, L. (2008). *The Financial Crisis and Global Imbalances: Two Sides of the Same Coin*. Speech at the Asia Europe Economic Forum, 9 December, Beijing. <http://www.bis.org/review/r081212d.pdf>, accessed on 10 August 2010.

Bini Smaghi, L. (2013). *Austerity: European Democracies Against the Wall*. Brussels: CEPS Paperbacks.

Bini Smaghi, L., and Micossi, S. (1990). 'Monetary and Exchange Rate Policy in the EMS with Free Capital Mobility'. *The European Monetary System in the 1990s*, London/New York: Longman, pp. 120–55.

Blundell-Wignall, A. (2012). 'Solving the Financial and Sovereign Debt Crisis in Europe'. *OECD Journal: Financial Market Trends*, 2: 201–24.

Boccuzzi, G. (2015). *The European Banking Union: Supervision and Resolution*. Basingstoke: Palgrave.

Bordo, M. D. (1990). 'The Lender of Last Resort: Alternative Views and Historical Experience'. *FRB Richmond Economic Review*, 76 (1): 18–29.

British Bankers' Association (BBA) (2012). *BBA statement on European Commission Banking Union Proposals*. 12 September. <https://www.bba.org.uk/news/press-releases>, accessed on 14 July 2013.

Brummer, C. (2012). *Soft Law and the Global Financial System: Rule Making in the 21st Century*. Cambridge: Cambridge University Press.

Brunnermaier, M., Crockett, A., Goodhart, C., Persaud, A.D., and Shin, H.S. (2009). 'The Fundamental Principles of Financial Regulation'. *Geneva Reports on the World Economy*, 11.

Buckley, J., and Howarth, D. (2011). 'Regulating the So-Called "Vultures of Capitalism"'. *Journal of Common Market Studies*, 49 (s1): 123–43.

Buiter, W. (1999). 'Alice in Euroland'. *Journal of Common Market Studies*, 37 (2): 181–209.

Buiter, W., Corsetti, G., and Pesenti, P. (1998). *Financial Markets and European Monetary Cooperation*. Cambridge: Cambridge University Press.

Buiter, W., and Rahbari, E. (2012a). 'The European Central Bank as Lender of Last Resort for Sovereigns in the Eurozone'. *Journal of Common Market Studies*, 50 (2): 6–35.

Buiter, W., and Rahbari, E. (2012b). 'Looking into the Deep Pockets of the ECB'. *CEPR Discussion Paper*, 8974. May.

Bülbül, D., Schmidt, R. H., and Schüwer, U. (2013). 'Savings Banks and Cooperatives in Europe'. *SAFE Paper*, 5, Frankfurt: SAFE. <http://safe-frankfurt.de/uploads/media/Schmidt_Buelbuel_Schuewer_Savings_Banks_and_Cooperative_Banks_in_Europe.pdf>, accessed on 2 May 2015.

Bulmer, S., and Paterson, W. E. (2013). 'Germany as the EU's Reluctant Hegemon? Of Economic Strength and Political Constraints'. *Journal of European Public Policy*, 20 (10): 1387–405.

Bundesbank (various dates) 'Monthly Balance Sheet Statistics'. Frankfurt: Bundesbank. <https://www.bundesbank.de/Redaktion/EN/Standardartikel/Service/Reporting_systems/monthly_balance_sheet_statistics.html>.

Bundesbank (2014). *Compromise Reached over Resolution Fund*. 22 December. <https://www.bundesbank.de/Redaktion/EN/Topics/2014/2014_12_22_compromise_reached_resolution_fund.html>, accessed on 10 December 2015.

Busch, D., and Ferrarini, G. (2015). *The European Banking Union*. Oxford: Oxford University Press.

Buti, M., and Carnot, N. (2012). 'The EMU Debt Crisis: Early Lessons and Reforms'. *Journal of Common Market Studies*, 50 (6): 899–911.

BVR/VÖB/DSGV (2012). *Gemeinsames Positionspapier Zu Einem Einheitlichen Aufsichtsmechanismus Für Kreditinstitute Im Sinne Der Gipfelerklärung Der Mitglieder Des Euro-Währungsgebiets*. July. Berlin: Bundesverband der Deutschen Volksbanken und Raiffeisenbanken; Bundesverband Öffentlicher Banken Deutschlands, Deutscher Sparkassen- und Giroverband. <https://www.bvr.de/p.nsf/20C0CEB3DD976153C1257D25004867D7/$FILE/Positionspapier-AufsichtBVR_DSGV_VOEB_20120822.pdf>, accessed on 2 December 2015.

Caballero R., Farhi E., and Gourinchas P. (2008). 'An Equilibrium Model of "Global Imbalances" and Low Interest Rates'. *American Economic Review*, 98 (1): 358–93.

Campbell, A., Raymond LaBrosse, J., Mayes, D.G., and Singh, D. (2009). 'A New Standard for Deposit Insurance and Government Guarantees After the Crisis'. *Journal of Financial Regulation and Compliance*, 17 (3): 210–39.

Cannas, G., Cariboni, J., Kazemi Veisari, L., and Pagano, A. (2014). 'Updated Estimates of EU Eligible and Covered Deposits'. European Commission, <http://publications.jrc.ec.europa.eu/repository/bitstream/JRC87531/lbna26469enn.pdf>, accessed on 2 January 2016.

Carletti, E., Hakenes, H., and Schnabel, I. (2005). 'The Privatization of Italian Savings Banks: A Role Model for Germany?'. *Vierteljahrshefte zur Wirtschaftsforschung*, 74 (4): 32–50.

Carmassi, J., and Herring, J. R. (2013). 'Living Wills and Cross-Border Resolution of Systemically Important Banks'. *Journal of Financial Economic Policy*, 5 (4): 361–87.

Chang, M. (2013). 'Fiscal Policy Coordination and the Future of the Community Method'. *Journal of European Integration*, 35(3): 255–69.

Chey, H. K. (2007). 'Do Markets Enhance Convergence on International Standards? The Case of Financial Regulation'. *Regulation & Governance*, 1 (4): 295–311.

Christopoulos, D., and Quaglia, L. (2009). 'Network Constraints in EU Banking Regulation: The Case of the Capital Requirements directive'. *Journal of Public Policy*, 29 (2): 1–22.

Ciocca, P. (2005). *The Italian Financial System Remodelled.* Basingstoke: Palgrave.

Cobham, D. (2012). 'Central Banks and House Prices in the Run-Up to the Crisis'. *Oxford Economic Papers*, 65 (1): 42–65.

Committee for the Study of Economic and Monetary Union (1989). *Report on Economic and Monetary Union in the European Community (Delors Committee Report).* Brussels: CEC.

Constâncio, V. (2014). 'Banking Union and European Integration', Speech at the OeNB Economics Conference, Vienna, 12 May. <https://www.ecb.europa.eu/press/key/date/2014/html/sp140512.en.html>, accessed on 2 November 2015.

Cosimano, T. F., and Hakura, D. (2011). 'Bank Behavior in Response to Basel III: A Cross-Country Analysis'. *IMF Working Paper*, 119, <https://www.imf.org/external/pubs/ft/wp/2011/wp11119.pdf>, accessed on 2 November 2015.

Cotterill, J. (2010). 'Basel, Behind the Maginot Line'. *Financial Times*, Alphaville, 13 September.

Crédit Agricole (2014). 'Union bancaire: Crédit Agricole signale plusieurs inquiétudes autour de la supervision unique de la BCE'. *EasyBourse*, 14 May. <https://www.easybourse.com/bourse/international/article/28302/union-bancaire-credit-agricole-signale-plusieurs-inquietudes-autour-de-la-supervision-unique-de-la-bce.html>, accessed on 17 October 2015.

Cuñat, V., and Garicano, L. (2009). *Did Good Cajas Extend Bad Loans? The Role of Governance and Human Capital in Cajas' Portfolio Decisions.* FEDEA monograph.

Darling, A. (2009). Letter to Miroslav Kalousek, Czech Finance Minister. [letter] (Personal Communication), 3 March.

Darvas, Z., and Wolff, G. B. (2013). Should Non-Euro Area Countries Join the Single Supervisory Mechanism? *Danube*, 4 (2): 141–63.

De Grauwe, P. (2011). 'The European Central Bank as a lender of last resort'. *Vox*, 18 August. <http://www.voxeu.org/article/european-central-bank-lender-last-resort>, accessed on 12 September 2014.

De Grauwe, P. (2012). *Economics of Monetary Union*. Oxford: Oxford University Press.

De Grauwe, P. (2013). 'The European Central Bank as Lender of Last Resort in the Government Bond Markets'. *CESifo Economic Studies*, 59 (3): 520–35.

De Grauwe, P., and Ji, Y. (2012). *Mispricing of Sovereign Risk and Multiple Equilibria in the Eurozone*. CEPS Working Documents, Brussels. <https://www.ceps.eu/publications/mispricing-sovereign-risk-and-multiple-equilibria-eurozone>, accessed on 2 March 2015.

De Grauwe, P., and Papademos, L. (eds) (1990). *The European Monetary System in the 1990s*. London: Longman.

De Groen, W.P. (2014). 'Was the ECB's Comprehensive Assessment up to Standard?' *CEPS Policy Brief* 325. 10 November. Brussels: Centre for European Policy Studies, <https://www.ceps.eu/system/files/PB%20No%20325%20WPdG%20ECB%20Comprehensive%20Assessment.pdf>, accessed on 2 March 2015.

De Larosière, J., Balcerowicz, L., Issing, O., Masera, R., Mc Carthy, C., Nyberg, L., and Ruding, O. (2009). *The High-Level Group on Financial Supervision in the EU*. Chaired by Jacques de Larosiere, Report, 25 February. <http://ec.europa.eu/internal_market/finances/docs/de_larosiere_report_en.pdf>, accessed on 23 June 2012.

De Polis, S. (2015). *DGS Alternative Measures in Banking Crises Under the New EU Framework*. Banking Union WG Meeting, European Forum of Deposit Insurers, 26 June. <https://www.bancaditalia.it/pubblicazioni/interventi-vari/int-var-2015/de polis-260615.pdf>, accessed on 22 December 2015.

De Witte, B. (2011). 'The European Treaty Amendment for the Creation of a Financial Stability Mechanism'. *European Policy Analysis*, 6, June. <http://www.sieps.se/sites/default/files/2011_6epa.pdf>, accessed on 12 October 2014.

De Witte, B. (2012). 'European Stability Mechanism and Treaty on Stability, Coordination and Governance: Role of the EU Institutions and Consistency with the EU Legal Order', in European Parliament, *Challenges of Multi-tier Governance in the European Union*, p. 14–17, <http://www.europarl.europa.eu/document/activities/cont/201210/20121003ATT52863/20121003ATT52863EN.pdf>, accessed on 6 January 2016.

De Witte, T., and Beukers, T. (2013). 'The Court of Justice Approves the Creation of the European Stability Mechanism Outside the EU Legal Order: Pringle'. *Common Market Law Review*, 50 (3): 805–48.

Deeg, R. (1999). *Finance Capitalism Unveiled: Banks and the German Political Economy*. Ann Arbor: University of Michigan Press.

Deeg, R. (2005). 'Change from Within: German and Italian Finance in the 1990s', in W. Streeck, and K. Thelen (eds), *Beyond Continuity: Institutional Change in Advanced Political Economies*. Oxford: Oxford University Press, pp. 169–202.

Deeg, R. (2010). 'Institutional Change in Financial Systems', in G. Morgan, J. L. Campbell, C. Crouch, O-K. Pedersen, and R. Whitley (eds), *The Oxford Handbook of Comparative Institutional Analysis*. Oxford: Oxford University Press, pp. 312–51.

Deeg, R., and Donnelly, S. (2016). 'Banking Union and the Future of Alternative Banks: Revival, Stagnation or Decline?', *West European Politics*, 39 (3): 585–604.

Deloitte (2013). *Commission Sets Out Plans for Single Resolution Mechanism in Banking Union—New Single Resolution Board Proposed*. Posted on 10 July 2013. <http://blogs.

deloitte.co.uk/financialservices/2013/07/eu_commission_sets_out_plans_for_srm_in_banking_union.html>, accessed on 16 July 2014.

Deloitte (2014). 'Structural Reform of EU banking—Rearranging Pieces'. *EMEA Centre for Regulatory Strategy*. <http://www2.deloitte.com/content/dam/Deloitte/uk/Documents/financial-services/deloitte-uk-fs-structural-reform-eu-banking-april-14.pdf>, accessed on 4 March 2015.

Demirgüç-Kunt, A., Kane, E. J., and Laeven, L. (2006). 'Deposit Insurance Design and Implementation: Policy Lessons from Research and Practice'. *World Bank Policy Research Working Paper Series*, June. <http://siteresources.worldbank.org/DEC/Resources/Deposit_Insurance_Design_and_Implementationc.pdf>, accessed on 23 November 2015.

Demirgüç-Kunt, A., Kane, E. J., and Laeven, L. (2008). 'Determinants of Deposit-Insurance Adoption and Design'. *Journal of Financial Intermediation*, 17 (3): 407–38.

Demirgüç-Kunt, A., Kane, E. J., and Laeven, L. (2014). 'Deposit Guarantee Database'. IMF Working Paper, WP/14/118, July. <https://www.imf.org/external/pubs/ft/wp/2014/wp14118.pdf>, accessed on 3 September 2015.

Deutsche Bank (2010). *Response to the Consultative Document of the BCBS—'Strengthening the Resilience of the Banking Sector'*. 16 October. <http://www.bis.org/publ/bcbs165/cacomments.htm>, accessed on 2 September 2013.

Deutsche Bank (2012). 'EU Banking Union: Do it Right, Not Hastily!'. *EU Monitor: European Integration*, 23 July. Frankfurt: DB Research. <http://www.dbresearch.de/PROD/DBR_INTERNET_EN-PROD/PROD0000000000291512/EU+Banking+Union%3A+Do+it+right,+not+hastily!.pdf?kid=dbr.inter_ghpen.headline>, accessed on 12 January 2014.

Domanski, D., and Sushko, V. (2014). 'Rethinking the Lender of Last Resort: Workshop Summary'. BIS Working Paper, 79, <http://www.bis.org/publ/bppdf/bispap79.pdf>, accessed on 6 January 2016.

Donnelly S. (2014). 'Power Politics and the Undersupply of Financial Stability in Europe'. *Review of International Political Economy*, 21 (4): 980–1005.

Dragomir, L. (2010). *European Prudential Banking Regulation and Supervision: The Legal Dimension*. Abingdon: Routledge.

Drudi, F., Durré, A., and Mongelli, F. P. (2012). 'The Interplay of Economic Reforms and Monetary Policy: The Case of the Eurozone'. *Journal of Common Market Studies*, 50 (6): 881–98.

Dutch Banking Association (2013). *Position Paper Single Resolution Mechanism*. <https://www.nvb.nl/media/document/000938_pospapsrm.pdf>, accessed on 4 March 2014.

Dutch Ministry of Finance (2013). 'Response to Consultation on Bank Structural reform'. <http://ec.europa.eu/internal_market/consultations/2013/banking-structural-reform/docs/contributions/public-authorities/the-netherlands-ministry-of-finance_en.pdf>, accesed on 27 August 2015.

Dyson, K. H. (1994). *Elusive Union: The Process of Economic and Monetary Union in Europe*. London: Longman.

Dyson, K. H. (2000). *The Politics of the Eurozone*. Oxford: Oxford University Press.

Dyson, K. H. (2010). 'Norman's Lament: the Greek and Euro Area Crisis in Historical Perspective'. *New Political Economy*, 15 (4): 597–608.

Dyson, K. H. (2013). 'Sworn to Grim Necessity? Imperfections of European Economic Governance, Normative Political Theory, and Supreme Emergency'. *Journal of European Integration*, 35 (3): 207–22.

Dyson, K. H. (2014). *States, Debt and Power: 'Saints' and 'Sinners'*. Oxford: Oxford University Press.

Dyson, K. H., and Featherstone, K. (1996). 'Italy and EMU as "Vincolo Esterno": Empowering the Technocrats, Transforming the State'. *South European Politics and Society*, 1 (2): 272–99.

Dyson K. H., and Featherstone, K. (1999). *The Road to Maastricht*. Oxford: Oxford University Press.

Dyson, K. H., and Quaglia, L. (2010). *European Economic Governance and Policies: Commentary on Key Historical and Institutional Documents*. Oxford: Oxford University Press.

Dyson, K. H., and Sepos, A. (2010). *Which Europe? The Politics of Differentiated Integration*. Basingstoke: Palgrave Macmillan.

ECOFIN (Council of Ministers) (2012). *Council Agrees Position on Single Supervisory Mechanism*. 17739/12, PRESSE 528. 13 December. <http://www.consilium.europa.eu/uedocs/cms_data/docs/pressdata/en/ecofin/134265.pdf>, accessed on 27 August 2014.

ECOFIN (Council of Ministers) (2013). *Council Agrees General Approach on Single Resolution Mechanism*, 21 November. <http://www.consilium.europa.eu/uedocs/cms_data/docs/pressdata/en/ecofin/140190.pdf>, accessed on 22 August 2015.

ECOFIN (Council of Ministers) (2014). Single Resolution Fund: *Council Agrees on Bank Contributions*. Press Release, ST 16645/14; Presse 634, 9 December. <https://www.consilium.europa.eu/uedocs/cms_data/docs/pressdata/en/ecofin/146129.pdf>, accessed on 27 October 2015.

ECOFIN (Council of Ministers) (2015). *Proposal for a Regulation of the European Parliament and of the Council on Structural Measures Improving the Resilience of EU Credit Institutions*. EF 121 ECOFIN 528 CODEC 910, 10150/15, 2014/0020 (COD), 19 June. <http://www.consilium.europa.eu/en/press/press-releases/2015/06/pdf/st10150-en15_pdf/>, accessed on 27 October 2015.

Eglene, O. (2011). *Banking on Sterling: Britain's Independence from the Euro Zone*. New York: Lexington Books.

Eichengreen, B. J., (1987). 'Hegemonic Stability Theories of the International Monetary System'. *National Bureau of Economic Research*, Working Paper no. 2193.

Eichengreen, B. J., (1997). 'Saving Europe's Automatic Stabilisers'. *National Institute Economic Review*, 159 (1): 92–8.

Eichengreen, B. J., and Frieden, J. (eds) (1994). *The Political Economy of European Monetary Unification*. Boulder, Colorado: Westview.

Eichengreen, B. J., Wyplosz, C., Branson, W. H., and Dornbusch, R. (1993). 'The Unstable EMS'. *Brookings Papers on Economic Activity*, pp. 51–143.

Eichengreen, B. J., (2000). *Can the Moral Hazard Caused by IMF Bailouts be Reduced?*, 1, Centre for Economic Policy Research.

Elgie, R. (2002). 'The Politics of the European Central Bank: Principal-Agent Theory and the Democratic Deficit'. *Journal of European Public Policy*, 9 (2): 186–200.

Elliott, D. J. (2012). 'Key Issues on European Banking Union Trade-Offs and Some Recommendations'. *Global Economy and Development Working Paper 52*. Washington, DC: Brookings Institution.

Emerson, M., Gros, D., and Italianer, A. (eds) (1992). *One Market. One Money*. Oxford: Oxford University Press.

Epstein, R. (2014). 'Assets or Liabilities? The Politics of Bank Ownership'. *Review of International Political Economy*, 21 (4): 765–89.

Epstein R., and Rhodes, M. (2016). 'The Political Dynamics behind Europe's New Banking Union'. *West European Politics*, 39 (3): 415–37.

Epstein, R. A., and Rhodes, M. (2014). *International in Life, National in Death? Banking Nationalism on the Road to Banking Union*. KGF, Working Paper No. 61, December, Brussels. <http://userpage.fu-berlin.de/kfgeu/kfgwp/wpseries/Working-PaperKFG_61.pdf>, accessed on 12 May 2015.

European Stability Mechanism (ESM) (2011). Treaty Establishing the European Stability Mechanism, signed on 2 February 2012, <http://www.esm.europa.eu/about/legal-documents/ESM%20Treaty.htm>.

Euro Group (2012). *Eurogroup Statement*. 21 February. <http://www.efsf.europa.eu/attachments/2012-02-21%20Eurogroup%20statement%20Bailout%20for%20Greece.pdf>, accessed on 30 October 2014.

Euro Group (2013). *Statement of Eurogroup and ECOFIN Ministers on the SRM backstop*. 18 December. <http://www.consilium.europa.eu/press/press-releases/2013/12/pdf/Statement-of-Eurogroup-and-ECOFIN-Ministers-on-the-SRM-backstop/>, accessed on 30 October 2014.

European Association of Co-operative Banks (2013a). *Key Statistics as of 31-12-13* (Financial Indicators). <https://www.globalcube.net/clients/eacb/content/medias/key_figures/2013_Key_Financial_Figures_FINAL_31.03.2015.pdf>, accessed on 30 October 2014.

European Association of Co-operative Banks (2013b). Draft EACB Response to the Commission Consultation on Reforming the Structure of EU Banking Sector, 11 July, <http://ec.europa.eu/internal_market/consultations/2013/banking-structural-reform/docs/contributions/registered-organisations/european-association-of-co-operative-banks_en.pdf>, accessed on 2 May 2014.

European Banking Authority (EBA) (2015a). *EBA Report on Convergence of Supervisory Practices*. April. London: EBA. <https://www.eba.europa.eu/documents/10180/950548/Supervisory+convergence+report.pdf/9f49ddf9-232f-4062-b34e-ff671d440081>, accessed on 30 November 2015.

European Banking Authority (EBA) (2015b). *Guidelines on Methods for Calculating Contributions to Deposit Guarantee Schemes*. EBA/GL/2015/10. May. London: EBA. <https://www.eba.europa.eu/documents/10180/1089322/EBA-GL-2015-10+GL+on+methods+for+calculating+contributions+to+DGS.pdf>, accessed on 4 December 2015.

European Central Bank (ECB) (2007a). *Monthly Bulletin*, Frankfurt, February. <https://www.ecb.europa.eu/pub/pdf/mobu/mb200702en.pdf>, accessed on 24 November 2014.

European Central Bank (ECB) (2007b). 'Reply to Letter from ECSDA to ECB on Target 2 Securities', February, Frankfurt. <https://www.ecb.europa.eu/paym/t2s/pdf/feedback/ECB-012.pdf>, accessed on 9 April 2014.

European Central Bank (ECB) (2008a). *Monthly Bulletin*. December, Frankfurt: ECB. <https://www.ecb.europa.eu/pub/economic-bulletin/mb/html/index.en.html>, accessed on 30 June 2014.

European Central Bank (ECB) (2008b). *Financial Stability Review*. December, Frankfurt. <https://www.ecb.europa.eu/pub/fsr/html/index.en.html>, accessed on 5 September 2015.

European Central Bank (ECB) (2012a). *Financial Integration Report*. April. Frankfurt: ECB. <https://www.ecb.europa.eu/pub/pdf/other/financialintegrationineurope201204en.pdf>, accessed on 4 October 2014.

European Central Bank (ECB) (2012b). *Verbatim of the Remarks Made by Mario Draghi*. 26 July. <https://www.ecb.europa.eu/press/key/date/2012/html/sp120726.en.html>, accessed on 28 October 2014.

European Central Bank (ECB) (2012c). *Introductory Statement to the Press Conference (with Q & A)*, Presented by Mario Draghi, President of the ECB and Vítor Constâncio, Vice-President of the ECB. December <https://www.ecb.europa.eu/press/pressconf/2012/html/is121206.en.html>, accessed on 25 May 2015.

European Central Bank (ECB) (2013). *Banking Structures Report*. November. <https://www.ecb.europa.eu/pub/pdf/other/bankingstructuresreport201311en.pdf>, accessed on 28 October 2014.

European Central Bank (ECB) (2014a). SSM Quarterly *Report: Progress in the Operational Implementation of the Single Supervisory Mechanism Regulation*. 2014/2. Frankfurt am Main: <https://www.bankingsupervision.europa.eu/ecb/pub/pdf/ssmqr20142en.pdf>, accessed on 30 December 2014.

European Central Bank (ECB) (2014b). *Asset Quality Review: Phase 2 Manual*. March (Frankfurt: ECB), <https://www.bankingsupervision.europa.eu/ecb/pub/pdf/assetqualityreviewphase2manual201403en.pdf>, accessed on 11 June 2015.

European Commission (1990). One Market, One Money. *European Economy*, 44: 68.

European Commission (1994). *Directive on Deposit-Guarantee Schemes*. 94/19/EC, 30 May.

European Commission (2007). *Scenario Analysis—Estimating the Effects of Changing the Funding Mechanisms of EU Deposit Guarantee Schemes*. <http://ec.europa.eu/internal_market/bank/docs/guarantee/interim_report_en.pdf>, accessed on 22 October 2015.

European Commission (2010a). *Proposal for a Directive on Deposit Guarantee Schemes [recast]*. COM/2010/0368 final, 12 July. <http://eur-lex.europa.eu/LexUriServ/LexUriServ.do?uri=COM:2010:0368:FIN:EN:PDF>, accessed on 3 June 2013.

European Commission (2010b). *Impact Assessment Proposal for a Directive on Deposit Guarantee Schemes*. <http://ec.europa.eu/internal_market/bank/docs/guarantee/20100712_summary_ia_en.pdf>, accessed on 2 October 2015.

European Commission (2012a). *A Legislative Proposal for a Regulation Conferring Strong Powers on the ECB for the Supervision of all Banks in the Euro Area, With a Mechanism for Non-Euro Countries to Join on a Voluntary Basis*. MEMO/12/662. <http://eur-lex.europa.eu/legal-content/EN/ALL/?uri=CELEX:52012PC0511,>, accessed on 16 February 2013.

European Commission (2012b). *A Legislative Proposal for a Regulation Aligning the Existing Regulation on the EBA to the New Set-up for Banking Supervision in Order to Make Sure that EBA Decision-Making Remains Balanced and that EBA Continues to Preserve the Integrity of the Single Market*. MEMO/12/662. <http://eur-lex.europa.eu/legal-content/EN/ALL/?uri=CELEX:52012PC0512>, accessed on 27 August 2014.

European Commission (2012c). *Communication from the Commission to the European Parliament and the Council: 'A Roadmap Towards a Banking Union'*. COM (2012) 510 final, 12 September. <http://eur-lex.europa.eu/legal-content/EN/ALL/?uri=CELEX:52012DC0510>, accessed on 21 March 2014.

European Commission (2012d). *A Communication Outlining the Commission's Overall Vision for the Banking Union, Covering the Single Rulebook and the Single Supervisory Mechanism, as Well as the Next Steps Involving a Single Bank Resolution Mechanism*. MEMO/12/662. <http://ec.europa.eu/finance/general-policy/committees/index_en.htm>, accessed on 27 August 2014.

European Commission (2012e). *Commissioner Barnier Appoints Members of a High-level Expert Group on Possible Reforms to the Structure of the EU Banking Sector*. MEMO/12/129, 22 February. <http://europa.eu/rapid/press-release_MEMO-12-129_en.htm?locale=en>, accessed on 16 February 2013.

European Commission (2012f). *New Crisis Management Measures to Avoid Future Bank Bail-Outs*. IP-12-570. <http://europa.eu/rapid/press-release_IP-12-570_en.htm?locale=en>, accessed on 27 October 2014.

European Commission (2012g). *Bank Recovery and Resolution Proposal: Frequently Asked Questions*. <http://europa.eu/rapid/pressReleasesAction.do?reference=MEMO/12/416&format=HTML&aged=0&language=EN&guiLanguage=en>, accessed on 16 February 2013.

European Commission (2013). *Commission Proposes Single Resolution Mechanism for the Banking Union*. 10 July 2013. <http://europa.eu/rapid/press-release_IP-13-674_en.htm>, accessed on 22 October 2015.

European Commission (2014a). *Commission Adopts Detailed Rules on Contributions of Banks to Resolution Funds*. 21 October 2014. <http://europa.eu/rapid/press-release_IP-14-1181_en.htm?locale=en>, accessed on 23 October 2015.

European Commission (2014b). *Proposal for a Regulation of the European Parliament and of the Council on Structural Measures Improving the Resilience of EU Credit Institutions*. COM (2014) 43 final, 2014/0020 (COD). 29 January. <http://eur-lex.europa.eu/legal-content/EN/TXT/PDF/?uri=CELEX:52014PC0043&from=EN>, accessed on 20 October 2015.

European Commission (2014c) Deposit Guarantee Schemes—Frequently Asked Questions, <http://europa.eu/rapid/press-release_MEMO-14-296_en.htm?locale=en>, accessed on 6 January 2016.

European Council (2012a). *European Council 28/29 June, Conclusions*. EUCO 76/12, 29 June. <http://www.consilium.europa.eu/uedocs/cms_Data/docs/pressdata/en/ec/131388.pdf>, accessed on 27 August 2014.

European Council (2012b). *The European Council Agrees on a Roadmap for the Completion of Economic and Monetary Union*. 14 December. <http://www.consilium.europa.eu/uedocs/cms_data/docs/pressdata/en/ec/134320.pdf>, accessed on 27 August 2014.

European Parliament (EP) (2010). *Report on Basel II and Revision of the Capital Requirements Directives (CRD 4)*. Committee of Economic and Monetary Affairs, Brussels, 21 September. <http://www.europarl.europa.eu/sides/getDoc.do?type=REPORT&reference=A7-2010-0251&language=EN>, accessed on 24 January 2014.

European Parliament (EP) (2012). *Draft Report on the Proposal for a Regulation of the European Parliament and of the Council on Prudential Requirements for Credit Institutions and Investment Firms*. COM (2011)0452—C7-0417/2011–2011/0202(COD). Committee on Economic and Monetary Affairs, Rapporteur: Othmar Karas. <http://www.europarl.europa.eu/sides/getDoc.do?type=REPORT&reference=A7-2012-0171&language=EN>, accessed on 17 June 2014.

European Parliament (EP) (2014a). *MEPs' Statement on the Work on the Single Resolution Mechanism for Banks*. Economic and Monetary Affairs Press Release, 9 January. <http://www.europarl.europa.eu/news/pl/news-room/20140109IPR32201/MEPs'-statement-on-the-work-on-the-single-resolution-mechanism-for-banks>, accessed on 25 March 2015.

European Parliament (EP) (2014b). *Parliament Negotiators Rescue Seriously Damaged Bank Resolution System*. 20 March. <http://www.europarl.europa.eu/news/de/news-room/20140319IPR39310/Parliament-negotiators-rescue-seriously-damaged-bank-resolution-system>, accessed on 24 April 2015.

European Savings Banks Group (2013). Key Figures. <http://www.wsbi-esbg.org>, accessed on 30 September 2014.

Featherstone, K. (2011). 'The JCMS Annual Lecture: The Greek Sovereign Debt Crisis and EMU: A Failing State in a Skewed Regime'. *Journal of Common Market Studies*, 49 (2): 193–217.

Febelfin (2013). 'ECOFIN Reaches Agreement on General Approach on Single Resolution Mechanism', 24 December. <https://www.febelfin.be/en/eu-flash-single-resolution-mechanism-bank-recovery-and-resolution-brrd-deposit-guarantee-scheme-bank>, accessed on 24 June 2015.

Feldstein, M. (1997). 'EMU and International Conflict'. *Foreign Affairs*, 76 (6): 60–73.

Ferran, E. (2014). 'European Banking Union and the EU Single Financial Market: More Differentiated Integration, or Disintegration?' *University of Cambridge Faculty of Law Research Paper*, 24. <http://papers.ssrn.com/sol3/papers.cfm?abstract_id=2426580>, accessed on 13 April 2015.

Ferran, E., and Babis, V. (2013). 'The European Single Supervisory Mechanism'. *Journal of Corporate Law Studies*, 13: 255–85.

Finance Watch (2014). *EU Bank Stress Tests and AQR Show the Need for a Binding Leverage Ratio*. 29 October. <http://www.finance-watch.org/press/press-releases/965>, accessed on 27 August 2015.

Financial Services Authority (FSA) (2009). *The Turner Review: A Regulatory Response To The Global Banking Crisis*. March. <http://www.fsa.gov.uk/pubs/other/turner_review.pdf>, accessed on 2 April 2015.

Financial Stability Board (FSB) (2008). *Report of the Financial Stability Forum on Enhancing Market and Institutional Resilience*. 7 April. <http://www.fsb.org/wp-content/uploads/r_0804.pdf?page_moved=1,>, accessed on 13 April 2014.

Financial Stability Board (FSB) (2011). *Key Attributes Of Effective Resolution Regimes For Financial Institutions*. November. <http://www.fsb.org/wp-content/uploads/r_111104cc.pdf?page_moved=1>, accessed on 14 May 2015.

Financial Stability Board (FSB) (2012). *FSB Publishes Peer Review on Deposit Insurance Systems*. Press release, Ref no: 13/2012. 8 February. <http://www.financialstabilityboard.org/wp-content/uploads/pr_120208.pdf>, accessed on 26 November 2014.

Finnish Ministry of Finance (2012). *Joint Statement of the Ministers of Finance of Germany, the Netherlands and Finland*. Press Release 175/2012. 25 September, <http://vm.fi/en/article/-/asset_publisher/joint-statement-of-the-ministers-of-finance-of-germany-the-netherlands-and-finland>, accessed on 27 August 2015.

Fitoussi, J. (1993). *Competitive Disinflation: The Mark and Budgetary Politics in Europe*. Oxford: Oxford University Press.

Fonteyne, W. (2007). *Cooperative Banks in Europe: Policy Issues*. IMF Working Paper, WP/07/159. Washington: IMF. <https://www.imf.org/external/pubs/ft/wp/2007/wp07159.pdf>, accessed on 2 December 2015.

Fratianni, M., and J. Von Hagen (1992). *The European Monetary System and European Monetary Union*. Boulder: Westview Press.

French and German Governments (2013). *Consultation on Reforming the Structure of the EU Banking sector*. Joint German and French response. <http://ec.europa.eu/internal_market/consultations/2013/banking-structural-reform/contributions_en.htm>, accessed on 26 July 2014.

French Banking Federation (FBF) (2010). *Comments on the Consultative Documents Published by the BCBS*, 16 October. <http://www.bis.org/publ/bcbs165/cacomments.htm>, accessed on 3 December 2012.

French Banking Federation (FBF) (2012). *The FBF Favours a Single Supervision Mechanism for European Banks* (Original as 'La FBF est favorable à une supervision européenne unique des banques'). 12 September. Paris: Fédération Bancaire Française. <http://www.fbf.fr/en/press-room/press-releases/the-fbf-favours-a-single-supervision-mechanism-for-european-banks>, accessed on 26 November 2015.

French Senate (2013). *Proposition de règlement du Parlement européen et du Conseil établissant des règles et une procédure uniformes pour la résolution des établissements de crédit et de certaines entreprises d'investissement dans le cadre d'un mécanisme de résolution unique et d'un Fonds de résolution bancaire unique, et modifiant le règlement (UE) n° 1093/2010 du Parlement européen et du Conseil*. <http://www.senat.fr/ue/pac/E8533.html>, accessed on 26 November 2015.

Frieden, J. (1994). 'Making Commitments: France and Italy in the European Monetary System, 1979-85', in B. Eichengreen and J. Frieden (eds), *The Political Economy of European Monetary Unification*. Boulder: Westview Press, pp. 25–47.

Frieden, J. (1996). 'The Impact of Goods and Capital Market Integration on European Monetary Politics'. *Comparative Political Studies*, 29 (2): 193–222.

Fund for the Guarantee of Deposits and Resolution (FDGR) (2015). 'Le FGDR gère 3 types de garanties', <https://www.garantiedesdepots.fr/fr/garanties-du-fgdr/la-garantie-des-depots>, accessed on 2 September 2015.

Garcia, G., and Prast, H. (2003). 'Depositor and Investor Protection in the EU and the Netherlands: A Brief History'. *Journal of European Economic History*, 32 (3): 307–48.

Garcia, G., and Prast, H. (2004). *Depositor and Investor Protection in the Netherlands: Past, Present and Future*. Amsterdam: De Nederlandsche Bank. <http://www.dnb.nl/binaries/OSVolNr2_tcm46-146642.pdf>, accessed on 6 December 2015.

Garicano, L. (2012). 'Five Lessons from the Spanish Cajas Debacle for a New Euro Wide Supervisor', in T. Beck (ed) *Banking Union for Europe: Risks and Challenges*. London: CEPR, pp. 77–84.

Gavilán Hernández de Cos, P., Jimeno, J. F., and Rojas, J. A. (2011). 'The Crisis in Spain: Origins and Developments', in M. Beblavy, D. Cobham, and L. Odor (eds), *The Euro Area and The Financial Crisis*. Cambridge: Cambridge University Press.

German Banking Industry Committee (2010). 'Opinion to Directorate General Internal Market and Services: Consultation Paper on Reforming the Structure of the EU Banking Sector'. 13 July, <https://die-dk.de/media/files/GBIC_Opinion_CP_Reforming_Structure_EU_Banking_Sector_100713_B1GDAfe.pdf>, accessed on 14 July 2015.

German Federal Government (2015). *The EMU Needs a Stronger Banking Union, but Must Get it Right*. Non paper, 8 September, on file with the authors.

German Law Journal (2013). Special Issue the ESM before the Courts, 14 (1).

German Law Journal (2014). Special Issue the OMT, 15 (1).

Giannini, C. (1999). 'Enemy of None But a Common Friend of All? An International Perspective on the Lender-Of-Last-Resort Function'. *International Monetary Fund Working Paper*, 10. <https://www.imf.org/external/pubs/ft/wp/1999/wp9910.pdf>, accessed on 19 August 2015.

Giavazzi, F., and Giovannini, A. (1989). *Limiting Exchange Rate Flexibility: The European Monetary System*. Massachusetts: MIT Press.

Giavazzi, F., Micossi, S., and Miller, M. (1988). *The European Monetary System*. Cambridge: Cambridge University Press.

Giavazzi, F., and Pagano, M. (1988). 'The Advantage of Tying One's Hands: EMS Discipline and Central Bank Credibility'. *European Economic Review*, 32 (5): 1055–75.

Giordano, F. (2007). *Storia del Sistema Bancario Italiano*. Roma: Doninzelli.

Gocaj, L., and Meunier, S. (2013). 'Time Will Tell: the EFSF, the ESM, and the Euro Crisis'. *Journal of European Integration*, 35 (3): 239–53.

Goodhart, C. A. E. (1995). *The Central Bank and the Financial System*. Boston: MIT Press.

Goodhart, C. A. E. (1999). 'Myths about the Lender of Last Resort'. *International Finance*, 2 (3): 339–60.

Goodhart, C. A. E., and Eric, A. (2000). *Which Lender of Last Resort for Europe?* Central Banking Publications.

Goodhart, C. A. E., and Schoenmaker, D. (1995). 'Should the Functions of Monetary Policy and Banking Supervision be Separated?'. *Oxford Economic Papers*: 539–60.

Goodhart, C. A. E., and Schoenmaker, D. (2014). 'The ECB as Lender of Last Resort?'. *DSF Policy Brief*, 36. <http://voxeu.org/article/ecb-lender-last-resort>, accessed on 19 August 2015.

Goyal, R., Brooks, P. K, Pradhan, M., Tressel, T., Dell'Ariccia, G., Leckow, R., Pazarbasioglu, C., and IMF Staff Team (2013). *A Banking Union for the Euro Area*. Washington: International Monetary Fund. <https://www.imf.org/external/pubs/ft/sdn/2013/sdn1301.pdf>, accessed on 19 August 2015.

Greenspan, A. (1996). *Remarks by Chairman Alan Greenspan at the Annual Dinner and Francis Boyer Lecture of the American Enterprise Institute for Public Policy Research.* 5 December. <http://www.federalreserve.gov/boarddocs/speeches/1996/19961205.htm>, accessed on 24 April 2013.

Gren, J. (2015). 'Integration Through Differentiation Uneasy Interactions of the (Bank) Single Market and the Banking Union', *Studia Diplomatica Egmont,* Vol. LXVII, Issue 2.

Gren, J., Howarth, D., and Quaglia, L. (2015). 'Supranational Banking Supervision in Europe: The Construction of a Credible Watchdog'. *Journal of Common Market Studies,* 53 (S1): 181–99.

Grilli, V. (2012). *Parliamentary Hearing of the Treasury Minister.* December. <http://documenti.camera.it/_dati/leg16/lavori/stencomm/06/audiz2/2012/1211/INTERO.pdf>, accessed on 14 October 2015.

Gros, D. (2012a). *The Treaty on Stability, Coordination and Governance in the Economic and Monetary Union* (aka Fiscal Compact). CEPS Commentary, 8 March. <https://www.ceps.eu/system/files/DG%20Fiscal%20Compact.pdf>, accessed on 14 October 2014.

Gros, D. (2012b). 'The Single European Market in Banking in Decline – ECB to the Rescue?', in T. Beck (ed), *Banking Union for Europe—Risks and Challenges.* London: CEPR, pp. 49–54.

Gros, D. (2012c). 'Macroeconomic Imbalances in the Euro Area: Symptom or Cause of the Crisis?' CEPS Policy Briefs. Centre for European Policy Studies, No. 266, April, <https://www.ceps.eu/publications/macroeconomic-imbalances-euro-area-symptom-or-cause-crisis>, accessed on 4 September 2014.

Gros, D., Alcidi, C., and Giovanni, A. (2012). 'Central Banks in Times of Crisis: The FED vs. the ECB'. *CEPS Policy Brief,* 276. 11 July. <https://www.ceps.eu/publications/central-banks-times-crisis-fed-vs-ecb>, accessed on 14 October 2014.

Gros, D., and Mayer, T. (2010). 'How to Deal with Sovereign Default in Europe: Create the European Monetary Fund Now!'. *CEPS Policy Brief,* 202. <http://papers.ssrn.com/sol3/papers.cfm?abstract_id=1610303>, accessed on 19 September 2015.

Gros, D., and Schoenmaker, D. (2012). 'A European Deposit Insurance and Resolution Fund: An Update'. *DFS Policy Paper,* 26. Amsterdam: Duisenberg School of Finance. <https://www.ceps.eu/publications/european-deposit-insurance-and-resolution-fund-update>, accessed on 18 November 2015.

Gros, D., and Schoenmaker, D. (2014). 'European Deposit Insurance and Resolution in the Banking Union'. *Journal of Common Market Studies,* 52 (3): 529–46.

Gros, D., and Thygesen, N. (1998). *European Monetary Integration: From the European Monetary System Towards Monetary Union.* London: Longman.

Grossman, E. (2006). 'Europeanization as an Interactive Process: German Public Banks Meet EU State Aid Policy'. *Journal of Common Market Studies,* 44 (2): 325–48.

Grossman, E., and Woll, C. (2014). 'Saving the Banks. The Political Economy of Bailouts'. *Comparative Political Studies,* 47 (4): 574–600.

Group of Thirty (2009). *Financial Reform: A Framework for Financial Stability.* <http://fic.wharton.upenn.edu/fic/Policy%20page/G30Report.pdf>, accessed on 14 May 2013.

Gutierrez, E. (2008). 'The Reform of Italian Cooperative Banks: Discussion of Proposals'. *International Monetary Fund Working Paper*, WP/08/74, Washington. <https://www.imf.org/external/pubs/ft/wp/2008/wp0874.pdf>, accessed on 2 December 2015.

Haas, P. (1992). 'Introduction: Epistemic Communities and International Policy Coordination'. *International Organization*, 46 (1): 1–35.

Hackenthal, A. (2004). 'German Banks and Banking Structure' in J. P. Krahnen and R. H. Schmidt (eds), *The German Financial System*. 2nd edn. Oxford: Oxford University Press, pp. 7 1–105.

Hackethal, A., and Schmidt, R. H. (2005). 'Structural Change in the German Banking System?'. *Working Paper Series/Johann-Wolfgang-Goethe-Universität Frankfurt am Main, Fachbereich Wirtschaftswissenschaften: Finance & Accounting*, 147.

Hall, P. (1993). 'Policy Paradigm, Social Learning and the State: The Case of Economic Policy Making in Britain'. *Comparative Politics*, 25: 275–96.

Hall, P. (2014). 'Varieties of Capitalism and the Euro Crisis'. *West European Politics*, 37 (6): 1223–43.

Hampl, Mojmír (2015). 'Banking Union: The Perspective of One Non-SSM Member State', Vice-Governor, Czech National Bank ESE Conference, Prague, 1 October, on file with the authors.

Hardie, I., and Howarth, D. (2009). 'Die Krise but Not La Crise?: The Financial Crisis and the Transformation of German and French Banking Systems'. *Journal of Common Market Studies*, 47 (5): 1017–39.

Hardie, I., and Howarth, D. (eds) (2013). *Market-Based Banking, Varieties of Financial Capitalism and the Financial Crisis*. Oxford: Oxford University Press.

Hardie, I., Howarth, D., Maxfield, S., and Verdun, A. (2013). 'Banks and the False Dichotomy in the Comparative Political Economy of Finance'. *World Politics*, 65 (4): 691–728.

Hardie, I., and Macartney, H. (2016). *West European Politics*. Forthcoming.

Hardie, I., and Maxfield, S. (2013). 'Market-Based Banking as the Worst of All World: Illustrations from the United States and United Kingdom', in I. Hardie and D. Howarth (eds) (2013). *Market-Based Banking, Varieties of Financial Capitalism and the Financial Crisis*. Oxford: Oxford University Press.

Hefeker, C. (1998). *Interest Groups and Monetary Integration: The Political Economy of Exchange Regime Choice*. Boulder: Westview Press.

Heipertz, M., and Verdun, A. (2012). *Ruling Europe: The Politics of the Stability and Growth Pact*. Cambridge: Cambridge University Press.

Heisenberg, D. (1999). *The Mark of the Bundesbank: Germany's Role in European Monetary Cooperation*. Boulder: Lynne Rienner Publisher.

Hennessy, A. (2014). 'Redesigning Financial Supervision in the European Union (2009–2013)', *Journal of European Public Policy*, 21 (2): 151–68.

Herring, R. J. (2007). 'The Rocky Road to Implementation of Basel II in the United States'. *Atlantic Economic Journal*, 35 (4): 411–29.

Higgins, M., and Klitgaard, T. (2011). 'Saving Imbalances and the Euro Area Sovereign Debt Crisis'. *Current Issues in Economics and Finance*, 17 (5), <https://www.newyorkfed.org/medialibrary/media/research/current_issues/ci17-5.pdf>, accessed on 29 December 2015.

High-Level Expert Group on Reforming the Structure of the EU Banking Sector (HLEG) (2012), *Final Report.* Chaired by Erkki Liikanen, October, <http://ec.europa.eu/finance/bank/docs/high-level_expert_group/report_en.pdf>, accessed on 6 January 2016.

Hill, C. (2015). 'Q & A on the Green Paper on Building a Capital Markets Union', <http://europa.eu/rapid/press-release_MEMO-15-4434_en.htm>.

Hodson, D. (2013). 'The Eurozone in 2012: "Whatever It Takes to Preserve the Euro?" *Journal of Common Market Studies*, 51 (S1): 183–200.

House of Commons, European Scrutiny Committee (2010). *9th Report Session 2010–11.* London. <http://www.publications.parliament.uk/pa/cm201011/cmselect/cmeuleg/428-ix/428ix.pdf>, accessed on 20 December 2015.

House of Lords (2012a). *European Banking Union: Key issues and Challenges.* London. <http://ec.europa.eu/dgs/secretariat_general/relations/relations_other/npo/docs/united_kingdom/2012/com20120280_510_511_512/com20120280_510_511_512_lords_opinion_en.pdf>, accessed on 20 December 2015.

House of Lords (2012b). *European Union Committee—Twenty-Fifth Report—The Euro Area Crisis.* 7 February. London. <http://www.publications.parliament.uk/pa/ld201012/ldselect/ldeucom/260/26002.htm>, accessed on 20 December 2015.

House of Lords (2014a). *Genuine Economic and Monetary Union and the Implications for the UK.* London. <http://www.parliament.uk/business/committees/committees-a-z/lords-select/eu-economic-and-financial-affairs-and-international-trade-sub-committee-a/inquiries/parliament-2010/genuine-economic-monetary-union/>, accessed on 20 December 2015.

House of Lords (2014b). 'Bank Structural Reform', Correspondence with Minister <http://www.parliament.uk/documents/lords-committees/eu-sub-com-a/BankStructuralReform/Bank-Structural-Reform-Correspondence.pdf>, accessed on 7 September 2015.

Howarth, D. (2001). *The French Road to European Monetary Union.* Palgrave: London.

Howarth, D. (2007). 'Making and Breaking the Rules: French policy on EU "Gouvernement Économique"'. *Journal of European Public Policy*, 14 (7): 1061–78.

Howarth, D. (2012). 'Defending the euro: Unity and disunity among Europe's central bankers', in J. Hayward and R. Würzel (eds) *European Disunion: Between Sovereignty and Solidarity.* Basingstoke: Palgrave Macmillan, pp. 131–45.

Howarth, D. (2013). 'France and the International Financial Crisis: the Legacy of State-led Finance'. *Governance*, 26 (3): 369–95.

Howarth, D., and Loedel, P. (2005). *The European Central Bank: The New European Leviathan*? Basingstoke: Palgrave Macmillan.

Howarth, D., and Quaglia, L. (2013a). 'Banking Union as Holy Grail: Rebuilding the Single Market in Financial Services, Stabilizing Europe's Banks and "Completing" Economic and Monetary Union'. *Journal of Common Market Studies*, 51 (1): 103–23.

Howarth, D., and Quaglia, L. (2013b). 'Banking on Stability: The Political Economy of New Capital Requirements in the European Union'. *Journal of European Integration*, 35 (3): 333–46.

Howarth, D., and Quaglia, L. (2014). 'The Steep Road to Banking Union: The Setting up of the Single Resolution Mechanism', *Journal of Common Marker Studies Annual Review*, 50 (s1): 125–40.

Howarth, D., and Quaglia, L. (2015a). 'The Comparative Political Economy of Basel III in Europe'. *Edinburgh School of Law Research Paper* No. 2015/19, *Europa Working Paper* No 2015/03. <http://papers.ssrn.com/sol3/papers.cfm?abstract_id=2630555>, accessed on 13 December 2015.

Howarth, D., and Quaglia, L. (2015b). 'The New Intergovernmentalism in Financial Regulation and European Banking Union', in C. Bickerton, D. Hodson, and U. Puetter (eds), *The New Intergovernmentalism.* Oxford University Press, Oxford, pp. 146–62.

Howarth, D., and Quaglia, L. (2016). 'International Banking, Alternative Banks, and the Single Supervisory Mechanism'. *West European Politics*, 39 (3), pp. 438–61.

Huertas, T. (2009). 'The Rationale for and Limits of Bank Supervision', *Speech LSE Financial market Group*, January. <http://www.lse.ac.uk/fmg/documents/events/conferences/2009/regulatoryResponse/1170_Huertas.pdf>, accessed on 23 December 2014.

Huertas, T., and Nieto, M. (2014). 'How Much is Enough? The Case of the Resolution Fund in Europe'. *VoxEU.* 18 March. <http://voxeu.org/article/ensuring-european-resolution-fund-large-enough>, accessed on 25 June 2015.

ING (2010). *ING Position Paper on Capital & Liquidity Reform Proposals.* 16 April. <https://www.bis.org/publ/bcbs165/ing.pdf>, accessed on 12 January 2015.

ING (2013). *2012 Annual Report of ING Bank.* <http://www.ing.com/Investor-relations/Annual-Reports.htm>, accessed on 12 January 2015.

ING (2014). *ING Bank Annual Report 2014.* Amsterdam: ING Bank.

ING (2015). *2014 ING Annual Report of ING Bank.* <http://www.ing.com/Investor-relations/Annual-Reports.htm>, accessed on 2 January 2016.

International Monetary Fund (IMF) (2005). 'Global Imbalances: A Saving and Investment Perspective'. In *World Economic Outlook.* September. <https://www.imf.org/external/pubs/ft/weo/2005/02/pdf/chapter2.pdf>, accessed on 23 December 2015.

International Monetary Fund (IMF) (2008). *Country Report Euro Area Policies: Article IV.* Consultation, No. 08/262, August. <http://www.imf.org/external/pubs/ft/scr/2008/cr08262.pdf>, accessed on 5 December 2015.

International Monetary Fund (IMF) (2011a). *United Kingdom: Staff Report for the 2011 Article IV Consultation—Supplementary Information.* IMF Country Report No. 11/220. July. <http://www.imf.org/external/pubs/ft/scr/2011/cr11220.pdf>, accessed on 16 February 2013.

International Monetary Fund (IMF) (2011b). *United Kingdom: Crisis Management and Bank Resolution Technical Note.* IMF Country Report No. 11/228. July. <https://www.imf.org/external/pubs/ft/scr/2011/cr11228.pdf>, accessed on 16 February 2013.

International Monetary Fund (IMF) (2011c). *France: Selected Issues Paper.* IMF Country Report No. 11/212. July. <https://www.imf.org/external/pubs/ft/scr/2011/cr11212.pdf>, accessed on 16 February 2013.

International Monetary Fund (IMF) (2011d). *Germany: Technical Note on Crisis Management Arrangements.* IMF Country Report No. 11/368. December 2011. <https://www.imf.org/external/pubs/ft/scr/2011/cr11368.pdf>, accessed on 23 March 2013.

International Monetary Fund (IMF) (2012a). *Spain: The Reform of Spanish Savings Banks Technical Notes.* IMF Country Report No. 12/141. June. <https://www.imf.org/external/pubs/ft/scr/2012/cr12141.pdf>, accessed on 2 May 2013.

International Monetary Fund (IMF) (2012b). *Spain: Financial Stability Assessment.* IMF Country Report No. 12/137. June. <https://www.imf.org/external/pubs/ft/scr/2012/cr12137.pdf>, accessed on 3 April 2013.

International Monetary Fund (IMF) (2012c). *IMF Calls on Eurozone to Take Determined Action in Response to Crisis.* IMF Survey Online, Economic Health Check. 18 July. <http://www.imf.org/external/pubs/ft/survey/so/2012/int071812a.htm>, accessed on 5 October 2012.

International Monetary Fund (IMF) (2012d). *France: Financial Stability Assessment.* IMF Country Report No. 12/137, December. <https://www.imf.org/external/pubs/ft/scr/2012/cr12341.pdf>, accessed on 13 March 2014.

International Monetary Fund (IMF) (2013a). *A Banking Union for the Euro Area: Technical Background Notes.* 13 February. <http://www.imf.org/external/pubs/ft/sdn/2013/sdn1301technt.pdf>, accessed on 2 March 2013.

International Monetary Fund (IMF) (2013b). *Technical Note on Deposit Insurance.* Financial Sector Assessment Programme, European Union, March, IMF Country Report No. 13/66, March. <https://www.imf.org/external/pubs/ft/scr/2012/cr12341.pdf>, accessed on 17 November 2013.

International Monetary Fund (IMF) (2013c). *Italy: Technical Note on Interconnectedness and Spillover Analysis on Italy.* <https://www.imf.org/external/pubs/ft/scr/2013/cr13347.pdf>, accessed on 13 June 2014.

International Monetary Fund (IMF) (2014). *Euro Area Policies: 2014 Article IV Consultation-Staff Report, Press Release, and Statement by the Executive Director,* <https://www.imf.org/external/pubs/ft/scr/2014/cr14198.pdf>, accessed on 12 January 2015.

International Monetary Fund (IMF) (2015). *The Report on Central and Eastern Europe: New Member States (NMS) Policy Forum, 2014, Cluster Consultations—Common Policy Frameworks and Challenges.* IMF Country Report No. 15/97. <https://www.imf.org/external/pubs/ft/scr/2015/cr1597.pdf>, accessed on 4 September 2015.

International Monetary Fund (IMF) *Financial Stability Indicators.* IMF elibrary. <http://data.imf.org/?sk=f15905b8-c65e-4aff-abc8-41c925a3aad7&sId=1390030323199&ss=1390030323199>, accessed repeatedly between January 2013 and November 2015.

Ioannou, D., Leblond, P., and Niemann, A. (2015). 'European Integration and the Crisis: Practice and Theory'. *Journal of European Public Policy,* 22 (2): 155–76.

Issing, O. (2003). 'Monetary and Financial Stability: Is there a Trade-off?' *BIS Papers,* 18: 16–23. <http://www.bis.org/publ/bppdf/bispap18.pdf>, accessed on 14 November 2015.

Italian Banking Association (ABI) (2010). *ABI Comments on Consultative Documents Issued by Basel Committee on Banking Supervision 'Strengthening the Resilience of the Banking Sector' and 'International Framework for Liquidity Risk Measurement, Standards and Monitoring'.* April. <https://www.bis.org/publ/bcbs165/italianbankinga.pdf>, accessed on 2 March 2013.

Italian Banking Association (ABI) (2013). Response to the DG Internal Market and Services Consultation Paper 'Reforming the Structure of the EU Banking Sector', July, <http://ec.europa.eu/internal_market/consultations/2013/banking-structural-

reform/docs/contributions/registered-organisations/associazione-bancaria-italiana-abi-_en.pdf.>, accessed on 29 November 2015.

Italian Government (2013). *Response to Consultation on Structural Measures for the Banking Industry* on file with the authors.

Italian Senate (2013). *Esame degli atti comunitari COM (2013) 266 (Proposta di direttiva sui conti di pagamento) e COM(2013)520 (Proposta di Regolamento sul Sistema Unico di Risoluzione).* <https://www.bancaditalia.it/pubblicazioni/interventi-vari/int-var-2013/Audizione-Szego-17-10.pdf>, accessed on 4 December 2015.

Jabko, N. (1999). 'In the Name of the Market: How the European Commission Paved the Way for Monetary Union'. *Journal of European Public Policy*, 6 (3): 475–95.

James, S. (2016). 'The Domestic Politics of Financial Regulation: Informal Ratification Games and the EU Capital Requirement Negotiations'. *New Political Economy*, 21(2), 187–203.

Jassaud, N., and Kang, K. (2015). *A Strategy for Developing a Market for Nonperforming Loans in Italy*. IMF Working Paper, WP/15/24. <http://www.imf.org/external/pubs/ft/wp/2015/wp1524.pdf>, accessed on 2 January 2016.

Jobst, A. A., and Gray, D. F. (2013). 'Systemic Contingent Claims Analysis—Estimating Market-Implied Systemic Risk'. *IMF Working Paper,* WP/13/54 <https://www.imf.org/external/pubs/ft/wp/2013/wp1354.pdf>, accessed on 14 June 2015.

Johnson, J., and Barnes, A. (2014). 'Financial Nationalism and its International Enablers: The Hungarian Experience'. *Review of International Political Economy*, 22 (3): 535–69.

Jones, E. (2012). 'Italy's Sovereign Debt Crisis'. *Survival*, 54 (1): 83–110.

Jones, E. (2013). 'Getting to Greece: Uncertainty, Misfortune, and the Origins of Political Disorder'. *European Political Science*. 12: 294–304.

Juncker, J-C. (2015). *Completing Europe's Economic and Monetary Union*. [Five Presidents' Report] <http://ec.europa.eu/priorities/economic-monetary-union/docs/5-presidents-report_en.pdf>, accessed on 8 December 2015.

Kaiser, S. (2012). 'Anzeigeaktion gegen die Bankenunion: Kampf um die deutschen Spargroschen', Spiegel Online, 13 September. <http://www.spiegel.de/wirtschaft/soziales/sparkassen-und-volksbanken-kaempfen-gegen-bankenunion-a-855706.html>, accessed on 21 October 2015.

Kaltenthaler, K. (1998). *Germany and the Politics of Europe's Money*. Durham: Duke University.

Kaltenthaler, K. (2002). 'German Interests in European Monetary Integration'. *Journal of Common Market Studies*, 40 (1): 69–87.

Kapstein, E. B. (1989). 'Resolving the Regulator's Dilemma: International Coordination of Banking Regulations'. *International Organization*, 43 (2): 323–47.

Kapstein, E. B. (1992). 'Between Power and Purpose: Central Bankers and the Politics of Regulatory Convergence'. *International Organization*, 46(1): 265–87.

Kindleberger, C. P. (1973). *The Formation of Financial Centers: A Study in Comparative Economic History*. International Finance Section Department of Economics, Princeton University. <https://www.princeton.edu/~ies/IES_Studies/S36.pdf>, accessed on 18 May 2013.

King, M. R., and Sinclair, T. J. (2003). 'Private Actors and Public Policy: A Requiem for the New Basel Capital Accord'. *International Political Science Review*, 24 (3): 345–62.

Knedlik, T., and Von Schweinitz, G. (2012). 'Macroeconomic Imbalances as Indicators for Debt Crises in Europe'. *Journal of Common Market Studies*, 50 (5): 726–45.

Knight, A. (2010). *Speech in Paris on Capital Requirements and International Regulation.* September 13. <https://www.bba.org.uk/policy/financial-and-risk-policy/prudential-capital-and-risk/bank-capital/angela-knight-speech-in-paris-on-capital-requirements-and-international-regulation/>, accessed on 18 May 2013 & March 2016.

Knight, J., and Wang, W. (2011). 'China's Macroeconomic Imbalances: Causes and Consequences'. *The World Economy*, 34 (9): 1476–506.

Koalitionsvertrag (2013). 'Deutschlands Zukunft gestalten Koalitionsvertrag zwischen CDU, CSU und SP', *18. Legislaturperiode*. <http://www.bundesregierung.de/Content/DE/_Anlagen/2013/2013-12-17-koalitionsvertrag.pdf?__blob=publicationFile>, accessed on 19 June 2014.

Kremers, J., Schoenmaker, D., and Wierts, P. (eds) (2003). *Financial Supervision in Europe.* Cheltenham: Edward Elgar.

Kudrna, Z. (2012). 'Cross-Border Resolution of Failed Banks in the European Union after the Crisis: Business as Usual'. *Journal of Common Market Studies*, 50 (2): 283–99.

Lane, P. R. (2012). 'The European Sovereign Debt Crisis'. *Journal of Economic Perspectives*, 26 (3): 49–68.

Lannoo, K. (2013). 'Bank Bonus Compromise Bodes Ill for the Single Supervisory Mechanism'. *CEPS Commentary*. 8 March, Brussels. <https://www.ceps.eu/publications/bank-bonus-compromise-bodes-ill-single-supervisory-mechanism>, accessed on 11 October 2015.

Lapavitsas, C. (2012). *Crisis in the Eurozone*. London: Verso Books.

Lastra, R. (2013). 'Banking Union and Single Market: Conflict or Companionship', *Fordham International Law Journal*, 36 (5): 1190–222.

Lehmann, A., and Nyberg, L. (2014). 'Europe's Banking Union in the Global Financial System: Constructing Open and Inclusive Institutions'. EBRD Working Paper No. 175, October, London: EBRD. <http://www.ebrd.com/documents/oce/europes-banking-union-in-the-global-financial-system-constructing-open-and-inclusive-institutions.pdf>, accessed on 4 December 2015.

Loedel, P. (1999). *Deutsche Mark Politics: Germany in the European Monetary System.* Boulder: Lynne Rienner.

Ludlow, P. (2010). 'In the Last Resort. The European Council and the Euro Crisis'. *Briefing Note 7*. <http://www.eurocomment.be/?p=182#more-182>, accessed on 18 October 2013 [link now defunct].

Lyngen, N. (2012). 'Basel III: Dynamics of State Implementation'. *Harvard International Law Journal*, 53 (2): 519–35.

Lynn, M. (2010). *Bust: Greece, the Euro and the Sovereign Debt Crisis*. London: John Wiley & Sons.

Mabbett, D., and Schelkle, W. (2015). 'What Difference Does Euro Membership Make to Stabilization? The Political Economy of International Monetary Systems Revisited'. *Review of International Political Economy*, 22 (3): 508–34.

MacDougall, D. (1977). Report of the Study Group on the Role of Public Finance in European Integration. Brussels: Commission of the European Communities. <http://www.cvce.eu/content/publication/2012/5/31/c475e949-ed28-490b-81ae-a33ce9860d09/publishable_en.pdf>, accessed on 4 January 2015.

Mackintosh, J. (2015). 'Playing Morality with Greek Markets', *Financial Times*, 15 July.

Manghetti, G. (2011). 'Do Savings Banks Differ from Traditional Commercial Banks?' In World Savings Banks Institute/European Savings Banks Group, *200 Years of Savings Banks: A Strong and Lasting Business Model for Responsible, Regional Retail Banking*, Brussels: WSBI/ESBG, pp. 141–56: <http://www.savings-banks.com/SiteCollectionDocuments/Perspectives%2063.pdf>, accessed on 2 November 2015.

Marc, F. (2013). 'Proposition de résolution sur le Mécanisme de résolution unique: nouvelle étape de l'Union bancaire'. Rapport au Sénat, 398, au nom de la commission des finances, <http://www.senat.fr/rap/l13-398/l13-3981.pdf>, accessed on 24 February 2015.

Marcussen, M. (2000). *Ideas and Elites*. Aalborg: Aalborg University.

Marsh, D. (2013). *Europe's Deadlock: How the Euro Crisis Could be Solved-and Why it Won't Happen*. Yale: Yale University Press.

Marzinotto B., Pisani-Ferry J., and Sapir A. (2010). 'Two Crises, Two Responses'. *Bruegel Policy Brief*, 1, 22 March. <http://bruegel.org/2010/03/two-crises-two-responses/>, accessed on 14 December 2015.

Masciandaro, D., and Nieto, M. (2014). *Governance of the Single Supervisory Mechanism: Some Reflections*. Baffi Center Research Paper, no. 149. <https://www.researchgate.net/publication/259946847_Governance_of_the_Single_Supervisory_Mechanism_Some_Reflections>, accessed on 24 August 2015.

Masciandaro, D., Nieto, M., and Quintyn, M. (2009). 'Financial Supervision in the EU: Is there Convergence in the National Architectures?', *Journal of Financial Regulation and Compliance* 17 (2): 86–92.

Mayes, D. G. (2004). 'Who Pays for Bank Insolvency?'. *Journal of International Money and Finance*, 23(3): 515–51.

Mayes, D. G., Halme, L., and Liuksila, A. (2001). *Improving Banking Supervision*. Basingstoke: Palgrave.

McKinnon, R. (1963). 'Optimum Currency Areas'. *American Economic Review*, 53: 717–24.

McNamara, K. R. (1998). *The Currency of Ideas: Monetary Politics in the European Union*. Ithaca, NY: Cornell University Press.

McNamara, K. R. (1999). 'Consensus and Constraint: Ideas and Capital Mobility in European Monetary Integration'. *Journal of Common Market Studies*, 37 (3): 455–76.

Merler, S., and Pisani-Ferry, J. (2012). 'Sudden Stops in the Euro Area'. *Bruegel Policy Contribution*, No. 2012/06. <http://bruegel.org/2012/03/sudden-stops-in-the-euro-area-2/>, accessed on 28 July 2015.

Mero, K., and Piroska, D. (2016). 'The Persistence of National Banking Systems: Banking Union and Financial Nationalism.' IBS Working Paper 1/2016 (February). <http://www.ibs-b.hu/data/downloads/2016/03/18/Mero_and_Piroska_IBS_WP_on_Banking_Union.pdf>, accessed on 24 May 2016.

Mersch, Y. (2013a). 'Europe's Ills Cannot Be Healed by Monetary Innovation Alone'. *Financial Times*, 24 April.

Mersch, Y. (2013b). *Neueste politische Entscheidungen zur Bankenunion und ihre Auswirkungen auf die EZB als Aufsichtsbehörde*. Speech at Generalversammlung der Österreichischen Bankwissenschaftlichen Gesellschaft (BWG). 24 September, Wien. <http://www.ecb.europa.eu/press/key/date/2013/html/sp130924_1.de.html>, accessed on 24 July 2014.

Micossi, S. (2012). 'Unholy Compromise in the Eurozone and How to Right it'. *CEPS Policy Brief*, 277. <http://aei.pitt.edu/35911/1/PB278_SM_Unholy_Compromise.pdf>, accessed on 24 August 2015.

Micossi, S., Carmassi, J., and Peire, F. (2011). 'On the Tasks of the European Stability Mechanism'. *CEPS Policy Brief*, 235. <http://aei.pitt.edu/30039/1/PB_No_235_Micossi_et_al_on_the_ESM-2.pdf>, accessed on 23 September 2015.

Mink, M., and De Haan, J. (2013). 'Contagion During the Greek Sovereign Debt Crisis'. *Journal of International Money and Finance*, 34: 102–13.

Mishkin, F. S. (2011). 'Monetary Policy Strategy: Lessons from the Crisis'. *National Bureau of Economic Research Working Paper*, 1675. <https://www.imf.org/external/np/seminars/eng/2011/res2/pdf/fm.pdf>, accessed on 6 January 2016.

Moloney, N. (2011). 'The European Securities and Markets Authority and Institutional Design for the EU Financial Market–A Tale of Two Competences: Part (1) Rule-Making'. *European Business Organization Law Review*, 12 (1): 41–86.

Moravcsik, A. (1993). 'Preferences and Power in the European Community: A Liberal Intergovernmentalist Approach'. *Journal of Common Market Studies*, 31 (4): 473–524.

Moravcsik, A. (1998). *The Choice for Europe*. London: UCL Press.

Moscovici, P. (2012). *Pierre Moscovici's Speech at Bruegel Annual Meeting*. Opgehaald van Bruegel. <http://www.bruegel.org/nc/blog/detail/article/883-pierre-moscovicis-speech-%20at-bruegel-annual-meeting>, accessed on 27 July 2013.

MTIE (2013). 'Hungary Govt Aims to Raise Domestic Ownership of Banking Sector to at Least 50 pt'. Orban. *MTI—EcoNews*, 12 March.

Münchau, W. (2014). 'Europe Should Say No to a Flawed Banking Union'. *Financial Times*, 16 March.

Mundell, R. (1961). 'Theory of Optimum Currency Areas'. *American Economic Review*, 51: 509–17.

Mussari, G. (2012). *Parliamentary Hearing*. December. <https://www.abi.it/DOC_Info/Audizioni-parlamentari/Audizione_Unione_bancaria-Camera_5_12_2012.pdf>, accessed on 5 November 2015.

Netherlands Government (2012). *Translation of Parliamentary Letter of 1 October 2012 in which the Netherlands' Position is Outlined with Regard to the European Commission's Proposals for a Single Supervisory Mechanism as Well as with Regard to Direct Recapitalization of Banks by the ESM and Possible Further Steps towards a Full Banking Union*. 1 October. <https://www.rijksoverheid.nl/binaries/rijksoverheid/documenten/brieven/2012/10/01/english-translation-of-letter-european-banking-supervision-and-direct-recapitalization-of-banks-from-the-esm/english-translation-of-letter-to-parliament-on-european-banking-supervision-and-direct-recapitalization-of-banks-from-the-esm.pdf>, accessed on 5 December 2015.

Netherlands Government (2013a). *Consultation by the Commission on the Structural Reform of EU Banking Sector—Response of Netherlands.* 9 July. <http://ec.europa.eu/internal_market/consultations/2013/banking-structural-reform/contributions_en.htm>, accessed on 8 July 2014.

Netherlands Government (2013b). *Kabinetsreactie op het voorstel van de Europese Commissie voor de oprichting van een Europees resolutiemechanisme.* 9 September. Eerste Kamer der Staten-Generaal. <https://www.eerstekamer.nl/eumobiel/behandeling/20130909/brief_regering_kabinetsreactie_op_2/info>, accessed on 8 July 2014.

Niemann, A., and Ioannou, D. (2015). 'European Economic Integration in Times of Crisis: A Case of Neofunctionalism?'. *Journal of European Public Policy,* 22 (2): 196–218.

Noyer, C. (2012). *Basel III—CRD4: Impact and Stakes.* Speech at the ACP conference. June 27. <http://www.banque-france.fr/uploads/tx_bdfgrandesdates/Conference-ACP-27-june-2012.pdf>, accessed on 15 March 2013.

Obstfeld, M. (2012). 'Financial Flows, Financial Crises, and Global Imbalances'. *Journal of International Money and Finance,* 31 (3): 469–80.

Obstfeld, M., and Peri, G. (1999). 'Regional Nonadjustment and Fiscal Policy: Lessons for EMU'. *National Bureau of Economic Research Working Paper,* 6431. <https://core.ac.uk/download/files/153/6881378.pdf>, accessed on 3 August 2015.

Padoa-Schioppa, T. (1982). 'Capital Mobility: Why is the Treaty Not Implemented?', in T. Padoa-Schioppa (ed), *The Road to Monetary Union in Europe* (1994). Oxford: Clarendon Press.

Padoa-Schioppa, T. (2007). Letter to Fernando Teixeira dos Santos, President of the ECOFIN Council, 26 November, Italian Ministry of Economy.

Pagoulatos, G., and Quaglia, L. (2013). 'Turning the Crisis on its Head: Sovereign Debt Crisis as Banking Crisis in Italy and Greece', in I. Hardie and D. Howarth (eds), *Market-Based Banking, Varieties of Financial Capitalism and the Financial Crisis.* Oxford: Oxford University Press, pp. 179–200.

Panetta, F. (2004). *Il Sistema Bancario Italiano Negli Anni Novanta: Gli Effetti Di Una Trasformazione.* Bologna: Il Mulino.

Papadia, F. (2014). 'Lending of Last Resort? A European Perspective'. *BIS Papers,* 79. <http://www.bis.org/publ/bppdf/bispap79.pdf>, accessed on 10 November 2015.

Paterson, W. E. (2011). 'The Reluctant Hegemon? Germany Moves Centre Stage in the European Union'. *Journal of Common Market Studies,* 49 (1): 57–75.

Pauly, L. (2008). 'Financial Crisis Management in Europe and Beyond', *Contribution to Political Economy,* 27 (1): 73–89.

Pisani-Ferry, J. (2012). 'The Euro Crisis and the New Impossible Trinity'. *Bruegel Policy Contribution* 2012/01. <http://bruegel.org/2012/01/the-euro-crisis-and-the-new-impossible-trinity-2/>, accessed on 12 August 2015.

Pisani-Ferry, J. (2013). 'The Politics of Moral Hazard'. *Project Syndicate.* 30 March. <http://www.project-syndicate.org/commentary/cyprus-and-the-politics-of-moral-hazard-in-europe-by-jean-pisani-ferry>, accessed on 24 February 2015.

Prudential Regulatory Authority (PRA) (2014). *Depositor Protection.* PRA Consultation Paper, CP20/14. <www.bankofengland.co.uk/pra/Documents/publications/cp/2014/cp2014.pdf>, accessed on 28 March 2015.

Putnam, R. (1988). 'Diplomacy and Domestic Politics: The Logic of the Two-Level Game'. *International Organization*, 42 (3): 427–60.

Quaglia, L. (2004). 'Italy's Policy Towards European Monetary Integration: Bringing Ideas Back In?'. *Journal of European Public Policy*, 11 (6): 1096–111.

Quaglia, L. (2008). 'Committee Governance in the Financial Sector in the European Union', *Journal of European Integration*, 30 (3): 565–80.

Quaglia, L. (2010a). *Governing Financial Services in the European Union*. London: Routledge.

Quaglia, L. (2010b). 'Completing the Single Market in Financial Services: The Politics of Competing Advocacy Coalitions', *Journal of European Public Policy*, 17 (7): 1007–22.

Quaglia, L. (2014). *The European Union and Global Financial Regulation*. Oxford: Oxford University Press.

Quaglia, L., Eastwood, R., and Holmes, P. (2009). 'The Financial Turmoil and EU Policy Co-operation in 2008'. *Journal of Common Market Studies*, 47 (1): 63–87.

Quaglia, L., and Royo, S. (2015). 'Banks and the Political Economy of the Sovereign Debt Crisis in Italy and Spain'. *Review of International Political Economy*, 22 (3): 485–507.

Rabobank (2010). *International Framework for Liquidity Risk*. AB/hr/basel 100413. <https://www.bis.org/publ/bcbs165/rabobank.pdf>, accessed on 14 April 2013.

Rabobank (2011). *Basel III: Tough but Realistic*. Special Report 2011/01. <https://economics.rabobank.com/publications/2011/january/basel-iii-tough-but-realistic/>, accessed on 14 April 2013.

Rabobank (2013). *The Single Resolution Mechanism: Position Paper*. November. <https://www.rabobank.com/en/images/20131204-PP-Single-Resolution-Mechanism.pdf>, accessed on 24 March 2014.

Rajan, R. (2012). 'The True Lessons of the Recession'. *Foreign Affairs*, 91 (3): 69–79.

Rajoy, M. (2012). *Intervención del presidente del Gobierno en el Pleno del Congreso de los Diputados para informar sobre los Consejos Europeos de los días 22 y 23 de noviembre, y de los días 13 y 14 de diciembre de 2012*. 19 December. Madrid. <http://www.congreso.es/public_oficiales/L10/CONG/DS/PL/DSCD-10-PL-83.PDF#page=34>, accessed on 14 September 2014.

Rajoy, M. (2013). *Discurso del presidente del Gobierno en la inauguración de la reunión del Grupo de Reflexión sobre el futuro de la Unión Europea Palma de Mallorca*. 19 July. Madrid. On file with the authors.

Rajoy, M. (2014). *Intervención del presidente del Gobierno en el Pleno del Congreso de los Diputados para informar sobre el Consejo Europeo de Bruselas de los días 19 y 20 de diciembre de 2013*. On file with the authors.

Reinhart, C., and K. Rogoff (2009). *This Time is Different: Eight Centuries of Financial Folly*. Oxford and Princeton: Princeton University Press.

Ringe, W.G. (2015). 'Capital Markets Union for Europe—A Political Message to the UK', *Oxford Legal Studies Research Paper*, 26/2015, March. <http://papers.ssrn.com/sol3/papers.cfm?abstract_id=2575654>, accessed on 13 January 2016.

Risse, T., Engelmann-Martin, D., Knope, H. J., and Roscher, K. (1999). 'To Euro or Not to Euro? The EMU and Identity Politics in the European Union'. *European Journal of International Relations*, 5 (2): 147–87.

Rodrigues, J., and Reis, J. (2012). 'The Asymmetries of European Integration and the Crisis of Capitalism in Portugal'. *Competition & Change*, 16 (3): 188–205.

Rommerskirchen, C. S. (2014). *Fiscal Policy Coordination in Times of Economic and Financial Crises*. PhD thesis, University of Edinburgh.

Royo, S. (2011). *Portugal in the 21st Century: Politics, Society and Economics*. Lanham, MD: Lexington Books.

Royo, S. (2013a). 'How did the Spanish Financial System Survive the First Stage of the Global Crisis?' *Governance* 26 (4): 631–56.

Royo, S. (2013b). 'A Ship in Trouble: The Spanish Banking System in the Midst of the Global Financial System Crisis: The Limits of Regulation', in I. Hardie, and D. Howarth (eds), *Market-Based Banking, Varieties of Financial Capitalism*. Oxford: Oxford University Press.

Royo, S. (2013c). *Lessons from the Crisis in Spain*. New York: Palgrave.

Sabatini, G. (2013). *Proposta di Regolamento del arlamento europeo e del Consiglio che fissa norme e procedure uniformi per la risoluzione delle crisi degli enti creditizi e di talune imprese di investimento nel quadro del meccanismo unico di risoluzione delle crisi e del Fondo unico di risoluzione delle crisi bancarie*. COM (2013) 520. 10 October. <https://www.abi.it/DOC_Info/Audizioni-parlamentari/Audizione_RegolamentoRisoluzioneCrisiBancarie.pdf>, accessed on 27 November 2015.

Saccomanni F. (2013). *Letter of Italian Finance Minister Saccomanni to the other* Finance Ministers. 13 December. On file with the authors.

Sadeh, T. (2006). *Sustaining European Monetary Union: Confronting the Cost of Diversity*. Boulder: Lynne Rienner.

Sadeh, T. (2009). 'EMU's Diverging Micro Foundations—A Study of Governments' Preferences and the Sustainability of EMU'. *Journal of European Public Policy*, 16 (4): 545–63.

Sadeh, T., and Verdun, A. (2009). Explaining Europe's Monetary Union – A Survey of the Literature', *International Studies Review*, 11 (2): 277–301.

Salines, M., Glöckler, G., and Truchlewski, Z. (2012). 'Existential Crisis, Incremental Response: The Eurozone's Dual Institutional Evolution 2007-2011'. *Journal of European Public Policy*, 19 (5): 665–81.

Sandholtz, W., and Sweet, A. S. (eds) (1998). *European Integration and Supranational Governance*. Oxford: Oxford University Press.

Santander (2014). Santander UK plc 2013 Annual Report; available at <http://www.aboutsantander.co.uk/documents/sanuk-2013-annual-report.pdf>, accessed on 1 December 2015.

Schild, J. (2015). *Leading Together or Opposing Each Other? Germany, France and the European Banking Union*. Paper presented for the 14th Biennial Conference of the European Union Studies Association, 5–7 March, Boston. <https://eustudies.org/conference/papers/download/125>, accessed on 23 November 2015.

Schiller, R. J. (2005). *Irrational Exuberance*. Princeton: Princeton University Press.

Schimmelfennig, F. (2015). 'Liberal Intergovernmentalism and the Euro Area Crisis'. *Journal of European Public Policy*, 22 (2): 177–95.

Schimmelfennig, F. (2016). 'A Differentiated Leap Forward: Spillover, Path-Dependency, and Graded Membership in European Banking Regulation', *West European Politics,* 39 (3): 483–502.

Schmidt, V. A., and Radaelli, C. M. (2004). 'Policy Change and Discourse in Europe: Conceptual and Methodological Issues'. *West European Politics*, 27 (2): 183–210.

Schmitz, B., and Von Hagen, J. (2012). 'Current Account Imbalances and Financial Integration in the Euro Area'. *Journal of International Money and Finance*, 30 (8): 1676–95.

Schmitz, S. (2012). 'The Liquidity Coverage Ratio Under Siege'. *Economonitor*. 9 December. <http://www.economonitor.com/blog/2012/07/the-liquidity-coverage-ratio-under-siege>, accessed on 2 June 2014.

Schoenmaker, D. (2011). 'The Financial Trilemma'. *Duisenberg School of Finance—Tinbergen Institute Discussion Paper*. TI 11-019/DSF 7, <http://papers.tinbergen.nl/11019.pdf>, accessed on 6 January 2016.

Schoenmaker, D., (2013). *Governance of International Banking: The Financial Trilemma*. Oxford: Oxford University Press.

Schoenmaker, D., and Peek T. (2014). 'The State of the Banking Sector in Europe'. *OECD Economics Department Working Papers* 1102, January. <http://www.oecd-ilibrary.org/economics/the-state-of-the-banking-sector-in-europe_5k3ttg7n4r32-en?crawler=true>, accessed on 12 September 2015.

Sibert, A. (2012). *Monetary Policy, the Provision of Financial Stability and Banking Supervision,* Directorate General for Internal Policies, European Parliament, December, <http://www.europarl.europa.eu/document/activities/cont/201212/20121210ATT57792/20121210ATT57792EN.pdf>, accessed on 6 January 2016.

Signorini, M. (2012). *Parliamentary Hearing of the Direttore Centrale of the Bank of Italy*. October 2012. <https://www.bancaditalia.it/pubblicazioni/interventi-vari/int-var-2012/unione_bancaria_signorini.pdf>, accessed on 4 December 2015.

Simmons, B. A. (2001). 'The International Politics of Harmonization: The Case of Capital Market Regulation'. *International Organization*, 55 (3): 589–62.

Simpson, C. (2013). *The German Sparkassen (Savings Banks): A Commentary and Case Study*. London: Civitas (Institute for Civil Society). <http://www.civitas.org.uk/content/files/SimpsonSparkassen.pdf>, accessed on 20 March 2015.

Sinn, H. W. (2012). TARGET losses in case of a euro breakup, 22 October 2012, Vox, <http://www.voxeu.org/article/target-losses-case-euro-breakup>, accessed on 15 March 2015.

Sinn, H. W. (2014). 'Austerity, Growth and Inflation: Remarks on the Eurozone's Unresolved Competitiveness Problem'. *The World Economy*, 37 (1): 1–13.

Sinn, H. W., and Wollmershäuser, T. (2012). 'Target-Salden und die deutsche Kapitalbilanz im Zeichen der europäischen Zahlungsbilanzkrise'. *Ifo Working Paper*, 149. <http://econpapers.repec.org/scripts/redir.pf?u=http%3A%2F%2Fwww.cesifo-group.de%2Fportal%2Fpage%2Fportal%2FDocBase_Content%2FWP%2FWP-Ifo_Working_Papers%2Fwp-ifo-2012%2FIfoWorkingPaper-149.pdf;h=repec:ces:ifowps:_149>, accessed on 14 October 2014.

Smith, M. (2001). 'In Pursuit of Selective Liberalization: Single Market Competition and its Limits'. *Journal of European Public Policy*, 8 (4): 519–40.

Spanish Banking Association (2010). *The Spanish Banking Association Comments to the Basel Committee on Banking Supervision Consultative Document.* 16 April. <https://www.bis.org/publ/bcbs165/spbac.pdf>, accessed on 3 January 2013.

Spanish Government (2013). *Response to Consultation on Structural Measures for the Banking Industry*, on file with the authors.

Spendzharova, A. (2012). 'Is More "Brussels" the Solution? New European Union Member States' Preferences about the European Financial Architecture', *Journal of Common Market Studies* 50(2): 315–34.

Spendzharova, A. (2014). 'Banking Union Under Construction: The Impact of Foreign Ownership and Domestic Bank Internationalization on European Union Member-States' Regulatory Preferences in Banking Supervision'. *Review of International Political Economy*, 21 (4): 949–79.

Spendzharova, A., and Bayram, N. (2016). 'Banking Union Through the Back Door? The Impact of European Banking Union in Sweden and the Baltic States'. *West European Politics*, 39 (3): 565–84.

Speyer, B. (2013). 'EU Banking Union: Right Idea, Poor Execution'. *Deutsche Bank Research, EU Monitor European Integration.* 4 September. <https://www.dbresearch.com/PROD/DBR_INTERNET_EN-PROD/PROD0000000000319670/EU_Banking_Union%3A_Right_idea,_poor_execution.PDF>, accessed on 18 October 2015.

Stegeman, R., and van der Meer, J. (2012). 'The Netherlands: Losing Sleep Over Basel III'. *International Financial Law Review (IFLR)*, 31 January. <http://www.iflr.com/Article/2970361/The-Netherlands-Losing-sleep-over-Basel-III.html>, accessed on 6 January 2016.

Story, J., and Walter, I. (1997). *Political Economy of Financial Integration in Europe: The Battle of the Systems*. Manchester: Manchester University Press.

Szago, B. (2013). Parliamentary Hearing 'The SRM regulation', 17 October: <https://www.senato.it/application/xmanager/projects/leg17/attachments/documento_evento_procedura_commissione/files/000/000/564/Audizione_Bruna_Szego_Banca_Italia.pdf>, accessed on 12 August 2015.

Talani, L. S. (2000). *Betting For and Against EMU: Who Wins and Who Loses in Italy and in the UK from the Process of European Monetary Integration*. London: Ashgate.

Thompson, H. (1996). *The British Conservative Government and the Exchange Rate Mechanism 1979–94*. London: Pinter.

Tsingou, E. (2008). 'Transnational Private Governance and the Basel Process: Banking Regulation and Supervision, Private Interests and Basel II'. In J-C. Graz and A. Nölke (eds) *Transnational Private Governance and its Limits*: pp. 58–68.

Tucker, P. (2014). 'The Lender of Last Resort and Modern Central Banking: Principles and Reconstruction'. *BIS Paper*, 79. <http://www.bis.org/publ/bppdf/bispap79b_rh.pdf>, accessed 25 June 2015.

UK Government (2014). *UK Non Paper on Securitization: Executive Summary to the UK Response to the EU securitisation consultation*, available at <https://ec.europa.eu/eusurvey>, accessed on 7 January 2016 and on file with the authors.

Underhill, G. R. D. (1998). 'The Making of the European Financial Area: Global Market, Integration and the EU Single Market for Financial Service', in G. R. D. Underhill (ed), *The New World Order in International Finance*. London: Macmillan.

Underhill, G. R. D. (2012). 'The Political Economy of Eventual Banking Union', in T. Beck (ed), *Banking Union for Europe: Risks and Challenges*. London: CEPR, pp. 137–51. (See also <http://www.voxeu.org/article/political-economy-eventual-banking-union>, accessed on 2 March 2015.)

Underhill, G. R. D., and Zhang, X. (2008). 'Setting the Rules: Private Power, Political Underpinnings, and Legitimacy in Global Monetary and Financial Governance'. *International Affairs*, 84 (3): 535–54.

Unicredit (2010). *UniCredit Group's Reply to the Basel Committee on Banking Supervision's Consultative Document on 'Strengthening the Resilience of the Banking Sector'*. <https://www.bis.org/publ/bcbs165/unicreditcapita.pdf>, accessed on 2 May 2013.

Valiante, D. (2014). 'Framing Banking Union in the Euro Area: Some Empirical Evidence'. *CEPS Working Document* 388. <https://www.ceps.eu/publications/framing-banking-union-euro-area-some-empirical-evidence>, accessed on 15 October 2015.

Van Rompuy, H. (2012a). *Towards a Genuine Economic and Monetary Union: Report by President of the European Council Herman Van Rompuy* [Four Presidents' Interim Report]. EUCO 120/12, PRESSE 296, PR PCE 102; Brussels, 26 June. Available at <http://www.consilium.europa.eu/en/workarea/downloadasset.aspx?id=17220>, accessed on 13 April 2015.

Van Rompuy, H. (2012b). *Towards a Genuine Economic and Monetary Union*. [Four Presidents' Report], 5 December. <http://www.consilium.europa.eu/uedocs/cms_Data/docs/pressdata/en/ec/134069.pdf>, accessed on 9 May 2015.

Verdun, A. (1996). 'An "Asymmetrical" Economic and Monetary Union in the EU: Perceptions of Monetary Authorities and Social partners?'. *Journal of European Integration*, 20 (1): 59–81.

Verdun, A. (1998). 'The Institutional Design of EMU: A Democratic Deficit?', *Journal of Public Policy*, 18 (2): 107–32.

Verdun, A. (1999). 'The Role of the Delors Committee in the Creation of EMU: An Epistemic Community?'. *Journal of European Public Policy*, 6 (2): 309–28.

Verdun, A. (2002). 'Merging Neofunctionalism and Intergovernmentalism: Lessons from EMU', in A. Verdun (ed), *The Euro: European Integration Theory and Economic and Monetary Union*, pp. 9–28.

Verdun, A. (2015). 'A Historical Institutionalist Explanation of the EU's Responses to the Euro Area Financial Crisis'. *Journal of European Public Policy*, 22 (2): 219–37.

Véron, N. (2012). *Briefing Paper for the European Parliament*. <http://veron.typepad.com/main/2012/10/briefing-paper-for-the-european-parliament.html>, accessed on 10 June 2015.

Véron, N. (2014). 'Defining Europe's Capital Markets Union', *Bruegel Policy Contribution*, 2014/12. <http://bruegel.org/2014/11/defining-europes-capital-markets-union/>, accessed on 14 September 2015.

Véron, N. (2015). 'Europe's Capital Markets Union and the New Single Market Challenge'. 30 September 2015, <http://bruegel.org/2015/09/europes-capital-markets-union-and-the-new-single-market-challenge/>.

Véron, N., and Wolff, G. B. (2013). 'From Supervision to Resolution: Next Steps on the Road to European Banking Union', *Bruegel Policy Contribution*, 2013/04.

<http://bruegel.org/2013/02/from-supervision-to-resolution-next-steps-on-the-road-to-european-banking-union/>, accessed on 17 April 2015.

Vona, S., and Bini Smaghi, L. (1988). 'Economic Growth and Exchange Rates in the European Monetary System: Their Trade Effects in a Changing External Environment'. In F. Giavazzi, S. Micossi and M. Miller (eds), *The European Monetary System*. Cambridge: Cambridge University Press, pp. 140–77.

Walsh, J. (1994). 'International Constraints and Domestic Choice: Economic Convergence and Exchange Rate Policy in France and Italy', *Political Studies*, 42 (2): 243–58.

Walsh, J. (2000). *European Monetary Integration and Domestic Politics. Britain, France and Italy*. London: Lynner Rienner.

Werner, Pierre (1970). 'Report to the Council and the Commission on the Realisation by Stages of Economic and Monetary Union in the Community (Werner Report)'. *Bulletin of the European Community*, Supplement 11, Brussels.

West European Politics (2016). *The Politics of Supranational Bank Supervision in Europe*. special issue (guest editors D. Howarth and H, Macartney), 39 (3): 415–604.

Whelan, K. (2011). 'Ireland's Sovereign Debt Crisis'. *UCD Centre for Economic Research Working Paper Series*, WP11/09. May. <http://researchrepository.ucd.ie/handle/10197/6384>, accessed on 12 May 2014.

Wolf, D. (2002). 'Neofunctionalism and Intergovernmentalism Amalgamated: The Case of EMU', in A. Verdun (ed), *The Euro: European Integration Theory and Economic and Monetary Union*, Lanham, MD: Rowman & Littlefield, pp. 29–50.

Woll, C. (2014). *The Power of Inaction: Bank Bailouts in Comparison*. Ithaca: Cornell University Press.

Wood, D. (2005). *Governing Global Banking*. Aldershot: Ashgate.

Wymeersch, E. (2014). 'The Single Supervisory Mechanism or "SSM", Part One of the Banking Union'. *ECGI—Law Working Paper*, 240/014, February. <http://papers.ssrn.com/sol3/papers.cfm?abstract_id=2397800>, accessed on 13 October 2014.

Wyplosz, C. (2011). 'An Open Letter to Dr Jens Weidmann'. *VoxEU*. 18 November. <http://voxeu.org/index.php?q=node/7296>, accessed on 11 May 2013.

Wyplosz, C. (2012). 'Banking Union as a Crisis Management Tool', in T. Beck (ed), *Banking Union for Europe: Risks and Challenges*. London: CEPR, pp. 17–22.

Xiao, Y. (2009). 'French Banks Amid the Global Financial Crisis'. *IMF Working Paper*, WP/09/201, September.

Yiangou, J., O'Keeffe, M., and Glöckler, G. (2013). 'Tough Love': How the ECB's Monetary Financing Prohibition Pushes Deeper Euro Area Integration'. *Journal of European Integration*, 35 (3): 223–37.

Zahariadis, N. (2012). 'Complexity, Coupling and Policy Effectiveness: The European Response to the Greek Sovereign Debt Crisis'. *Journal of Public Policy*, 32 (2): 99–116.

Zaring, D. (2015). 'Legal Obligation in International Law and International Finance'. *Cornell International Law Journal*, 48 (1): 175–217.

Zavvos, G. S., and Kaltsouni, S. (2015). 'The Single Resolution Mechanism in the European Banking Union: Legal Foundation, Governance Structure and Financing', in M. Haentjens and B. Wessels (eds), *Research Handbook on Crisis Management in the Banking Sector*. Cheltenham: Edward Elgar.

Zenios, S. (2015). 'Fairness and Reflexivity in the Cyprus Bail-In'. *Wharton Financial Institutions Center Working Paper*, 14-04.

Zentraler Kreditausschuss (ZKA) (2010). *Strengthening the Resilience of the Banking Sector.* Position Paper on the Consultative Document of the Basel Committee. April 16. <https://www.bis.org/publ/bcbs165/zkrac.pdf>, accessed on 19 January 2015.

Zysman J. (1983). *Governments, Markets and Growth.* Ithaca, NY: Cornell University Press.

Index

Note: Detailed information pertaining to countries is to be found under the specific countries.